MRS SAPPHO

Mrs SAPPHO

The Life of C.A. Dawson Scott
Mother of International P.E.N.

MARJORIE WATTS
with a Foreword by
Francis King

Duckworth

First published in 1987 by
Gerald Duckworth & Company Limited
43 Gloucester Crescent, London NW1

ISBN 0 7156 2183 1

British Library Cataloguing in Publication Data

Watts, Marjorie
  Mrs Sappho : the life of C.A. Dawson Scott,
'Mother of International P.E.N.'
  1. Dawson Scott, C.A. — Biography
  2. P.E.N.   3. Writers — Great Britain
  — Biography
  I. Title
  806'01   PR6007.A8/

ISBN 0-7156-2183-1

Photoset in North Wales by
Derek Doyle & Associates, Mold, Clwyd
Printed and bound in Great Britain by
Unwin Brothers Limited, Old Woking

Contents

Plates

(between pp. 50 and 51)

William Edward Dawson, 1802-1899
Dr John Armstrong, 1805-1890
Amy Dawson aged about 14
Amy Dawson aged about 25
Sappho in 1901 aged 36
Sappho in 1910 aged 45, with the author aged 11
Scottie in R.A.M.C. uniform, 1914
Charlotte Mew in about 1923 (National Portrait Gallery)
May Sinclair and her cat, Tommy (Mansell Collection)
Selma Lagerlöf (National Portrait Gallery)
Anatole France (National Portrait Gallery)
Joseph Conrad
Rebecca West (Mansell Collection)
Karel Čapek (National Portrait Gallery)
Ernst Toller (BBC Hulton Picture Library)
Stacy Aumonier (National Portrait Gallery)
Ezra Pound (National Portrait Gallery
Menu for the first P.E.N. Club dinner
John Galsworthy with some of the international writers present at the
    first P.E.N. Congress, London 1923 (Mansell Collection)
The first P.E.N. Congress, London 1923
Henry Nevinson (National Portrait Gallery)
H.G. Wells and members of the Bombay P.E.N. Centre
John Galsworthy, Sappho and Hermon Ould at the Polish Congress
    in 1930
Sappho at Levorna in about 1932
Sappho and Colonel Arthur Lynch in about 1933

This book is dedicated affectionately to all Sappho's descendants

Christopher Dawson Scott
Frances Dawson Scott

Toby Dawson Scott
Robert Dawson Scott

Marjorie-Ann Lowenstein
Oliver Lowenstein
Stephen Lowenstein

Simon Watts
Richard Watts
Alison Watts
Rebecca Watts

Julyan Watts
Serge Watts

and

Kristina Anderson, her great-great-granddaughter

Foreword

It was in an innocent age, at the turn of the century, that Mrs Dawson Scott, later to achieve international fame as 'The Mother of the P.E.N. Club', acquired the nickname Sappho. 'I suppose that she was a lesbian?' foreign P.E.N. members now often say to me; and I then have to explain that, married and the mother of children, she became 'Sappho' merely because her first published work had been an epic poem about the poet (the second was a poem entitled *Idylls of Womanhood*) and because at that period her girlish ambition was to become 'the Sappho of this age'.

Sadly, despite an encouraging letter from Browning in her youth and encouraging reviews from people less distinguished in her later years, Mrs Dawson Scott never fulfilled her ambition, her poetry being altogether too diffuse and derivative. But she wrote richly plotted, strenuous novels, some of which, set in the Cornwall which she so much came to love and which she adopted as her own, still repay a reading. But her chief claims to remembrance are her founding of the international writers' organisation P.E.N. and her vivid comments, in her diaries and letters to her daughter, on so many of the leading authors of her time.

The founding of P.E.N. was an astonishing achievement for such a person. Unlike Queen Marie of Roumania, who was one of P.E.N.'s early members, Sappho had no great influence and no large fortune at her disposal. Nor, unlike another early member and a friend, Rebecca West, did she have international fame or indeed much fame of any kind, except among other writers. What she achieved, she achieved merely through perseverance, good sense, enthusiasm and a capacity for loyal friendship and hard work. (These, incidentally, are qualities all passed on to her daughter, Marjorie Watts, author of this book, who was the first secretary of P.E.N. for a period of six years and who, in her eighties, is still energetically involved in its activities.)

Like many visionaries, Sappho could often be a trial to her associates. As Rebecca West summed her up with characteristic crispness in a speech at a P.E.N. teaparty at Claridge's in 1927: 'There isn't probably a person in London who hasn't called Sappho a pest. But, as you get to know her, you realise she is a lovable pest.'

(How Sappho, who was present, responded to this somewhat dubious compliment, her daughter does not record.) It was by being 'a lovable pest' that this plump, ardent woman enlisted John Galsworthy's essential support as the first President of P.E.N., a post to which he brought an idealistic self-dedication; indefatigably organised fund-raising activities; and instigated the setting-up of P.E.N. Centres all over the world.

Commenting on people often her literary but rarely her moral superiors, Sappho shows sharpness of observation and a delightful irreverence. Of Ezra Pound she writes: 'A silly-looking, fatuous face, topped by wild, wiry hair, no doubt much more interesting than he looks'; of H.G. Wells, 'So commonplace-looking that, in a crowd, he managed to resemble everybody else.' After reading *Howard's End*, she refers, in all innocence, to its author as 'Miss Forster', and goes on to append the verdict of her unliterary doctor husband: 'Another of these damned old maids talking about things of which they know nothing.'

On Sappho's death, a younger woman novelist, G.B. Stern, whom she had befriended and encouraged, wrote of her: 'There was about her an indestructible quality of sturdy optimism; remarkable considering that life seemed to spend most of its time knocking her down and forgetting to help her up again.' It is this sturdy optimism that, above all her other qualities, emerges from Marjorie Watts' affectionate but always clear-sighted and unsentimental book. A remarkable woman has been remembered in the way that she herself, modest and candid, would surely have wished and that every reader should enjoy.

Francis King
President, International P.E.N.

1

The Beginning

1. The Child

Baby Maude was to have her mid-day meal in the kitchen, but in future Kate would dine with Papa and Mamma. Kate knew Papa enjoyed her eager chatter, and she ran into the dining room with her lips already parted on the tale of her morning's activities.

Mamma was speaking.

The atmosphere of the room was permeated with emotions which the child recognised, without understanding why, as dangerous. With her heart beating quickly, she climbed on to her chair.

The round of roast beef stood before Papa. Everything was as usual, except Mamma.

Once or twice before Kate had seen her with heightened colour and glassy eyes, eyes which looked but did not see. During the time between, however, the child forgot.

When Mamma was what Kate, still too young to have a large vocabulary, termed 'funny', tension filled the room in which she sat, and waves of it, flowing out, filled the house. Mamma, upon whom you counted to do and say the same sort of things as other people, was no longer to be relied upon. You could not guess what she might do next, only that it would be unpleasant – and perhaps painful.

Mamma, staring down the table at Papa, was speaking in a loud voice. 'I don't and I never have ...' She continued: 'It doesn't hurt anybody to hear the truth ...'

'You wanted to get away from Gravesend ...' He put a plate in front of Kate with a quiet, 'Eat your dinner.' The child, perched on two music books, felt herself to be unnecessarily conspicuous. The only refuge in the large bright room was below her feet – among the red and black hassocks a little girl would have been neither seen nor heard.

A row built up between the adults, and, in the child, fear grew. If the 'very dreadful' were to happen, she would sink a little, slide down ...

The quarrel reached its peak when Papa said sarcastically, '*I* never take anything stronger than soda-water ...' The smoulder broke into flame ... Mamma screamed. She snatched at the knife on the bread trencher and ran round the table. Papa fled. 'Don't be a fool,' he

shouted, the stronger voice cutting through her shrieks. She reached his
empty chair and stopped. 'Sit down,' he cried roughly, and, after a
little, she obeyed ... and broke into tears. 'You have been so good to me
... the kindest man that ever lived ... only – I've lost – I've lost –'

'You've plenty left. Why don't you make the best of it?'

'I'm not that sort.' Though he remained silent, she could read his
mind and she thought how difficult it was, once the habit had been
formed, to break it. 'I will give it up. I *will*, Ben, I promise.'

Kate had vanished, and neither thought to look for her in the tented
obscurity of 'under the table'.

The above is an extract from the opening chapter of an unfinished
autobiographical novel which my mother, 'the child' of the story,
wrote about sixty years later in 1934. She must have been between 5
and 6 at the time of this incident, and it made such a deep impression
on her and was so fixed in her memory, together with the feelings of
fear it engendered, that she used to describe it to us children over and
over again in precisely the same words. But she told us that 'Mamma
snatched the carving knife' – much more exciting – whereas in the
book she wrote so many years later, it became the 'bread knife'. This
would be much more likely, since Papa was wielding the carving knife.

Papa and Mamma were my grandparents, Ebenezer Dawson and
his first wife, Catharine Mason Armstrong, but 'The Child', my
mother, whose story this is, derived so little from her parents and so
much from her two grandfathers, that to understand her life one must
begin by knowing something of theirs – of Dr John Armstrong on her
mother's side, and William Edward Dawson, on her father's.

2. The Armstrongs

Dr John Armstrong was born in Manorhamilton, in the county of
Leitrim, in 1805, his father keeping a general store and farming land
originally donated to his ancestors for their services on the side of the
English around the time of the Battle of the Boyne in 1690.

Before they migrated to Ireland during the sixteenth and
seventeenth centuries, the Armstrongs lived on the borders of
Scotland and England, and their main occupation – and means of
livelihood – was, together with other border clans, harrying the
English, burning their farms and stealing their cattle and women.

As the Border became too uncomfortable for this wild clan of
'rievers and robbers', some of them went to the Netherlands, where
they fought courageously, and others settled in Ireland. By the time
Dr John was born the scattered branches of the family had become
reasonably law-abiding and mostly devout Methodists – his

grandparents having come under the influence of John Wesley during one of his many visits to Ireland.

John Armstrong was an outstandingly intelligent boy who, in spite of almost non-existent opportunities, still managed to achieve an unbalanced but high standard of education from Catholic priests who visited his village, intermingled with short periods from time to time at small schools started by educationalists. His father wanted him to become a Methodist minister, but the boy was determined to become a doctor – his mother was widely known in his rural area as a herbal healer. At the age of 13 he took an exam at the Apothecary's Hall in Dublin in 'Virgil's Georgics', 'Horace', the 'Greek Testament' and 'Lucian', which he passed, he wrote, 'at a hand gallop'. He was then apprenticed to a local doctor and 'helped' with his patients!

Aged 16 John became a student at the College of Surgeons at Richmond Hospital, Dublin and also at the Rotunda Lying-in Hospital, and after three years went to London with hardly any money and an introduction to a Dr James Hunter, of Islington Green, who was also a Methodist.

From then on he battled to achieve his ambition with tenacity and persistence until finally, without money and sometimes half-starved, he qualified at St Bartholomew's Hospital in 1828 and got a post as assistant to a Dr Park – a relation of the traveller, Mungo Park – at Gravesend. His starting salary was £60 a year and he was 23.

John Armstrong became partner to Dr Park and later took on the practice. He remained at Gravesend as a much-loved G.P. for the rest of his life, serving for a period as Mayor.

In addition to his profession, Dr John had literary interests and wrote philosophical and medical articles for scientific journals, thus acquiring a wide circle of friends. He had a lot of Irish charm, a feeling for history and a gift for story-telling, and he left the story of his life in manuscript. His little granddaughter, my mother, loved him dearly and was fascinated by the tales he told of his Armstrong ancestors and their wild and wicked ways. Looking back, she was sure he was psychic, as she considered she was, but the many incidents in his life which she would explain in psychic terms, he unfailingly attributed to 'God's will' or to 'the intervention of the Lord'.

In 1837 Dr John married Anne Hawe Mason, daughter of John Mason, the Book Steward of the Methodist Conference, whose portrait and bust can still be seen at the Methodist Archives and Research Centre in the City Road, London.

John Armstrong and Anne Hawe Mason had nine children, of whom my grandmother, Catharine Mason Armstrong – 'Mamma' – was the eldest daughter. Unhappily Anne died, aged thirty-seven, of what seems to have been a brain tumour, when the youngest of her nine children was a few months old, and my grandmother fourteen. Dr John did not re-marry, and his sister-in-law, Karen-happuch Mason, joined the household at 38, Harmer Street, Gravesend – still a doctor's house in 1980 – and cared for the large family.

Dr John died in 1890 aged 85.

3. The Dawsons

My mother's other grandfather, William Edward Dawson, was born in 1802 and died in 1899, aged 97. Thus these two long-lived Victorians were contemporary.

The Dawsons were all farmers in Holt, Norfolk, until one son came to London and bought land in Plumstead which his son William Edward inherited in 1817, when he was 15. In 1827 he married his Norfolk first cousin Susanna and they had eight children. It was a Methodist family and Susanna was reputed to be psychic. There is a story told of her being unwilling to travel by train to Norfolk on a certain day, but going quite happily the next day. On arrival at Holt she and William learned that the day before there had been a train accident in which a number of people were killed. 'I knew it,' said Susanna.

William Edward left no written account of his life, but, since he became a well-known public figure, a distinguished citizen of Plumstead and owner of a successful pottery works, official records provided a great deal of information.

He was a Commissioner for the Queen's Taxes (1834), Highway Surveyor, Guardian of Lewisham and Woolwich Unions … He held public unpaid office for 40 years, and, on the spot where his pottery stood, there was at one time a Dawson Street. Like the Armstrongs, the Dawsons were staunch Methodists, and in 1862 William Edward gave £500 – far more than any other contributor – towards building Plumstead Common Methodist Church, bombed during the war and now known as Trinity Methodist Church.

William Edward also brought a successful action against The Queen's College, Oxford, who were the freeholders of Plumstead Common and were intending to sell large plots of this 'common land'. The case – 'Invasion of their rights, as tenants of the Manor' – went to Appeal, and the Provost and Scholars of The Queen's College were ordered to remove all fences and to pay the costs.

In 1864 William Edward's youngest son, my grandfather, Ebenezer Dawson, married Catharine Mason Armstrong, and my mother was their eldest child.

My mother learned from her mother's sister, who lived until 1927, that her own mother Catharine had not wanted to marry Ebenezer, a kind but rather stupid suitor 2 years younger than herself, but the pressures from the two Methodist families had been too much for her. And those first years of marriage must have been a shattering experience.

Catharine Amy, called Amy, was born in August 1865, 10 months after the marriage, followed by two little boys, who both died as infants. Finally Ellen Maude, (Nellie) arrived in January, 1869, and survived. Thus Catharine gave birth to four children in 3 years and 5 months. It is not surprising that fairly early in her unhappy married life she started to drink. My mother told us horrifying stories of her childhood – of being hit by her mother with her riding crop, of being asked by her father to 'look for the black bottle Mamma keeps hidden in her room', of the bread knife incident. She would never admit to having any happy memories of her childhood and had no loving thoughts of her mother.

William Edward had also bought land at Dulwich, where he had a second pottery. Gothic Lodge, Dulwich, where Amy and Nellie were born and lived with their parents, was on a hill adjoining the pottery works that Ebenezer managed for his father. Later the site was known as Dawson Hill, and now there is a huge block of flats there called Dawson Heights. At the local library no one knew why the flats had been named *Dawson* Heights ... 'Because they were built on Dawson Hill, I suppose ...'

Catharine died in January, 1877, aged 37, when Amy was 11 and Nellie 7. Her death was said to be caused by 'apoplexy'.

2

Childhood

Ebenezer re-married a year after Catharine died, in 1878, and his bride was 21, the second eldest of sixteen children of an impecunious widow, Mrs Sarah Ancell. Again, this girl, another Catherine, but known as Kate, was not in love with Ebenezer. She had wanted to marry a poor curate, but was persuaded to accept the young widower, ostensibly for the sake of his two motherless little girls, but also, I am sure, because it was a good match, and her widowed mother hoped that some of the well-to-do attributes of such a marriage would rub off on to other members of Kate's impoverished family, as indeed they did. Kate was deeply religious, and she finally agreed to the marriage as being 'her duty', but my mother remembered seeing the young girl on her wedding day, seated weeping at her dressing table. It must have been a tough assignment, from which she got little comfort, except through the conviction that she was obeying God's will.

Amy was, from all accounts, a dynamic and gifted child – articulate, intelligent and questioning. She also had an explosive temper which, later, her children experienced, although this may have developed owing to the frustration of her early life. In appearance she had straight brown hair, deepset grey eyes, high cheek bones, a lovely, creamy skin, a 'blobby' – as she called it – nose and a wide generous mouth.

Amy wrote of her young stepmother:

> She was 21, and I was 12, and we had no point of contact ... she thought me an undisciplined, self-confident child.

One of Amy's grandsons, who was born a few months after she died, and one of her great-grandsons, seem to have inherited many of her characteristics, and the one I know best, my own son, was an exhausting, albeit enchanting, child to 'bring up'. I therefore contemplate Amy's childhood and the difficulties of the adults who tried to cope with her with understanding and sympathetic concern for both. The normal questions asked by an intelligent child were never answered truthfully: she was put off with the Victorian camouflage, and her lively and enquiring mind must have been in a frustrated turmoil.

By the time she reached early middle age, Amy had become a first-class organiser. As a child she probably tried to organise and boss everyone in her immediate vicinity, which could not have endeared her to her family or teachers in 1877. Like other unusual children born into not very intelligent families, Amy could not help being awkward and troublesome.

Had she been a happy child, she would have been an attractive little girl, but a photograph taken when she was about 14 or 15 shows something of her inner distress in its turned-down mouth and suspicious, angry eyes.

Poor Kate, her unwilling young stepmother, who never had any children of her own, must have been driven to despair by such a child, who, after her chaotic early childhood, soon became unmanageable. Mrs Ancell, Kate's widowed mother, supported her large family by running a small boarding school, and to this 13-year-old Amy was soon sent. Her descriptions of this establishment were reminiscent of Jane Eyre's school – nasty and inadequate food, petty rules, a low standard of education instilled by unqualified teachers and, above all, Mrs Ancell, whom Amy hated.

It would take an unusually intelligent and sympathetic teacher even in these days, over a hundred years later, to cope with such a damaged child, and Mrs Ancell was certainly not that. Amy must have been a sore trial to her.

After a time her little sister Nellie joined her at this school and began to sleep-walk occasionally. Nellie was a pretty, gentle little girl, liked by her teachers, who were concerned about this habit. She became the centre of attention and everyone made a fuss of her, and Amy, although she loved Nellie and protected her, was yet jealous of her popularity and thought she was sleep-walking on purpose, in order to gain attention. She decided to put an end to such silly behaviour, so she placed a bath of cold water beside Nellie's bed, into which the child duly tumbled and awoke screaming ... and Amy was once more in disgrace. No wonder she said later that she was 'always in trouble'. However, Nellie never walked in her sleep again.

The only pleasant facet of Amy's boarding school existence was that she soon became popular with the other girls. She already had the gift of story-telling and used to keep her dormitory mates entranced night after night, as she invented tales of adventure for their delight. She also wrote verse, and a source of resentment against the authorities was that she was not allowed to have a paper and pencil to write down the lines as they came into her head. She was told to wait till the morning, by which time of course the verses were forgotten. One night, when she had one of those moments of inspiration, she pricked her arm and wrote the verses out in her blood, to the admiring awe of the other girls.

In 1880, aged 15 and after two years of misery, Amy left the 'horrible school' and went to an Anglo-German College in Camberwell where she learnt German and met a group of intelligent, hard-working girls, both German and English, with whom she had something in common. At last she had the chance to learn something of the world outside her own narrow circle. She also began to think about a country other than her own, and some of those German girls became her life-long friends. But she was not allowed to invite them to her home, because her stepmother did not approve of them – although only schoolgirls of 15 or 16, if Amy liked them, they were bound to be intelligent and thoughtful, and probably rebelling against the established order.

One source of comfort for Amy was her large concourse of first cousins – 32 Armstrongs and 24 Dawsons, 56 in all; and since Amy and Nellie were the only members of these two big families to be left without a mother while still young, they were probably made welcome in a number of homes, which may account for Amy's deep interest in and knowledge of her many relations. She left carefully documented genealogical tables of her own and her husband's families from which family trees going back hundreds of years have been correctly deduced.

One of her Dawson aunts had married a Cornishman, Tom Lowry, and lived in Camborne, where Amy stayed as a girl. And there she became great friends with her first cousin, Henry Dawson Lowry, who was 4 years younger. H.D. Lowry became quite a well-known minor poet, expressing a Cornishman's love of his county in many charming lyric poems, some of which were published in 1904 by Elkin Mathews in *The 100 Windows*. The cousins had much in common – their sense of alienation from their conventional families, their mutual aspirations to become writers ...

Amy left the Camberwell school aged nearly 17 and lived at home for a short time, but did not fit in. Her stepmother, Kate, still only 26, therefore decided to send her to a finishing school run by four spinster sisters, who guaranteed to turn her step-daughter into a 'young Lady' and a 'good woman'.

Amy did not mind going. Life with Ebenezer and Kate was dull and uncomfortable. Before his first wife died he had himself begun to drink too much, and the habit was increasing. His daughter was glad of any change, and, although the 'finishing school' was hardly a happy milieu, it at least widened her experience.

There were twenty girls there from well-to-do Victorian homes, whose main interest was 'what your father was and how many horses and servants he kept?' Her school mates talked mostly of the young men they had met – they were curious about sex and crudely instructed. Amy was totally ignorant of this subject and, although exceedingly interested, she was also alarmed and troubled. She decided she would not marry – and yet realised that all her aunts were happy women, with a deep affection for their husbands and children. Inexplicable!

She poured out her bewilderment in verse – her theme was Papa's behaviour at home – she had forgotten Mamma – and the sins of the universe rested on male shoulders. The subject was 'Hypatia', and she told the story of Hypatia's love for Orestes, but how her father, long since dead, interposed between them an old promise:

Your duty
Shall fill your life
Shall be your all until we meet again.
And with it linked a vague remembrance came
Of vows
That grave philosophy should take the place
Of Mother, Husband, Children in my life.

Her own wish to avoid marriage showed itself in the poem, the most ambitious she had yet attempted, her wish not to be troubled by sex, not to marry.

Through a friend of Papa's, 'Hypatia' was sent to Robert Browning, with a request for his criticism, and the following letter, in the poet's fine, sharp writing, was eventually received:

19, Warwick Crescent, W.
June 9. [1882-3?]

Dear Miss R .... I see a very considerable promise of ability in 'Hypatia'; there is proof of much 'in the bud' as one would say, which presumably may expand into a considerable flower. The inevitable want is of *originality* – whether of subject or of mode of treatment: nothing here but has been thought and similarly written about before: yet the quality is just what is required nowadays to give distinction to a poem, the mechanical part of poetry being a very ordinary acquisition at present. At the same time there is much aspiration and always a subject underlying the treatment, however conventional the latter may be.

I can only say – the poem may be a prelude to much – on condition that its author resolutely asks herself – 'Is what I am about to write a true and earnest feeling of mine? Is it already before the world in an adequate presentment? And – if the feeling is attributed to other men of other times – as in this case – 'Is the feeling true to the people, place and age I suppose it born among?'

The best advice is that old one – 'Look in thy heart and write'. No harm can come of keeping that in mind.

Yours very sincerely,
Robert Browning.

The letter came in a grey envelope, bearing a blue coat of arms, the crest of a lion rampant and the motto 'Virtute', and Amy was greatly encouraged.

3

Girlhood

Amy returned from the finishing school aged nearly 19 to find the pattern of her home life as boring as before. The one difference was that Papa was drinking heavily and secretly, unwillingly aided by his coachman, who bought the drink. The drinking bouts got worse, the doctor was called in, and, whereas Ebenezer had always had a comfortable income, now he owed the tradesmen money, the servants their wages, and he did not give Kate enough cash even for necessities. She was frightened of his drunken fits, he began to have attacks of delirium tremens, and Amy had to help nurse him, which revolted her.

At last the final crisis came. When Ebenezer was very ill and delirious, one of his creditors distrained on him and sent in a bailiff. There was no money in the house, and poor Kate was forced to take the next train to Plumstead to seek help from her formidable father-in-law, William Edward Dawson, now over 80.

And that was the end. William Edward and his eldest son George came, paid the bailiffs and the servants' wages and looked into Ebenezer's affairs. In the separate branch of the family business at Dulwich where he had worked, he had not been suspected, but George discovered that for months no bricks had been made, no business done, no books kept. The only papers were unpaid bills – there were no assets.

William Edward, together with George, considered the situation. The old man owned the ground on which Ebenezer's business stood, and with his consent Ebenezer had let some of it on building leases. William Edward laid down his terms:

Ebenezer should have the ground rents of these leases, which would bring in £400 a year, and this would be paid to his wife, but out of this he must gradually repay his father the amount of his debts. The old man would not allow him to disgrace the family by going bankrupt. And William Edward had assessed his daughter-in-law correctly – she could be relied on not to give her husband money for drink, would think it her duty to stay with him and 'reclaim him'.

And this she did. Ebenezer, who was then only 44, seems to have been psychologically damaged by his drinking, and perhaps by the long strain of his life since he first married over twenty years previously, and I do not think he ever worked again. He and Kate moved to a small house in Sutton, living in poverty compared to what they had enjoyed, but gradually the ground rents increased in value, so that not only was the family well-to-do when I knew them in about 1905 and living in a big house with servants, but when Ebenezer died in 1928, aged 88, he left a fair sum – in ground rents – to me and my two brothers, his grandchildren.

When Ebenezer's affairs had been dealt with by his father and brother, and the family had settled down to their new and greatly reduced financial situation, Amy found herself a job as secretary-companion to an elderly, blind Professor Jennings and his semi-invalid daughter, Louey: he had fallen in love with the young girl's clear speaking voice, and her main duty was to read to him daily. Years later she wrote an undated account of her life with the Jennings:

> They paid me what was considered very good wages for a woman – £200 a year. I read aloud to him for several hours a day for four years and took him for long walks. The old man considered my education unfinished and interested himself in teaching me Greek, Latin and logic. But he did more than that for me. He had a fairly good library, and he gave me the run of it. I read voraciously – every sort of book. Once, when reading Byron, I discovered that the volume I was reading, which was the last on the shelf, came to an end in the middle of a poem. 'That edition has been there for 30 years,' said the Professor, 'and you are the first person to discover that there is a volume missing. That one is in my room, locked up.' The missing part was, of course, from Don Juan.

Amy and Nellie still lived at home in Sutton and, during her years with Professor Jennings, approximately from 1884 or 5 to 1889, Amy's relationship with her parents must have become more and more difficult. She was outspoken and could not refrain from shocking their friends; and she refused to go regularly to church and sit through family prayers twice a day. In 1885, when she was 19½, she started a 'Confession Book', in beautiful copper-plate hand-writing, in which she invited her friends to answer a number of questions. In her own 'confession' some of the answers she wrote are interesting:

1. *Describe your ideal woman.* Tall, dark, resolute-looking; bright eyes,

curly hair; intellectual; unconventional; original; brave; truthful; deeply read; true to friends; a wise wife; a woman of pure and noble feelings.

2. *Her ideal man* was similar to her ideal woman – Dark, strong, firm, curly-haired, pure-minded and with high and noble ideas; intellectual, truthful.
3. *If not yourself, who would you be?* The Sappho of this age.
4. *What is your pet aversion?* Twaddle – no – inaccuracy.
6. *What can you do best?* The wrong thing in the wrong place – I'm rather celebrated for doing that.
7. *To what end do you exist?* To witness for the truth.

She was already interested in the feminist movement and, having learnt Greek, she described in an undated memo the fate of her first book:

It was an epic poem on Sappho, the greatest of lyric poets. When it was finished I went up to London to try and place it. Valiantly I walked into Smith, Elder, in those days the House for poetry, and was received by a fierce, grey-haired man, who refused even to consider the manuscript. Epic poems, he told me harshly, were a drug in the market, and he rudely dismissed me. Eventually I paid Kegan Paul all my savings – £64 – to publish it. It got a column of praise in the Morning Post [8.10.89], and I thought my reputation made. In less than a month there was a fire at my publisher's warehouse, and – the firm not being responsible for my uninsured book – the edition was lost. All my savings.

Her account of those exciting beginnings continued:

However, still obsessed by my interest in feminism, I was hopefully writing 'Idylls of Womanhood' – stories of different women's lives – in verse.
    The old gentleman for whom I worked had known I was writing a book, but had not supposed it would ever be published. When he found it brought me a certain amount of notice, he did not consider it was suitable for a female member of his household to attract public notice and said Goodbye to me.
    I did not mind, for I had learned from him as much as he had to teach, and I wanted to go on. I went to see the Society of Authors[1]; Walter Besant was there and was benevolence itself. 'Lyric poems, my dear young lady?' he asked (but they weren't). I was very small and slight, with a white skin and grey eyes. He knew that such a young and

[1] This was in the very early days of the Society of Authors, which was founded in 1884, with Walter Besant as Chairman.

little creature should be writing little sweet spring songs. 'Well,' he said, 'there *is* a young publisher I know who will read your manuscript.' And he gave me an introduction to William Heinemann.

4

London in the Nineties

Amy had a little money saved, and she had also begun to earn small sums by her pen, as the following cutting from the *Herald* (Sutton) dated 12.12.88 shows:

> *Charades for Home Acting.* The series of half a dozen home charades by Miss C.A. Dawson, of Rushton Lodge, Benhill St, Sutton, came at an opportune moment (Christmas). The dialogues are interesting and appear to have been skilfully planned. Published by Woodford Fawcett & Co., London at 6d.

Amy's poem 'Sappho' had been published in 1889, and at about this time she found a small flat in London, where she lived by herself – free at last.

She continued to earn modest sums by her writing – poems, short stories, articles – living, she said, mostly on bananas, which were very cheap. She also sent Walter Besant's introduction to William Heinemann, who invited her to call at his ofice, and her description of her visit to him is included in Fred White's book, *William Heinemann: a memoir*, published by Cape, 1928.

> I remember so well that interview with William Heinemann – I only 21[1] and he not so very much older. I was scared almost to tears at meeting a real live publisher, and he was stammering hurriedly. Because of propriety, I had taken a maiden aunt with me, and we went up all those marble stairs at 21, Bedford St with throbbing hearts ... he became one of my dearest friends ...

She also noted that:

> He had just secured Hall Caine as a client. I was the first poet that he published [*Idylls of Womanhood*, 1892], and Hall Caine the first novelist.

[1] Amy was in fact 24 or 25 when she first met Heinemann, in about 1890.

From the day that 'Sappho' was published, Victorian Amy became known as Sappho to her contemporaries and friends, and from now on I shall call her by that name.

Many people have been puzzled as to why my mother took the name of 'Sappho', adding 'She wasn't a Lesbian, was she?' I have now looked up what is known about Sappho, and I am no longer mystified. In her Confession Book, compiled in 1885, when she was 19, she answers the question 'If not yourself, who would you be?' with 'The Sappho of this age'. And if one looks at the description of Sappho in Lesbos around 600 BC, the reason why my mother, a lifelong feminist, admired her is quite clear. As in Sparta, so shocking to later Athenians, aristocrats like Sappho were fed as well as men, educated too, and with freedoms of which later Athenians did not dream. It was in Lesbos, too, that Sappho established her School for women, where, as in Sparta and Gortyn in Crete, women managed the home and property, had the right of ownership and inheritance ... and so on. Although she was married and had a daughter, there is no doubt Sappho loved women as well as men, but she was my mother's heroine because of her vital personality, her poetry and her establishment of Women's Rights 2,600 years ago.

A year or two after 'Sappho' was published, her sister Nellie joined her in London, whilst their parents, horrified, arranged for prayers to be said in the local church at Sutton for 'two young girls who had been led astray'. And yet the two girls seem to have led blameless lives, which they enjoyed immensely. They met people with whom they could talk and argue, they did not have to go to church; Nellie was musical and had a small but lovely voice; she began to train as a singer. And the sisters soon got involved in Movements – the beginnings of Women's Suffrage particularly. Mainly through William Heinemann, who invited her to his literary luncheons, Sappho was now part of the stimulating world of London in the nineties.

I am indebted to Holbrook Jackson's book, *The Eighteen Nineties*, written in 1913, for an insight into that world and thereby an understanding of Sappho's excitement at being an insignificant member of it. This repressed, frustrated girl, who yet had an inborn desire to express herself in writing, suddenly found she was actually meeting and talking to the Great Ones of the period, whilst at the same time acquiring real friends who were also writers – Violet Hunt, long before her love affair with Ford Madox Hueffer – and that lively, charming gossip, Netta Syrett, a contributor to *The Yellow Book*, forgotten now, but the author of very many novels and children's books, Annie Besant, Flora Annie Steel ... Edmund Gosse, Whistler.

In 1890, aged 25, Sappho was contemporary with or a little younger than many of the *fin de siècle* giants – H.G. Wells, Charles Condor, Lionel Johnson, Henry Harland, W.B. Yeats, Israel Zangwill ... Barrie, Dowson. And only a few years older than Sappho ... Francis Thompson, Cunninghame-Graham, G.B. Shaw and Oscar Wilde, the last two born in 1856. Since Sappho had had two books of verse published and was an attractive, widely read young woman of a rebellious and original turn of mind, she was made welcome at parties and literary gatherings everywhere. To her it was a wonderful world, of which she could hardly have dreamed during the years she was secretary to Professor Jennings, but which he had unknowingly helped her to achieve.

Sappho was a voracious reader: no new work by any of the writers of the day came out unnoticed, and when, a few years later, in about 1904, after her marriage, she travelled up from Cowes in the Isle of Wight to attend the Women Writers' Dinners, she quickly renewed old friendships, many of which lasted through to the days of the To-Morrow Club (1917) and the P.E.N. (1921).

The sisters had a wide circle of friends, both in London and their home suburb of Sutton, and my mother had one serious suitor, a young doctor from Northern Ireland. He had the superb names of Horatio (after Nelson) Francis Ninian Scott and was descended from the Scottish border clan of that name. His ancestors (Scotts) and Sappho's (Armstrongs) may well have combined to harry the English two or three hundred years previously, but his family had developed along quite different lines. Young Doctor Scott had been educated at Portora Royal School, Enniskillen, and at Trinity College, Dublin. One of his ancestors, Gideon Scott, Clerk in Holy Orders, read the prayers before William III before the Battle of the Boyne, and others included Sheriffs, Bishops, Generals and any number of Rectors.

Horace Scott, a quiet, conventional young man, had been brought up, together with his three older sisters, by maiden aunts and a redoubtable great-aunt in Northern Ireland. His father was in the Indian Medical Service, and his mother was sister to Dr William Steel, headmaster of Portora School. Surgeon-Major Scott's profession took him to Australia, New Zealand and India, and there were periods when these parents were parted from their four children for between three and five years. My father's older sister, Maud, once described to me the misery and distress of her mother, when she had to return to India, leaving her children, especially her only son, then aged 5, knowing she would not see them for four or five years.

As he grew up my father had only one ambition – to go into the regular army like his father and both his grandfathers. He and all his relatives, as true Ulstermen, believed in the superiority of the British.

Unhappily my father was short-sighted and therefore not accepted by the army. His only hope was to join via the R.A.M.C., so he became a doctor, but was again rejected. His mother had died in 1889, when he was 14, and his father had re-married a young woman the age of his daughters. Horace was probably disappointed and lonely, without any sense of direction, and he went to England and took a locum's job at Sutton. There, at a tennis club, he met Sappho, who was visiting her parents, and was immediately attracted by her cheerful optimism, her flow of talk, her exuberance.

In their mutual lack of parental care, Horace and Sappho had something in common, but in all else their experiences and background were totally different. He had willingly accepted his social status, whereas she had rebelled against hers. With her admiration for her grandfather, Dr John, Sappho thought a doctor's career far more interesting and worthwhile than being a soldier. She said so and for a long time she would not agree to marry him. After all, he was hardly her ideal man, as set down in her 'Confession', although he was not ill-looking – of medium height, slim, brown-haired and with fine sensitive hands; he was also intelligent and broad-minded, considering his upbringing.

Sappho was not averse to going about with him and visiting his relations, who did not approve of her at all. They, too, had never come across such an odd unconventional creature, who wore outlandish bright-coloured clothes and had the queerest ideas. They were also deeply shocked by her professed atheism and her extraordinary friends. Sappho did not like her suitor's string of names and decided to call him 'Scottie', and Scottie and Sappho they became to all save their relatives for the rest of their lives.

Having discovered that Scottie liked travelling, Sappho persuaded him to go round the world as a ship's doctor. His family was greatly relieved and, when 'Horace' returned from his voyage, his sisters were disappointed that Sappho 'quite unnecessarily' renewed the friendship. However, I am sure the two had corresponded, and she had missed his companionship ... and there was no one else. She was nearly 31 and she probably wanted to marry. Also, for some inexplicable reason she had lost her gift for writing and no longer had this outlet for her emotions. She had, in fact, had no book published since *The Idylls of Womanhood* in 1892. So she adjusted to the idea of children and home-making with this chap who loved her and needed her.

They had very little in common. He liked the country, sailing and boats, and a quiet life. She was unhappy and awkward in boats, could not swim and liked the social contacts of living in a town. Yet she relied on his commonsense and advice, admired him as a good diagnostician and kind doctor and enjoyed his companionship. They were married on 6 June 1896.

5

Marriage

When Sappho and Scottie married, he had just become a partner in the firm of doctors who attended the royal family. The senior physician was Sir Francis Laking, and the most junior was Scottie, who had an impeccable family background, as well as good professional qualifications.

In 1896, when Scottie was appointed, Queen Victoria was still on the throne, and her large family of grandchildren and great grandchildren often stayed at Buckingham Palace and sometimes needed a doctor's care. Scottie attended visiting royal children – such as the future Duke of Windsor and Princess Mary – and the Palace servants. He and Sappho took a tall narrow house at 2, Bennet Street, St James's, and each morning he walked down St James's Street and across the park in a frock coat and top hat, to see if anyone at the Palace needed his care. Sappho already had many friends, and as one of the Royal doctors living in St James's, Scottie soon had a number of distinguished patients from the social and theatrical world. They kept two or three servants, and Sappho was free to entertain and be entertained, which suited her. And there was the palace and all its visitors, and the consequent royal and political gossip, as well as tales of literary personalities. Soon after her marriage – probably in late 1896 or '97, she and Scottie dined with William Heinemann at his 'Westminster flat with the flying friezes', and Sappho wrote of that dinner:

> Whistler was there and the (Edmund) Gosses, the Pennells, Flora Annie Steel ... Whistler did the talking. He sat on a round stool in the middle of the room after dinner and, whenever Edmund Gosse would have chipped in with a story, he was remorselessly silenced by the Bigger Man! Very good for him, some of us thought. Later, W.H. said, 'That dinner was unusual in that I asked husband and wives together, I prefer them apart – each cramps the other's style.'

Sappho agreed with him and, thirty years later, introduced a rule into the P.E.N. Constitution to obviate this situation (see p.104).

On 17 August 1898, Sappho wrote to her sister:

> 8 p.m. Scottie has just been summoned to attend the Duchess of York [later Queen Mary] at Buckingham Palace, as the senior partner had flu. Scottie is really, for once in his life, quite roused up. It is rather amusing to think of the difference between the Sutton practice and this ...
>
> Later: Half a dozen people called this afternoon, and I couldn't get any information from Scottie till after tea. It appears the Duchess had a touch of colic, but wanted to get down to Balmoral to-night ... The Duke was there and they were both very friendly and kind. Scottie says she is a fine-looking woman, and he is very small and insignificant. They both seemed to be exceedingly nice to him and shook hands with him when he went ...

I had arrived in December 1898, when Sappho was 33, and my brother Christopher was born in March 1901. By the following year our parents were arranging to move to the country, as the strain of living in London and trying to be part of his wife's social life was becoming too much for Scottie. He was hard-working and conscientious, but was not very strong and did not take kindly to the social obligations of his position. He wanted a quiet life and a peaceful home where he could, when not looking after his patients, put on his slippers and relax by his own fireside, there to read one of those solid books in which he delighted – Gibbon's *Decline and Fall*, or Prescott's *Conquest of Mexico*. Scottie, I later discovered, suffered from moods and depression, and I imagine that some aspects of his life provided good cause for these, even though people who suffer from depression need no cause. He apparently drank too much sometimes, which shattered his wife, who, because of her childhood memories, was obsessively anti-alcohol. Neither I nor my brothers can remember ever seeing my father drunk, but I can believe that he had a weak constitution and could not carry his drink: a couple would make him a bit merry – cheer him up. He was also secretive, and could not express his feelings and his needs even to his wife – in fact he was a depressive, about which little was known then.

I was 3½ when we left 2, Bennet Street, and the only personalities I remember are my mother, as a vague, plump, cosy comforter, and 'Millsie' (Mrs Mills), the cook. The kitchen in this tall thin house was at the bottom of some dark narrow stairs which led to the basement from ground level, and Millsie lived there with a big black cat. Usually I was upstairs in those large unidentifiable rooms where my parents and my unremembered nurse lived. But sometimes I escaped, or

Nurse, bored with her own company, took me down to the bright warm welcome of the kitchen and Millsie – of whom I have a clearer memory than of any other adult in that period of my life – sitting by the brightly polished black and steel kitchen range, with the big black cat on her knee and the red hearthrug and the red glow from the fire. I suppose it is fixed in my memory because to go down the dark kitchen stairs was an exciting adventure and only happened occasionally.

During the second world war I went to look at 2, Bennet Street and found it had been bombed. All the floors and street wall had been blown out, or demolished later, just the back wall left standing, with scraps of wall paper still attached. I looked down 'below stairs'. The kitchen range of 1901 had gone, and there was a rusty modern grate in its place. But in front of that grate was the floor space where Millsie had sat with her cat forty years before ...

The death of the Queen brought an historical era to an end and with it the first half of Sappho's life. She and Scottie, with their two children, moved to West Cowes in the Isle of Wight in the summer of 1902.

6

Cowes

In June 1904 Walter, who was nicknamed Toby, was born and, in order not to shock Scottie's patients, Sappho unwillingly allowed him to be christened – in London this had not been a problem for Christopher and me. Our family was then complete, although years later Sappho told me she had had fourteen miscarriages, most of them very early ones.

We only remained in Cowes for seven years, but I have colourful and mainly happy memories of this time. Our house backed on to the river Medina, where many yachts were moored, and we had our own jetty and rowing boat. My mother, who could not swim or row – she was, in fact, very clumsy in boats – yet thought these were valuable accomplishments. So she arranged for a first class swimming instructor to teach me to swim – which I did at 4 – and my father taught me to handle a boat. She was also terrified of cows and bullocks – they were all bulls to her! But she saw to it that I, aged about 9, learned to milk cows when we first stayed at Trevose farm in Cornwall, so that I and my brothers grew up totally unafraid of horned creatures.

The Cowes shipyards were active, building destroyers, and it was exciting to watch the speed trials of the newly constructed ships streaking through the sea. They were painted a brilliant cerise before they got their final dark grey coat.

Except for Sappho it was a fairly commonplace Edwardian middle-class household. We had a nursery with tall barred windows and a high fire-guard, a night nursery and a small room for me which looked down on to the garden, the river and the boats. On the floor below were bedrooms and then down again to the dining room, drawing room – again looking on to the sea – and finally the narrow back stairs leading to the big, stone-flagged kitchen, scullery and passages at garden level, where there were rows of bells which would summon the maids upstairs when their services were required. Here the cook and the house-parlourmaid reigned, whilst our nurse lived at the top of the house. Since my father drove to visit his patients in a dog-cart, we also had a horse and a coachman.

In addition to the garden and jetty, there was another joy for us – the stables, complete with coachhouse, loose box for the mare, hay-loft above, and the delicious-smelling harness room, where Perkins the coachman might be found. Lastly there was 13-year-old Peach, the dispensary boy, who delivered the medicines my father made up and helped clean the stables or run errands for the cook.

Quite an expensive household to maintain.

Sappho was not a physically strong woman – she had a weak back and became easily tired, although mentally she was so vital and energetic. She always had breakfast in bed, and we would come down from the nursery after our own breakfast and be regaled with choice bits of bloater or bacon from her tray. About the house and garden, and even in our boat, she wore trailing tea-gowns made of warm-coloured soft materials, mostly velvet, and woe betide us if we trod on her 'tail' or train – a sharp slap soon taught us to be careful. Sometimes, when we called in on her on our way up to the nursery from the garden, she would play an exciting game. Lying on her sofa with one leg tucked under her – out of sight – she would say in an awe-inspiring voice, 'Be careful, or Mr Left Foot will *get* you', and there would be a slight movement in the folds of her dress, as she wiggled a toe. We would back away in delicious fear and then come nearer again. 'Look out – look out – He's coming – Mr Left Foot is nearly out', with more violent movement of the hidden left foot, as we dashed away. We never actually *saw* Mr Left Foot – he remained a wonderful mystery.

When Sappho went calling in her brougham, she 'dressed'. She was plump, and she put on a stiff, boned corset, a 'proper' dress, and pretty size 2 shoes on her small feet. When she came home, the first thing she did was to get out of those corsets with a sigh of relief and relax into a gown.

As she spent so much time lying down, if we were over-tired or not very well, she would stretch herself on her big brass double bed, and we would climb up beside her. With an arm round each, before Toby was old enough to demand his share of her, and our heads pillowed on her soft, ample bosom, breathing her delicious, cosy mother smell, we invariably slept and awoke refreshed.

My brother Christopher thinks of her as 'fat and dumpy', but says he felt sorry for other boys who had thin, skinny mothers. She herself wanted to lose weight – perhaps it was thought that her figure had something to do with her many miscarriages – and on one occasion she said to me happily, 'Your father is going to put me on a diet so that I shall get nice and thin.' To her surprise I burst into tears. 'But I don't *want* you to get thin like so-and-so's mother – it wouldn't be nice to cuddle up to a thin mother. How could we go to sleep against you?'

I need not have worried. She never did get thin.

Our nurses were untrained country girls, whom we called by their first names. Contrary to most Edwardian employers, Sappho approved of 'followers', because she thought that a girl who was 'walking out' and intending to get married would be content and make the nursery happy for us. So we had a comfy, cheerful Lily for a couple of years followed by an equally pleasant Annie, who both left to get married; we used to visit them with the new Annie or Lily.

I only remember one horrid crisis in the nursery. When Toby was about a year old, Sappho wanted to have a holiday with Scottie, so she engaged a highly recommended Lady Nurse to take charge of us, with a nursery maid to help. The Lady Nurse was a horror! She was unkind and punitive, and we were helpless, being about 6½ and 4, but luckily she slipped up: the baby became ill, our parents were recalled, and it did not need the dirty feeding bottle in the nursery to tell Scottie that Toby had gastro-enteritis.

There was a frightening yet delicious atmosphere, and from the landing at the top of the stairs we heard Sappho furiously giving Nurse the works. She left the same day.

Sappho was greatly upset and asked me about the woman and what she had done and I told her. Sappho was an emotional woman and had tears in her eyes which frightened me a little, as she asked, 'If I hadn't come back and found out, would you have told me, darling?' I said 'No', and added, 'We thought you would be on *her* side.'

Sappho's relationship with her children was close, physically warm and mentally fascinating, but also too dominating, although, as children, we did not realise this. To us she was the centre of life, in spite of inevitable battles. Sappho believed that a mother must never give in to her child, and that the child's wishes and will *must* be subordinate to her own.

So far as I was concerned, I could never bear to be 'out' with Sappho for long. I knew that, in any quarrel with her, I would have to apologise before we could be friends again and, as this was important to me, I would say I was sorry for whatever the incident was and would at once be forgiven. I said the necessary words without delay and without meaning them, and all was well.

My elder brother Christopher, however, was as stubborn as

Sappho, and often did not give in, which resulted in furious rows
between them and real trouble in adolescence. He has told me of the
satisfaction he felt when, as a schoolboy, he got the better of her.

As for Toby, who was a particularly charming little boy, he became
adept and rather devious at getting his own way and, although they
had furious rows, in which Sappho lost her temper and he gradually
learnt to control his, by teasing and laughing at her in a loving way, he
usually got round her.

Sappho's temper was sudden and fierce. There was one awful
occasion when I, aged 9, was playing about in the stables with Peach.
We were chasing each other and he finally shut himself in the mare's
loose box to escape me, but I got a jug of water from the yard tap and
threw it over him through the bars. I felt very frightened and ran into
the garden and started weeding in my plot, a job I usually disliked.
But I could not avoid Nemesis! A stern voice called me, 'Marjorie,
come here,' and when I reached my august parent, she upbraided me,
'How dare you throw water at Peach? He is a poor boy who hasn't
many clothes, and he is soaked and will have to go home, and his
mother will be cross with him – you naughty little girl' – and while she
spoke she slapped my face and cuffed me about the shoulders. I ran
upstairs crying and finally sobbed myself to sleep. Later Sappho came
and forgave me, took me downstairs to have tea with her, and she and
Scottie took me out in our rowing boat.

I came to understand my father too late: I am sure he did not agree
with some of his wife's attitudes towards us, and had probably
intervened on this occasion.

Since there were no suitable schools for us in Cowes, we had a daily
governess, whom Sappho instructed as to what she was to teach us.
We were not allowed to believe in the New Testament, but were told
that the Bible was a wonderful book about, among others, a
remarkable people called the Jews, a kind of history, and that the
Books of the New Testament were written down many years after the
events described in them had taken place and were certainly very
inaccurate. Jesus was a great Teacher, but he was not a 'Fairy Man',
nor was He the Son of God; one, all-seeing God did not exist. We
were, in fact, brought up as atheists. We were also taught something
of comparative religions.

Sappho herself taught us to read before we had a governess, as later
I taught my own three children. We also learned the dates of the
Kings and Queens of England from William the Conqueror. Before
lessons started each morning, we said these through to Sappho as far
as we had learned them, and every so often added another one – it was

rather like the game 'I packed my Saratoga Trunk' – it was a great day when I was able to say finally and triumphantly, 'and Edward VII, our King now, 1901.' I learned these by rote and enjoyed doing so, and in my schooldays I was able to fit them into history, which became my favourite subject. I have found it a very useful piece of knowledge which I have never fogotten. The next thing was tables – 5 minutes each day before lessons, with the same result.

In the winter evenings Sappho used to read to us from her sofa in the big drawing room – Kipling's *Jungle Books* and *Just So Stories*, Jack London's *White Fang* and *Call of the Wild*; Dickens, Scott, and, earlier, *Struwwelpeter*, and, of course, the brothers Grimm, Hans Andersen and Andrew Lang's fairy tales – while I sat on a stool and learned to sew. Sappho was no dressmaker, but she liked doing fine embroidery with coloured silks, and she taught me to 'sew a fine seam', to hem, using tiny stitches, do drawn thread work and embroidery, to darn and patch – all before I was 9. As a result of this acquired skill, my sons and grandsons either bring or send me their favourite jerseys – even from America – to *mend*!

Although my step-grandmother Kate Dawson, and my grandfather, Ebenezer, disapproved of my mother and her writing, her atheism, her friends, and her methods of bringing up her children, yet Sappho had such a deep interest in her relations that she kept in touch, and we knew our grandparents quite well and stayed with them from time to time, both with Sappho and, as we grew older, alone. They lived in a large house on Bromley Common, Kent, opposite, in those days, fields, and they had three acres of garden, with ducks and chickens and a croquet lawn.

I am glad I had the experience of being part of that typical Victorian-cum-Edwardian household, so totally different from that of my parents. The house had everything that has ever been written about such an establishment in the period between 1900 and 1914 – the four-poster bed and dressing room, the big 'spare' room with another four-poster, the wide staircase ascending from the hall decorated with antlered heads, the dining room with the three green-velvet-seated chairs near the door on which the servants sat at morning and evening prayers, the two-tiered mahogany stand for Grandma's Bible and other religious books from which she read prayers, the lovely warm wooden-seated W.C. with a willow-patterned china bowl. But best of all was the fascinating back staircase, narrow and uncarpeted, leading to the servants' bedrooms above and down to the kitchen. The maids, of course, only used the front stairs when they were cleaning them, which they did at 6.30 a.m. or when they brought hot water for washing to the bedrooms in brass cans.

I slept in a small room leading from Grandpa's dressing room. It had a flowery wallpaper and one framed tract: 'It is I, Be Not Afraid.' Later, at school, whenever I was in doubt about the personal pronoun and was tempted to write 'me', I remembered that tract.

Mostly we had good plain food, but on one terrible day Grandma announced that as a treat the dinner was Lark Pudding, i.e. a sort of steak and kidney pudding, but with larks in it too – *larks!* I looked at my plate with horror and revulsion – I couldn't eat a mouthful. And Grandma said, 'Eat it up, Marjorie, you will love it – there are oysters in it too.' This was too much. I burst into tears, and ran out of the room. Luckily Sappho was there, and, although she was fairly ruthless about making us eat whatever she considered good for us, on this occasion she was sympathetic, explained something to Grandma and brought a less detestable dinner up to me in my room.

After three or four years at Cowes Sappho became very bored. The one great joy she derived from living there was her ever increasing delight in the sea. She had lived all her life in towns except for brief visits to Camborne in Cornwall as a girl, but at Cowes she learned to love the sea in all its changing moods and colours. For the rest of her life she needed to spend some months in every year within sight of the sea – preferably in Cornwall.

But she had few friends, although she made spasmodic efforts to do the conventional things, driving in her brougham to pay calls and leaving the appropriate number of visiting cards. When her calls were returned, she usually managed to say something unexpected and vaguely shocking to the visiting ladies.

One of her Dawson cousins was married to a Colonel Baker and lived in Portsmouth for a few years after 1900, and occasionally Sappho went over from Cowes in the paddle steamer to visit this family. There were three daughters, the youngest of whom, Enid, was about 17 in 1904, and she remembered 'Cousin Amy's' visits for three good reasons. First because she and her older sisters were not allowed to remain in the drawing room for tea, as the visitor might tell unsuitable or risqué stories, secondly because none of their friends were ever asked to meet Cousin Amy, since one never knew what she would say next, and lastly because the sisters – fully grown-up as they were, were not allowed to read her books after her first novel was published in 1907. Nevertheless they heard laughter and gaiety coming from behind the closed drawing room door, as the cousins gossiped. Scottie used to go on sailing holidays with their father, a regular army colonel, and often one or other of the sisters went as crew – there was no danger of *Scottie* corrupting them! He was remembered as quiet, kind and '*nice*'.

Such visits, however, were only an occasional diversion and although they helped, as did her love of the sea, they were not enough.

Sappho had time on her hands.

And suddenly her creative gift, which had lain dormant for fourteen years, returned, and she had the urgent desire once more to write.

7

First Novels

In 1907 Heinemann published Sappho's first novel, *The Story of Anna Beames*, and, at the same time, she began to write poetry again. She was delighted when the *Nation* published one of her poems, the first she had had published for nearly twenty years.

Other poems appeared in *Chambers' Journal*, and these came out in book form in 1912 with the title *Beyond*. One describes the sea and garden at Cowes:

The Sea-Gate

Holpen by sweet neglect
The yellow clock has faded to a ghost
And clover thickens in the sward. A path
Wanders by fern and foxglove to the sea,
And near the fading lavender, the gloom
Of ilex branches o'er a wall
Ruddy and low, branches above the pale
And glimmering margent of the tide.

Beyond the garden close – the derricks swing,
The fell destroyer shaping in the slips –

But here an ancient chymist who distilled
Elixir from the breeze, and softly turns
The green of poplar into gold.

Unlatch the gate –
The water trembles on the weedy stair ...

The theme of Sappho's first novel was the hypocritical attitude of society, especially men – the heroine's brothers – towards a woman who had broken the rules, i.e. had a baby when unmarried, even although their own lives did not bear looking into! She had good reviews and was welcomed by the *Nation* as 'a new writer (male) of original power, showing the gifts of a born novelist'. The *Standard* wrote: 'A gloomy and impressive piece of realism alight with sincerity, deep feeling and passion.'

Once *Anna Beames* was published, Sappho began to hanker for contact with her old friends, especially other writers, and she used fairly frequently to go to London for a few days, mostly alone, but sometimes with Scottie. She described how she arrived at the plot for her second novel:

> One night Scottie and I were sleeping at the Brunswick Hotel in Jermyn St after a theatre, and I dreamed I saw the story of 'The Burden' enacted before me in 3 acts. I woke up and remembered it very clearly; thinking it a good story, I wondered what the name could be. I slept again and dreamed that its name was 'The Burden'.

The plot of *The Burden* was again unconventional, a story of understandable adultery, described with sympathy for all the characters; Sappho's relations were deeply shocked when these first two books were published, and friends dating from those far-off days in Sutton were also shocked. She was, however, encouraged by her friend, William Heinemann, who wrote:

> You have made big strides in the art of storytelling. Your characters are exceedingly vivid – I have few books on my list of which I feel more confident than this one.

Sappho had remained fond of Louey Jennings, daughter of the Professor Jennings whose secretary she had been in 1883, but Louey belonged to that very section of narrow-minded self-deceivers whom Sappho's books criticised, and she could not be expected to approve of or understand them. Louey Jennings was nearly blind and books were read to her, but, having gathered something of the contents from her readers, she stopped the readings and must have made her disapproval clear to Sappho. When the latter conceived the plot of a later novel, *Madcap Jane*, which she referred to as 'a bit of nonsense, Trivia', she wrote and outlined the story to Louey, who replied:

> I am so glad you are writing a book for the Young Person. All the nice people I know prefer a clean healthy book to the other sort ... the novels I read in my teens have influenced my whole life and still come back to my mind with fresh pleasure.

This really roused Sappho and, in October 1909, she sent Louey a long letter which expressed exactly what she thought at that time. It also shows for what the forerunners of Women's Lib were fighting nearly eighty years ago:

Dearest Louey. ... the artist is always a moralist and thinker. If you
have read the Commission on the Censor, you will have seen that
writers claim to lead in the world of ethics, to be bringing fresh light to
bear upon the great problems, to be advocating a higher morality than
at present exists. It is the artist who tries gradually to accustom people
to the possibilities of a better state of things. He has the great ideas, and
the little people resist, but, for all that, gradually follow, and his ideas
sink into their minds and thus become part of the national heritage ...
the artist is teaching great truths, and the little everyday people are
turning their backs on him, preferring the comfort of their mediocrity.

Now, I claim in my humble way to be a true artist: My time is spent
in trying to teach a high morality in as beautiful a manner as I can. And
that my friend of many years should ... condemn my books without
reading them, seems to me an incomprehensible injustice ... You take
for granted that the people you know are 'nice'. Also that the influence
of those books you read in your teens was a good one, but I am proud to
say that many girls read my books ... and (could be) influenced
towards a greater righteousness. Against your 'nice' people, you must
set the critics of the big daily papers, who have labelled those very
books as 'of an intense spirituality, wholesome, profound moral
purpose, the book deals with bitter things without bitterness, with
sordid things cleanly', ... At least the critics see what I am trying to do.

Now I have spoken out ... Will you not read my books and try to do
me justice?'

Sappho was an optimist and remained so to the end of her life, and
she got no change out of Miss Jennings:

It has been a grief to me that I could not sympathise with your books.
From the reviews you quote it is clear some minds may find them
helpful – to all whom I have met they have been repulsive and
disgusting both in subject and treatment ... The present state of morals
in Society does not look as if much good has been done by making
public all that in my mother's time and in my girlhood it was thought
immodest to discuss, except in private ... I believe that the novels and
plays of this class have done the same sort of harm in England as
Wagner's operas have to young girls in Germany ... I cannot read your
books for myself, and I cannot ask my young reader to read anything I
should be ashamed of her hearing ... Always your friend, L. Jennings.

'An impossible letter', Sappho commented.

Between 1907 and 1914 Sappho wrote six novels, one of which,
Madcap Jane, of which Miss Jennings so approved, was a great success,
being reprinted in a Nelson edition of 10,000 copies.

In 1918 Sappho learned that the cheap edition of *Madcap Jane* had
sold 33,000 copies and that there was a possibility of filming it! 'What
shocking taste,' said she.

When her third novel, *Treasure Trove*, appeared in 1909, she considered it so blameless that she wrote:

To my Aunts, Great Aunts, Aunts-in-law and Step-Aunts, this book is respectfully dedicated.

Punch printed some verses about this book.

> I fancy Mrs Dawson Scott
>   Was troubled by a sort of doubt,
> In writing 'Treasure Trove', of what
>   She really meant to write about;
> Was it to prove ill-gotten gains
>   Bring no good luck and fly apace,
> Or was it that ancestral strains
>   Keep reappearing in the race?
>
> She writes of both, and though the one
>   Provides the name, the finer part
> Expounds the other, and it's done
>   With not a little skill and art.
>   Which being so, it's understood
>   My point implied no kind of blame;
> The Story (Heinemann) is good,
>   And, after all, what's in a name?

8

Southall

From Cowes Sappho kept in touch with quite a few old friends, partly through her immense correspondence but also by attending the occasional Women Writers' Dinners.

There she met again Mrs Annie Besant, of whom she commented:

> She had lovely white hair, but did not look intelligent, or even human or kind. Very different from Flora Annie Steel.

She had met the latter previously at William Heinemann's and had much in common with her, in particular an interest in psychic matters. Mrs Steel belonged to the Psychical Research Society and was experimenting with automatic writing, and Sappho described her as the dearest and most human of old ladies. She was also excited to meet an even older writer – Madame Belloc, mother of Hilaire and Marie Belloc (Lowndes), who had been a friend of George Eliot.

She was introduced to Beatrice Harraden, author of *Ships that Pass in the Night* (which sold 1,000,000 copies), 'tiny, with untidy grey hair and a weatherbeaten face'. She met Evelyn Underhill, the Imagist poet, and her friendship with May Sinclair started at one of those dinners, although she unflatteringly described May as 'a wee dry old maiden'. They were almost the same age, and Sappho later spoke of May differently.

Sappho and William Heinemann liked each other and when she was in London he sometimes took her out to lunch. She found him a charming and interesting companion, writing that she always preferred the cultured Jew to the ordinary Englishman:

> He is so much more critical, artistic and informed. Mr Heinemann seems to know everything, from the greatest living art critic, to the best man to ask to try Nellie's voice. He is shorter than I am, with fine hands and feet, and opaque green dark eyes. He is evidently a strong, ruthless, cautious, kind, sympathetic, eager person. He told me, 'I agree with Menchnikoff's idea about death. I live every moment of my life, and

when the end comes I shall be tired and glad to go. I do not believe
there is anything more than this. I hope I shall never have time to write
my reminiscences. I have had a wonderful life, wonderful ... the years
with Whistler.'

James McNeill Whistler had become close friends with the young
publisher towards the end of the 1880s, referring to him as 'publisher
and friend'. And Heinemann published Whistler's famous book *The
Gentle Art of Making Enemies*. After his wife died Whistler lived with
Heinemann for two years.

Mr Cazenove, Sappho's literary agent, passed on a comment by
Heinemann:

It is a great pity that Amy Dawson (reverting to her unmarried name)
lives at Cowes. I know the place – behind the times and out of date,
with no clever people for her to sharpen her wits against. It is bad for
her and shows in her work.

He need not have been concerned. Already, towards the end of
1908, Sappho and Scottie were considering a move from Cowes. There
were no suitable schools there and, progressive and modern as they
were, for the period, they could see no alternative education for their
two boys than a boarding preparatory school, with public school to
follow. And travelling to and from the Island three times a year for
holidays was too complicated. I, also, was beginning to think that
school would be more fun than a governess. We finally moved in the
middle of 1909.

In spite of her dislike of Cowes and its inhabitants, Sappho had
managed to live a full and quite interesting life there, particularly
during the last three years, after she again began to write. She had
had three novels published and two more accepted; she had had
encouraging reviews and was in touch with many other writers.

She also found time to read the books of her contemporaries:

Fraternity [by John Galsworthy] is the most delicate and lovely work,
like tiny fire opals set in a network of silver wire – exquisite. *Tono Bungay*
[by H.G. Wells] is a big fat blazing jewel, but I have never seen such
delicate fineness yet glow as *Fraternity* has ...

Just read *Howard's End*, by Miss Forster.[1] I like it – the vein of
thought, the indeterminate people, the soothing lack of incident, the
dreamy way in which it is written. The people aren't real, but it doesn't

---

[1] Apparently reviewers regarded Forster as a woman, just as Sappho's books were
sometimes attributed to a man.

matter. What incidents there are wouldn't have happened, but it
doesn't matter. You see it through a haze, and it's like a city in a dream
– glamoured.

Scottie is *not* pleased with it: 'Another of these damned old maids
talking about things of which they know nothing.' And that's true, too.

Sappho's interests were wide and not only concerned with
literature. Her imagination could be fired by almost any tale of
unkind or unfair treatment of an individual. For example, she rushed
to the defence of Netta Syrett, whose last book had been adversely and
with vitriolic fervour reviewed by Andrew Lang. And Sappho
extracted an unwilling apology from that redoubtable reviewer.

She attacked the Haymarket Stores who, after thirty years, had
sacked an employee for no reason save that he was getting old (50)
and had 'never been very competent'. He was to receive no pension,
and the Chairman, when tackled, wrote that 'he had studied the
interests of the *shareholders* in sacking an incompetent clerk'. This
roused Sappho even more, and she returned her membership card and
also campaigned among those of her friends who were members of the
Haymarket Stores to resign similarly.

Alongside this vigorous mental activity was her poor physical
health. It is surprising how she managed to cope with all her interests
– but she spent hours every day lying on a sofa, and she never walked
anywhere except into and around the garden; the coachman or Scottie
drove her to the harbour to catch the paddle steamer to Portsmouth,
and thence the train to London and a cab to her sister Nellie's flat.

I have never understood precisely what Sappho's ill-health was
about. I know she had a weak back and could not stand for long
without getting a severe backache, hence the long periods lying on a
sofa. Yet in Cornwall she could walk, or rather wander, for quite long
distances on the turf of the cliffs. And in the years when she was
organising her various 'Ideas' – from 1914 till her death in 1934 – she
travelled a great deal, attending annual P.E.N. Congresses all over the
world and taking part in endless exhausting committees. At home she
rarely sat on an upright chair, but was usually curled up on a sofa or
sitting on the floor leaning against that sofa. Her weak back must have
been genuine, whatever the cause, because I and one of my brothers
inherited it – to a lesser degree. And her sister Nellie had the same
weakness so badly that she looked slightly hunchbacked.

I think Scottie and Sappho were reasonably happy in their
marriage during those years. She had grown very fond of him, and she
relied on his affection, commonsense and support. She refers to him
constantly in her journals and, although he may not have been a very

positive figure in *our* lives, he was certainly important to his wife. Without his loving and experienced care, she might well have collapsed into invalidism.

In July 1909 all the arrangements for our move from Cowes were completed, the practice sold and the decision taken to buy another in a working-class neighbourhood at Southall, Middlesex.

Southall was then quite a small town, although the small-roomed, four-storied semi-detached Victorian house which went with the practice was near Norwood Green, an open space on the edge of the town within cycling distance of the flat Middlesex countryside. Christopher would go to a boarding school and Toby, who was 5 when we moved, could go with me by train – ten minutes – to a girls' private day school at Ealing Broadway, where they took a few small boys. Scottie could visit his patients on a bicycle, and Sappho would once more be within reach of London.

Two days before we left Cowes, Sappho's literary agent arranged for Arthur Waugh, of Chapman and Hall, father of Alec and Evelyn, who was holidaying at Shanklin in the Isle of Wight, to visit Sappho, even though the kitchen table stood in the hall, and the glass was spread out in the drawing room waiting to be packed.

Mr Waugh had written that it would be a pleasure to think that his firm was to have a chance of getting Sappho's name on their list. He had reviewed her last two books in the *Daily Telegraph* without knowing they were by a woman and had been deeply impressed by both.

Arthur Waugh's visit was a success, Sappho always being delighted to make a new friend, especially a man. She described him as

a pleasant and urbane stranger, about my own age, short, dark – quite *sweet* – iron grey hair, a smooth face.

She acquired a new or alternative publisher, since Heinemann said she was writing too fast.

From Cowes we went on holiday to Cornwall, and then after a couple of months in rooms at Fleet, Hants, we joined Scottie in Southall in December, 1909.

Sappho wrote a postscript on Cowes:

We left Cowes to-day. I have been glad of the quiet time there; it has enabled me to write 4 novels and 2 plays and some poetry. Cowes itself seems to me a dying place, dying because of its enervating air, which encourages in its inhabitants a sort of grasping, inhospitable slackness. Its upper classes are mean, narrow and out-of-date, clinging to exploded ideas and ancient prejudices. They kow-tow to Princess

Henry of Battenberg [then living at Osborne House], a priest-ridden and vain woman who is unpopular, while her faithless husband is greatly liked.

9

Cornwall

There's never a wave upon western beaches
  Falls and fades to a wreath of foam,
But takes at the last a voice that reaches
  Over the distance and calls me home.

And you, who love me, if you would know me,
  Come away to the Western sea,
The land that did make shall take and show me
  Better than I have seemed to be.

H.D. Lowry.

Sappho's Cornish cousin Henry Dawson Lowry had died in 1906 at the age of 37, which was a great grief to her, and in 1907 I was very ill with diphtheria, but recovered and needed a change of air. Sappho decided to renew her acquaintance with Henry's beloved Cornwall, and she and my father took me to Tintagel for ten magical spring days. Tintagel was then a totally unspoiled village, with its tiny cottage post office, one hotel and single shop; also the fascinating unrestored ruin of King Arthur's Castle on the wild and lonely cliffs. Sappho's early love of Cornwall, which had begun when she stayed as a girl in Camborne, returned and the following April we had rooms at Trevone Bay, near Padstow, for the Easter holidays.

In March 1909 she wrote:

It is a curious thing ... but since Henry's death, I have got back my power of writing poetry and grown a great love of Cornwall. I have also the greatest desire to push his poetry to greater recognition. Since he went on, I have been to Cornwall 4 times ... I am also writing about Cornwall.

It is almost as if he had combined with me in my work and that my new love of his county was in some way due to him. I have lately been very conscious of this. I long for Cornish seas and air ...

She found Trevone a charming spot. It was not as wild as Tintagel, but was, she wrote, 'a coast in the making'.

She was dead right, and this coast has now been 'made over' to the thousands of visitors, cars, dogs and caravans that spend their holidays there every year.

Although Sappho could walk on the cliffs as she never could on pavements, her usual way of travelling any distance was to hire a jingle and pony trap,[1] and a boy to drive it, until we were old enough to take his place. She drove all over the area, up and down the steep hills and along the lanes to where they met the sea and became coves and bays. In this way she discovered Trevose Head, with its lighthouse, and Trevose Farm nestling at its back. The farm was rented by a tenant farmer, Alfred Biddick, and adjoining the farmhouse was a six-roomed cottage in which one of the farm workers, Jim Tippett, lived with his wife Alice and their three children. Sappho booked their rooms for the six or seven weeks of the summer holidays: a long spell in Cornwall would give her a respite before the upheaval of the move to the new practice.

On 29 July 1909 we came to Trevose Cottage, which Sappho described:

> The cottage, part of the old farmhouse, is thick-walled with beamed ceilings and little 16-paned windows, and it has slate-flagged floors. The sea is there on either side of us – Mother Ivey and Harlyn Bays to the right and Booby's and Constantine Bays to the left. It is very beautiful and very lonely. I think perhaps we have at last found, amongst these good and honest people on this lovely headland, with its blunt nose thrust out to the West – The Ideal Spot.

We had, and our long love-affair with Cornwall began that year. Sappho knew it was in this wild and isolated land that she wanted to be and where she wanted her children to spend their holidays. From that time until the end of her life 25 years later she spent several months in each year near Trevose.

Those holidays in Cornwall when we were children were extremely happy. Short-tempered as she was, Sappho was always an interesting companion, and she told us wonderful stories and historical tales ... and boxed our ears on occasion. She found flint arrowheads in the rabbit diggings on the cliffs and told us about Early Man and the story of ruined Constantine Church, of the 'fougou' at Porthcothan (pronounced 'vugger'), of the remains of prehistoric dwellings at Tregudda – the homes of the Little People who lived there hundreds of

---

[1] A small square two-wheeled trap – open – used in Cornwall at that time.

years ago, and some of whose graves are in the prehistoric burial
ground at Harlyn.[2]

> Rhythms of lonely Constantine – the arc
> Of the wide bay, the billowy dunes, the long
> Atlantic roll.
>
> To look on the translucent green, the blue
> Deepening to purple where the weed is dense!
> To hear the homing call as the brave sweep
> Of wings is folded on a sea-girt rock!
> To lie in golden warmth, while tow'ring waves
> Break with a lazy roar along the beach –
> To lie and dream.
>
> A perfect dream! That I
> Might sleep for ever by the ruined church
> Whose threshold is the sacrificial stone
> Of a forgotten people, if such dream –
> Were mine.[3]

Sappho wore her tea-gowns even on her cliff wanderings, and
walked barefoot – so did we, and when during the 1914 war we had a
cottage of our own, we often slept out under the night sky. No tents for
us – 'stuffy places', said Sappho, and she did not believe that damp
sea mist was harmful. It often rained, but only when our pillows were
soaked, and cold wet pools collected under our shoulder blades did we
drag our bedding indoors.

The Tippetts and their three children lived during the summer in
their kitchen and one bedroom. We had the other four rooms, and
Mrs Tippett 'did' for us. She was a wonderful country cook and made
her own bread and 'splits' and yeast buns ... We had 'Cornish Roast'
– rabbit baked in a roasting tin with onion and bacon and covered
with potatoes – and pasties, hogs pudding and Cornish cream from
the farm at 3½d a quarter of a pound, butter at 9d a pound and eggs 13
a shilling.

Rabbits were mostly caught in 'gins' – horribly cruel traps – and
sometimes, as we got older and became aware of what was going on, if
we heard a trapped rabbit screaming at night, we would go and look
for it and either kill it quickly or let it go. Sappho, of course, pointed
out that rabbits formed part of the livelihood of the country people! I

[2] Now housed at Truro Museum.
[3] From *Beyond*, published by C.J. Glaisher in 1912.

am thankful the gins were outlawed, but then came myxomatosis, which was quite horrible – worse than the gins, I think. I cannot now bring myself to eat rabbit – but Cornish Roast really was delicious.

In 1909 we had all those lovely coves and cliffs around Trevose to ourselves. Every now and then another family would invade our favourite spots, and we would regard them with suspicion and dislike – there was no question of making friends in order to have other children to play with. This was *our* territory, and we had our own ploys and occupations and needed no alien children impinging on our world.

One of our especially favourite haunts was the area of uncultivated land behind Constantine dunes, which stretched east to the lane leading to the road to the lighthouse. There was not then a golf course, but there were patches of marshy ground where king-cups and many varieties of mint grew and masses of other wild flowers – yellow iris, viper's bugloss, blue flax and so many more that I have forgotten, as well as all the commoner varieties that still cling to the cliff tops – sea thrift in all shades of pink, ladies' fingers in yellow and orange-red masses, kidney vetch, bladder campion, the blue scyllas and blue and white violets. And the birds – larks, cuckoos, buzzards, yellow-hammers, cliff-chaffs – and butterflies! Sappho never came with us, which was a blessing, and she did not worry overmuch as to where we went or how we passed the days, although, if she had actually seen the cliffs we climbed and the caves we explored, she might have been more concerned. As it was we 'stravaged'[4] over the countryside as the mood took us and climbed the cliffs when 'we'd a mind to'.

All this was an accepted joy of our childhood, before the arrival of the golf course.

I am not a golfer, so I may be forgiven for my nostalgic longing for those pre-golf years. I know, of course, that instead of the golf course, we might easily have had houses and hotels, so in one sense I am grateful, if only some corners could have been left as habitats for the birds, butterflies and flowers. Don't golfers care about these things too?

Alice Tippett, in whose cottage we stayed, was a handsome, intelligent, hard-working and thrifty woman, though minimally educated. In 1910 the family lived on Jim's wages of 11s to 15s a week, and she saved anything extra she made by taking in washing, 'doing' for summer visitors and even by working in the fields for 9d a day. Encouraged by Sappho, she bought a piece of land above Constantine Bay and built herself a house with 7 bedrooms – but no bathroom, of

[4] Stravage is an Irish word meaning 'to wander without any exact aim'.

course, and an outside earth closet. Mrs Tippett could thus 'take in' two families, for whom she cooked separate meals, as well as feeding her own family. In 1913 we stayed there instead of at Trevose Cottage.

The pattern of life in Cornwall began to change even before the 1914 war. More families were coming to the area, but basically, the old magic was still there – no golf course yet, or golfers: freedom to roam everywhere barefoot, and as there were not many cars, cycling was safe along the dusty roads and was a delightful, venturesome and independent mode of transport.

10

The Women Writers' Dinners

In our new and rather unattractive house in Southall we had only one
servant, and no car to replace the horse and carriage we had at Cowes
– a very different life from the rather lavish establishments at 2,
Bennet Street, St James's and at Cowes. Scottie was very
unbusinesslike, and money slipped through his fingers: we were
clearly much less affluent, and there were now school fees to pay.
Sappho knew that he had had a private income when they married,
but not how much, and since she was in the dark as to the family
resources, she was probably extravagant: we seemed to go away to
Margate or to Cornwall – staying in lodgings – rather often, and this
must have been expensive. From that time on we were always hard
up.

After moving to Southall, school dominated my life. The uniform
was navy blue, with white blouses, but Sappho, whose sense of colour
was unusual, almost bizarre on occasion, was convinced that dark
blue did not suit me. She had found a 'little' dressmaker who made me
a coat and skirt of dark green heather mixture tweed, with a large flat
Tam o'Shanter of the same material, which was attached to the back
of my head with elastic and was decorated with a long red feather. I
was a new and inexperienced pupil at this fairly big school in January
1910, and I need not describe the agonies I went through at being the
only child not wearing uniform, and, even worse, appearing in such
peculiar clothes. Luckily I only had to endure this for one term, because
I grew taller and thankfully transferred into navy blue the following
winter.

There were other terrible moments engendered by my female
parent. She had found a 'little' shoemaker in Cornwall – a 'real
craftsman', who made excellent shoes very cheaply, but used near
yellow leather. Sappho had shoes made for me and, whilst all the other
girls wore black or dark brown, only *I* had bright yellow footgear!
This was such a horror for me that I used to arrange to arrive at school
two minutes before the bell for Assembly went, when the cloakrooms

were empty, change my shoes hurriedly and scurry into the hall just in time to be marked 'present'. But I could rarely overcome the problem of the morning 'break', when we were obliged to change back into outdoor shoes and walk or play in the garden: we were forbidden to remain in the cloakroom except on wet days. I prayed for rain, stayed as long as I dared in the lavatory and never told a soul of my misery.

Once settled at Southall, Sappho took up the threads of her writing and all that that entailed with renewed vigour.

Edward Garnett, who was at that time a reader for Duckworth's, had reviewed her books favourably, and Sappho and Scottie were invited to a lunch to meet him.

Jan. 10th, 1910. To-day it really happened – the gods materialised and my critic talked to me of Art. When we walked in, a tall grey figure rose from a chair and greeted us. He was altogether grey: wavy grey hair above a strongly-featured grey face above a long grey coat ... He is a slow speaker, a dreamer, but warms as time passes and can interject a humorous phrase. He says Wells is no artist, but a sociologist who embodies his theories in novels: and he pointed out that the suffragist part of Ann Veronica was just thrown in and not in keeping with A.V.'s character ...

Sappho's next novel, *Mrs Noakes, an Ordinary Woman*, was published in 1911, and she wrote of her heroine:

Poor Mrs Noakes died to-day. I, at her bedside, wept, and now she has gone to be typed. At the beginning of a novel, it seems such an enormous undertaking, and then, when it's all over, the long strain, you lean back restfully in your chair – 'Another little bit of work done! ... yes, and why? Why did I do it? Why am I so satisfied to have done it?'

In March 1912 she began to write a novel, *Ulalia*, a tragedy set in Elizabethan times, which she finished in July and sent to Heinemann. But now Sappho had a severe setback, as Heinemann did not want to publish it, and John Murray suggested she should alter the 'true' end of *Ulalia* and make it happy. 'The impertinence of these purveyors of literature,' wrote Sappho wrathfully. She was puzzled and hurt that no publisher seemed able to recognise the worth of what she considered by far her best book, even although it was recommended by Edward Garnett, her staunch admirer. He thought it quite admirable, 'the story held me throughout', and he suggested that the publisher, 'whoever he is', should plan to put a cheap edition on the market as soon as possible. But even after reading Garnett's comments, Heinemann still objected that the period was too remote, the diction too archaic ... *Ulalia* was never published.

1911 and 1912 were difficult years for the family, and Sappho was unusually depressed. She referred in her journal to the poet Francis Thompson, who spent his last few pence buying matches to sell at a profit ... 'it embitters the artist to read of such things', and she again wrote of

> My poor *Ulalia*. I have been suffering all this year because publisher after publisher has refused her. They [the publishers] are full of the spirit of commercialism – even William Heinemann, who once could see, says 'So tragic is the book, it would never find readers.'

She wrote of herself as growing slowly soured, disappointed, embittered.

And perhaps she was feeling particularly miserable and depressed when she went to some family gathering about then and met a Dawson Aunt who was a great bore and unfortunately talked at length about her son's ordination. And, wrote Sappho, '*This* disagreeable pig presently said, "I can't abide parsons." '

In October 1912, after three years of hard work, pulling strings and surmounting unforeseen difficulties, her own collected poems, *Beyond*, and H.D. Lowry's posthumous poems *A Dream of Daffodils*, were published. To buy his manuscript from the legatee and get the book out cost £46: and she had herself earned £41: she wondered why she had done it – 'Just another book on the Family Shelf.' In 1927 she found time to complete Henry's novel, *Wheal Darkness*,

> in order that so careful a picture of conditions in a Cornish mining district and of Methodism a quarter of a century ago, should not be lost.

Sappho's disappointment over *Ulalia* was only one of the troubles that beset the family during 1911-12. We had a succession of childish illnesses, starting with whooping cough, which Sappho caught; and while she and my brothers were recuperating in Margate, she got pneumonia and was whisked into a nursing home at great expense. But the worst thing was when Toby, aged 6, had an appendix operation and was found to have mysenteric glands, i.e. T.B. He had to stay for six months in an open-air nursing home – again in Margate – and was the cause of great anxiety, although finally he made a good recovery. His illness was very expensive and, to add to the gloom, our cook-general, a widow with three children, whom Sappho had taken as a kindness and had trusted with money to pay the weekly housekeeping books, was found *not* to have paid them, having spent the money on drink instead!

We have had to cut down on everything, and yet overdraw £150. Truly a terrible and saddening year.

Being in such financial trouble, Sappho cast around for ways of adding to the family income. Through Ward Muir, a journalist friend, she sold two short stories to the *Pall Mall Magazine* and, as she had no more stories in hand, wrote to the editor asking him to give her an idea how many stories he could anticipate accepting, since she was really a novelist. The Editor replied:

There is a very great demand for short stories, and I think you would find it paid you to cater for it fairly continuously. I venture to make a few suggestions: The stories should preferably have a strong love interest, and the scenes should be laid in the British Isles or, if abroad, the characters should be English. You should keep clear of all reference to religion, the more serious sort of sex questions, drunkenness and politics. The stories should of course all have a happy ending and be entirely wholesome throughout. Very little space should be wasted on local colour.

She could not carry out these kindly suggestions.

That summer of 1912, instead of going to Cornwall, we stayed at an old Mill House at Hasborough in Norfolk, because the bracing East Anglian air was thought to be good for Toby. Sappho had an Indian friend who had married an Englishwoman and had four very attractive children. The marriage had ended, and the children were at a loose end, so they came to Norfolk with us. She wrote:

My three children are like rocks which, without the introduction of some softer material, grind each other to pieces; the Ali children are of softer material, and the amalgamation produces pleasant results!

I don't suppose it occurred to her that she herself was part of the grinding process.

W.W. Jacobs and his wife and five children were also staying in Norfolk, quite near us, and the two families often joined forces. Mrs Jacobs was a very pretty woman, and the eldest daughter, Barbara, who later married Alec Waugh, was quite lovely. Sappho found W.W. a pleasant companion – 'a sensitive man who talked like he wrote, but his views were entirely old-fashioned – a neat, colourless man.'

Despite the anxieties of those two years, Sappho also noted down the problems of the period and her thoughts concerning them. In the forefront was the continuing battle for Women's Suffrage, and on 8 March 1912 she wrote:

Vivid and exciting accounts of the Suffragettes. Splendid organisation of the leaders. Each person told exactly which window to be broken, the minute of action. Scotland Yard Authorities at their wits end how to cope. Sending them to prison is no good, as Mrs Pankhurst at once proclaimed a hunger strike. Mrs W.W. Jacobs sentenced to a month with hard labour to-day, and her husband actually had the bad taste to stand up and say he 'was bitterly opposed to the Movement'. Museums and other public buildings closed for fear of the Suffs, who, however, would naturally not harm the Nation's treasures. London is full of humour, and everyone is lost in wonder at the pluck of the women.

11

The Bank House and Ulster

In April 1913 we moved to The Bank House, 6, King Street, Southall, which had bigger rooms and was more convenient, although situated between shops in the High Street. The Bank had moved to other premises, so the former bank offices made good consulting and waiting rooms for Scottie, and there was living accommodation above. We were only there until the war started in 1914, but the year was significant for me because I became aware that sometimes my parents were at odds with each other, and I minded this dreadfully. In the evenings Sappho usually sat on the floor of the sitting room, leaning against Scottie's knees, as he sat in an armchair; she would read or sew, and there would be occasional friendly comments between them. My brothers being by then both at boarding school, I was the only child at home, and I would sometimes leave my homework and come into the room with some query or bit of school gossip, and be welcomed. But on other evenings Sappho sat in the armchair *opposite* Scottie, and had a cross, unspeaking look, and I would feel unable to chatter and talk. And when I was in bed I would say to myself, 'I know there isn't a God, but if by chance there is One, *please* make Mother and Daddie all right together again and please don't let me have appendicitis!' (I had been very frightened when Toby had had his operation and had then been ill for so long.) I had no idea what was wrong between my parents, but I was deeply apprehensive. Later I came to know that there were two factors which may have accounted for this situation. Sappho suggested that it was usually because Scottie had been drinking too much for her peace of mind, and they quarrelled about that. The other factor, which I only learned about three or four years later during the war, was that at about that time my father had met in Southall a young working class woman who was unhappy in her marriage and who fell in love with him, and with whom he felt comfortable and at ease. She was a patient, and I only saw her once, at his funeral. Sappho was unaware of this affair in 1913, but the fact that it existed probably produced tensions.

49

One very exciting incident in the autumn of 1913 was the discovery of some mysterious parcels hidden in Scottie's dispensary.

He was an Ulsterman, and his ancestors in Northern Ireland had been as prolific as the Dawsons and Armstrongs were in England – great grandfather Scott had had twelve children, so my father had very many cousins, all staunch loyalists and mostly known to each other.

In November, 1913, Sappho wrote:

All the North of Ireland is arming and drilling – .303 rifles – to resist Home Rule.

and she listed a number of Scotts, Lyles and Steeles involved, adding:

They are all cousins except Canon Walter Scott, who is an uncle. The enthusiasm is great.

And she pasted into her journal this newspaper cutting:

The Ulster Crisis
Armed support from Great Britain

The Committee of the British League for the support of Ulster and the Union, of which Lord Willoughby de Broke is chairman, entertained at luncheon at the Hotel Cecil on Saturday over 150 honorary agents of the League from all parts of the Kingdom. The proceedings were private. Matters of organisation were discussed, as also the course of action which has been finally decided upon in order to assist the Loyalists of Ulster in the last extremity. Up to the present between 8 and 9 thousand men have been enrolled in England, Scotland and Wales, and more are enlisting daily. The following resolution was sent to Mr Bonar Law:

We, the Central Committee, and 150 agents for the British League for the support of Ulster and the Union, desire to inform the leaders of the Unionist Party that we are engaged in enrolling a large force of volunteers from England, Scotland and Wales to assist the Ulster Loyalists, and intend to proceed with this force to Ireland, to reinforce the ranks of the Ulstermen in the event of the Government employing the Army and the Navy to compel their submission, without consulting the constituencies at a General Election.

'Scottie,' wrote his wife, 'was one of the 150 at this luncheon party on 8 November. He is the Southall agent for the British League.'

It must have been about then that we found the arms. We occasionally invaded Scottie's dispensary when he was out and played

William Edward Dawson,
1802-1899

Dr John Armstrong,
1805-1890

Amy Dawson aged about 14

Amy Dawson aged about 25

Sappho in 1901 aged 36

Sappho in 1910 aged 45, with the
author aged 11

Scottie in R.A.M.C. uniform, 1914

Charlotte Mew in about 1923

May Sinclair and her cat,
Tommy

Selma Lagerlöf, the first woman to be
awarded the Nobel Prize for
Literature, 1909

Anatole France, founder and
President of the French P.E.N.
Centre

Joseph Conrad

The young Rebecca West, photographed by Hoppé: 'The head dress has a funny history. At that time I was overworked ... and entered the [P.E.N.] dinner on the wrong page of my diary. I settled in for a quiet evening and washed my hair, and suddenly someone rang up and I realised what I had done. A painter had been to see me two days before with a head dress that had been worn by an Irish actress he had been painting, and he had left it in the hall. I put it on over my damp straight hair and went forth to the dinner. Hoppé thought it was lovely ... Hence the photograph.

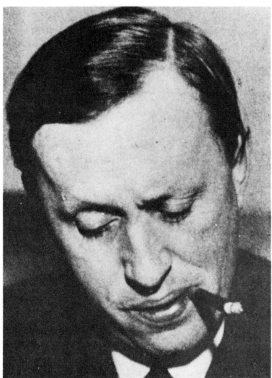

Karel Čapek

Ernst Toller

Stacy Aumonier

Ezra Pound

:: *The Pen Club.* ::

Menu.

Hors-d'Œuvre Variés

—

Petite Marmite à la Française

—

Turbot Mornay

—

Médaillon de Bœuf Bordelaise
Pommes Savoyarde
Haricots Verts au Beurre

—

Grouse Rôtie
Pommes Chips   Bread Sauce
Salade

—

Bombe Pralinée
Friandises

—

Café Double

October 5th, 1921

Menu for the first P.E.N. club dinner at the Florence Restaurant, Soho, October 5th 1921

John Galsworthy with some of the international writers present at the first P.E.N. Congress, London 1923. From left to right: Charles de Bos (France), Gregorio Marañon (Spain), Edwin Arlington Robinson (U.S.A.), J.G., Tor Hedberg (Sweden), unknown, Axel Brunius (Sweden)

The First P.E.N. Congress, London 1923

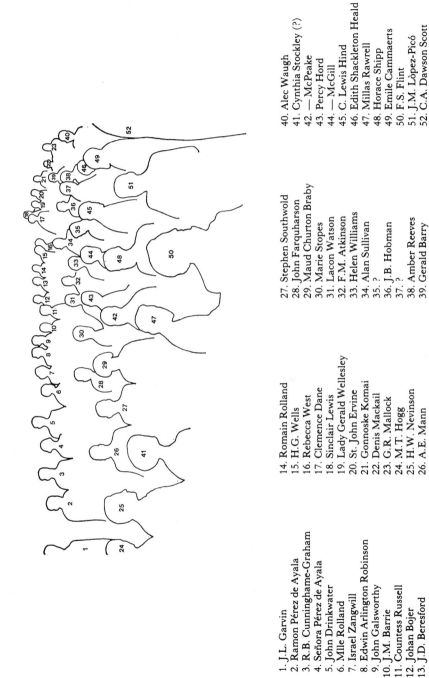

1. J.L. Garvin
2. Ramon Pérez de Ayala
3. R.B. Cunninghame-Graham
4. Señora Pérez de Ayala
5. John Drinkwater
6. Mlle Rolland
7. Israel Zangwill
8. Edwin Arlington Robinson
9. John Galsworthy
10. J.M. Barrie
11. Countess Russell
12. Johan Bojer
13. J.D. Beresford

14. Romain Rolland
15. H.G. Wells
16. Rebecca West
17. Clemence Dane
18. Sinclair Lewis
19. Lady Gerald Wellesley
20. St. John Ervine
21. Gonnoske Komai
22. Denis Mackail
23. G.R. Mallock
24. M.T. Hogg
25. H.W. Nevinson
26. A.E. Mann

27. Stephen Southwold
28. John Farquharson
29. Maud Churton Braby
30. Marie Stopes
31. Lacon Watson
32. F.M. Atkinson
33. Helen Williams
34. Alan Sullivan
35. ?
36. J.B. Hobman
37. ?
38. Amber Reeves
39. Gerald Barry

40. Alec Waugh
41. Cynthia Stockley (?)
42. — McPeake
43. Percy Hord
44. — McGill
45. C. Lewis Hind
46. Edith Shackleton Heald
47. Millas Rawrell
48. Horace Shipp
49. Emile Cammaerts
50. F.S. Flint
51. J.M. López-Picó
52. C.A. Dawson Scott

Henry Nevinson

H.G. Wells and members of the Bombay P.E.N. Centre

John Galsworthy, Sappho and Hermon Ould at the Polish Congress in 1930

Sappho at Levorna in about 1932

Sappho and Colonel Arthur Lynch in
about 1933

with his tiny scales and anything else lying about, and one day we looked in a low, floor-level cupboard and found a number of heavy parcels. We opened one and found – bayonets! We were excited and astonished, but Sappho must have explained their purpose satisfactorily and, presumably, told us to keep quiet. She clearly knew all about it, because in writing about my birthday party the following month – December 1913 – she said:

> During the tea-party Scottie's gun and bayonet for the Ulster trouble arrived, which was a little damping.

As it was only one gun, I imagine this was for his personal use, should he be called upon to be 'part of the armed support'.

In March 1914 she wrote:

> I went to Euston to see Scottie, laden with cartridges, off to Ireland. He had been busy for some time buying them and sending them over, and he is going to Portoferry to learn drilling and see how he can be useful to the Ulstermen. He said later that there was no customs examination: he could have hung the cartridges on his nose and walked out of the station.

It was not a very successful expedition, as Scottie, never strong, and then aged 49, caught a cold, insisted on drilling with the company, got worse and returned with a temperature of 104. Sappho nursed him for a few days nd then packed him off to Cornwall for the Easter holidays.

And Sappho? She probably did not want to interfere with something that was of such passionate interest to her husband, and she had many interests of her own. One of her cousins was a talented painter whose work was being shown at the Paris Salon, and during 1913 Kathie (Dawson) Giles began to paint a portrait of Sappho.

My mother had no appreciation of pictures, but she considered this painting of herself, by one of her favourite and most gifted Dawson cousins, thoughtfully and decided that she liked it. She could see that it was a beautiful picture, although she was not sure if it was like her. But the background was a rich blue-green and on a wall it seemed to glow. It had the colour which she lacked in her life and which was one reason why she so loved Cornwall ...

> Cornish seas, their blue, their dark green and purple, their peacock, their pale emerald laced with foam, the white flicker at the edge of the grey rock islets, and their flame sunsets.

The portrait was hung at the Women's International Art Club show in February 1914 and now hangs in the office of English P.E.N.

12

Charlotte Mew and May Sinclair

Sappho took her writing very seriously, but was usually willing to accept criticism from those whom she considered qualified to judge. She was also resilient and, after being depressed by a bad review or a rebuff such as she suffered over *Ulalia*, she would fairly soon regain her equanimity and cheerful optimism and start planning another novel or a poem or a gathering of friends.

Friends were important to her. She had many good women friends but she also greatly enjoyed masculine society. Except for the Women Writers' Dinners, she did not like organisations restricted to female membership and at her house one was sure to find more men than women at her tea-parties. People of both sexes were attracted to her and usually wanted to meet her again. She was invited to many parties and was always the centre of an animated group – talking, arguing, throwing in the outrageous conversational bomb – she could not be ignored.

I was 13 in 1912, and was now of an age to accompany Sappho on visits to her friends, to remember the people who came to the house and to have opinions about them, not always complimentary.

In the early summer of 1913, we had a house-warming party in the new house at Southall with its bigger rooms, to which thirty people, mainly writers, came down from London. Sappho had a new dress, and I thought she looked wonderful. It was black velvet, close fitting as to the bodice, but long and with a short train which swept the ground at the back. It was cut low, with no sleeves, showing her beautiful creamy arms and neck, and it was trimmed with tiny mother o'pearl shells and sequins. She wore a magnificent old French paste necklace, and her dark brown hair was piled high. She was 47.

Of all her guests, Sappho was particularly delighted that Violet Hunt and Ford Madox Hueffer were coming; her pleasure was communicated to me, and I also was excited and intrigued to meet these Famous Ones.

The behaviour of adults was not openly discussed with children in

1913, but I had gathered there was something unusual about Violet and
Ford – that they were in love, but not quite in the conventional way;
that Violet was very beautiful, and *he* was a *very* distinguished writer. I
expected I don't know what kind of a hero in Ford, a Prince Charming –
Instead, there was this big, rather fat and, to me, old and very
unattractive man who, to my horror, kissed me. I did think Violet was
beautiful, and *she* didn't seem old, but I could not imagine how she or
any other woman could love *him*.

There is a description of Ford in about 1909 by David Garnett quoted
in *The Life of Ford Madox Ford* by Frank Meshane: 'His fresh features,
the colour of raw veal, his prominent blue eyes and rabbit teeth.' This
coincides exactly with my own astonished memory of the great man.

Sappho's comment on the party was, 'Marjorie was surprised to see
what a magnificent host her father is ...' My father, like most of my
Irish relations, had charming manners and looked after his guests.

In 1913-14 Violet was obsessed by Ford and remained obsessed with
the memory of her life with him long after they parted. She told the
'marriage' story over and over again throughout the years. I think
Violet wanted so much to have been married to Ford in Germany, even
if the marriage was not legal in England, that she almost came to
believe it and ignored the little niggle of conscience that told her Ford
had faked a marriage ceremony.

In 1913-14 Ford wrote a series of articles in the *Outlook*, headed
'Literary Portraits', and in No. XXII (7 February 1914) he dealt
specifically with women novelists:

> The books that I wait for as they drift down the stream might well be
> those of Mrs W.L. George, Mrs Ada Leverson, Miss Violet Hunt, Mrs
> Dawson Scott or Miss May Sinclair. On the other hand I have to allow
> to pass me by the books of Mrs Mary E. Mann, of whom I have long
> had the greatest possible respect; or those of Mrs Margaret L. Woods,
> whose poetry I would put beside the work of anybody you could name:
> I have never had the pleasure of meeting *these* ladies.
>
> To Mrs George, then, I should look for powers of observation mated
> with an unusual courage of outspokenness; to Mrs Leverson to powers
> of observation, together with an unusual macabre seriousness and a
> hobgoblin power of making jokes. Mrs Dawson Scott has the
> appearance of possessing the 'the seein' eye', as the American legend
> has it, together with a sort of ponderous and impressive power in
> building up unbearable situations; and Miss Sinclair too has that
> perceptive organ, together with a deep seriousness.

In the autumn of that same year, when visiting Violet Hunt and
Ford at South Lodge, Campden Hill, Sappho was amazed when Ford
asked her to send him the manuscript of *Ulalia* saying he had influence

with some publishers and might be able to sell it: she had never been offered real help before! But even Ford was unsuccessful.

Sappho also met Ezra Pound in that pre-war era, but she was not very complimentary ... 'A silly-looking fatuous face, topped by wild, wiry hair, no doubt much more interesting than he looks.' At another party she also again met H.G. Wells and described him as being 'so commonplace looking that, in a crowd, he managed to resemble everybody else and was quite indistinguishable'.

In May 1912 Sappho met Charlotte Mew, described her as 'an imp with brains', invited her to tea and, as soon as she had read some of her verse, became an ardent admirer.

For two years, until July 1914, Sappho's and Charlotte's friendship was warm and, since she liked children, it spilled over into the poet's friendship for us, so that I, then aged 13, remember her very well. She was a queer, elfin little woman, shy and yet gay when she felt at ease, but often abrupt, 'farouche' and obstinate, and she could be downright rude, yet was attractive and lovable too. As she got to know us, she several times took us all three to the Zoo, or the Coliseum ... and we were delighted to go.

Early in 1913 Sappho wrote:

Have seen a good deal of Charlotte Mew and admire her verse very much – she is a queer mixture. I went to Evelyn Underhill's party and, meeting May Sinclair there, asked her to come and see me. I then invited Charlotte to meet her. She resisted, didn't want to meet clever people, but eventually agreed to come. May Sinclair arrived first and, when I told her Charlotte was coming, she was annoyed. 'But I want to talk about your books. I've just read *Mrs Noakes*, and now I'm going to read every word you've ever written.' However, when C.M. came I persuaded her to read *The Farmer's Bride*, and May was so won over that she deserted me and they left together and have since called on each other.

Although Sappho had already known Charlotte for nearly a year, from that date in February or March 1913 she was part of Sappho's circle, and she and May Sinclair did their utmost to get her work noticed by influential people. Sappho, especially, took her under her wing – that is, as much as such an independent, elusive, faery creature could be taken under a wing. Charlotte was not young – in 1913 she was 44 – although she had a youthful air, but she was certainly unknown and brilliant and thus qualified for Sappho's attention, who wrote: 'She has a wonderful young soul – neither quite boy nor quite girl.'

Although Charlotte tried to resist Sappho's efforts to publicise her and her poetry, she could not for long stand up to such an onslaught. Sappho was determined to obtain for her new friend the recognition that was her due. She and May Sinclair sent Charlotte's poems to Austin Harrison (editor of the *English Review*), Edward Garnett, Stephen Gwynne, Ford Madox Hueffer and many other contemporary literary lights.

Charlotte sometimes sent her poems to Sappho in manuscript, and during the summer holidays of 1913, she read some to us and wrote of our reactions:

> I read 'The Changeling' last, for every word of that is intelligible to a child, and it brought tears to all. Christopher (aged 11) with glistening eyes, begged to know the author; Toby (9) said it made him *feel* too much, and Marjorie (14) who already knew Charlotte, talked of her unusualness, her glowing charm.

In the September Sappho wrote:

> It is difficult for me to talk of liking or disliking a person, but I find in myself a keen desire for Charlotte's stimulating, irritating, keenly interesting society. Under the curious husk is a peculiarly sweet, humble nature.

When friends wrote to her praising or criticising Charlotte's poems, Sappho often repeated their remarks to the 'rude Charlotte', as she sometimes referred to her unamenable and awkward friend. And Charlotte was only half pleased, although on 18 July 1913 she wrote:

> Dear Mrs Sappho, I had a kind note from Miss Sinclair yesterday ... but saying that 'exception will be taken to the apparent lack of metrical technique' [in her verses]. Of course I *could* write smoothly if I chose. Miss Sinclair said she would send my things to Edward Garnett and Pound. I just replied that I don't want to make use of her. But, however it goes, I have firstly to thank *you* – and very sincerely do. In spite of my 'mountain way' I am an antiquely grateful person. I don't feel like more verse at the moment – the things I want to do are rather unmanageable, perhaps too big ...

On 16 March 1914 Sappho wrote:

> 'I think this ought to be a marked day in our lives. Charlotte came down [to Southall] to read her poems to Evelyn Underhill and Kathie Giles [the painter]. Charlotte sat with the little table before her, and on it were her papers and cigarettes, and she smoked all the time and, in her wonderful way, read us 5 poems. It was an enchanting hour! She was a little nervous when she began, but after the first poem forgot

herself. At the end Evelyn Underhill turned to me with, 'Magnificent!'

And Kathie said, 'I will go to the ends of the earth any time to hear your Charlotte tell her poems – she is a modern piper, and I will follow her piping.'

A day or two later Sappho heard from Evelyn Underhill:

50, Campden Hill Sq, March 18th. I feel as if I departed yesterday without saying a word to you, but really an hour with Miss Mew is like having whiskey in one's tea; my feet were clean off the floor. Heavens, what a tempest she produced. The most truly creative person I ever came near, I think. You were quite right about her, *of course* ...

Below is one of Charlotte's poems, not necessarily one of her best but interesting because of the note she added to the manuscript when she sent it to Sappho:

The Sunlit House

White, through the gate it gleamed and slept
In shuttered sunshine. The parched garden flowers
   Their scarlet petals from the beds unswept
   Like children unloved and ill-kept
     Dreamed through the hours.

Two blue hydrangeas by the blistered door burned brown
   Watched there, and no one in the town
     Cared to go past it night or day
     Though why this was they wouldn't say.

But I, the stranger, knew that I must stay.
   Pace up the weed-grown paths and down.
     Till one afternoon – there is just a doubt –
     But I fancy I heard a tiny shout –
     From an upper window a bird flew out –
      And I went my way.

I passed this house on a hot Guernsey road (with a rollicking party) one afternoon in '95, and have hung about it in thought, like the frog footman 'on and off for years and years'. Only suddenly 2 months ago I saw the little bound spirit inside. I *will not be psychic*, but please – one day – explain. CMM, 9, Gordon Sq, W.C.

Although Charlotte has become known now fifty years after her death and since the publication of Penelope Fitzgerald's admirable biography in 1984, she was almost unknown in 1912. Even then, however, Frank Swinnerton had written on page 257 of *The Georgian Literary Scene*:

> Her use of language is admirable; its suppleness enchants the ear; but what gives the poems perfection is a sincerity which finds fit words because the impulse to write, to tell, has been so intense.

But he added that Charlotte was a poet 'whose work, first published in 1916, belongs to the first world war', whereas all the poems he mentioned were written before 1914 and were collected and published by the Poetry Book Shop in 1916.

Between May 1912 and July 1914 Sappho received 23 letters from Charlotte. Then the correspondence ceased abruptly, and I think the reason is clear.

Charlotte was a lesbian, and Sappho was unaware of this. She had no idea that the special attraction she felt for Charlotte was more than normally emotional. Charlotte often lapsed into bad French, and Sappho took her comment ('Je n'aime pas vos romans, mais je vous aime') at its face value, and recorded in her journal in November 1913: 'Curious – little – dear. Surely, however, she will like my poor *Ulalia*?'

In the beginning Charlotte probably felt mildly attracted to Sappho, and this evoked an uncomprehending emotional response, but Charlotte's feeling for Sappho was quickly superseded by her deep attraction to May Sinclair.

By the summer of 1914 Sappho and May had become great friends, and there is a postcard from May dated 3 July 1914 in which she describes how to get to her house at 1, Blenheim Road, St John's Wood, and hopes to see Sappho about 4, 'so that we can talk'. No date is mentioned, but Sappho wrote:

> 12 July 1914. Spent afternoon and evening with May Sinclair. She is a dear, so gentle, conscientious, anxious – and so clever. A very sympathetic personality. She must have been a very pretty girl – she looks pretty still. I had thought we had nothing in common, but we talked like old friends.

On that day Sappho learned that Charlotte had been bothering and annoying May.

This was a great shock, and she wrote:

> All the geniuses I have met have been unsound sexually ... Ella d'Arcy was immensely over-sexed, practically a prostitute. Charlotte is evidently a pervert. Is then genius merely one form of sex? Genius

creates, just as sex does, and in genius perhaps the sex instinct is always atrophied, flawed, damaged, because all the real stuff is gone into the genius.[1]

I doubt if Sappho ever said anything to Charlotte – she would have found it difficult to find the right words, as she did a few years later when I asked some important questions. But in any case on 25 July we all went down to Cornwall for the summer holidays, after which the war disrupted our lives. There is no evidence that Charlotte and Sappho had any contact for some years, although Charlotte and May Sinclair remained friends. But in 1917, after she founded the To-Morrow Club, Sappho invited Charlotte to come and read her poems to the Club, and she refused.

In 1915 Mrs Harold Monro of the Poetry Bookshop came across one of Charlote's poems in the *Nation* and contacted the author. This led to the publication by the Poetry Bookshop of *The Farmer's Bride* in 1916, and Alida Monro and Charlotte became friends.

Charlotte committed suicide in 1927, and Messrs. Duckworth published her *Collected Poems* in 1953, to which Alida Monro contributed a long and moving 'memoir'. This contains several inaccuracies, mainly because Mrs Monro did not know Charlotte from 1912 to 1914 – two important years. She implied that Charlotte stopped being friendly with May Sinclair because the latter was a lesbian!

Even if there was not overwhelming evidence against this suggestion, there is the story told by May to Rebecca West and G.B. Stern that she had once been chased by a lesbian poetess into her bedroom where she 'had leaped over the bed 5 times to avoid her.' May talked about this openly, so that the story went round London. May added: 'I just said, "My good woman, you are simply wasting your perfectly good passion".' And in telling me this story Sappho said: 'That was Charlotte Mew, of course.'

Lesbian or not – and it must have been a very unhappy role to play in 1912 – Charlotte was a unique character, and I remember clearly the admiration and excitement that surrounded her: in my teens I loved her and her poems. The one person who did not join in the chorus of adulation was my father. Sappho wrote of the poem 'The Forest Road',

It's so deeply emotional – when I tried to read it to Scottie, I couldn't.

[1] The conviction that prostitutes were over-sexed was prevalent at that time. Most people now believe the contrary. Sappho's remarks about Ella d'Arcy are, I think, unfair and quite untrue.

He said, as usual, the essential thing: 'It makes you feel the writer is mad herself, to have drawn such a mad person so well.'

He did not know that Charlotte's brother and younger sister had been in asylums for many years and that this was a constant torment to her.

13

First World War

During those last few years of peace and a predictable future, Sappho had been preoccupied with her life as a wife, mother, writer and Cornwall. She had inherited from old William Edward Dawson an interest in land, had a flair for knowing what was potentially valuable, and had bought a few strips of land behind Constantine Bay at between £30 and £40 apiece. She had then designed a bungalow which was completed in the summer of 1914. It was called 'Wastehills', as the strip of land on which it was built was one of a number on the lane down to the Bay known locally as 'The Wastralls'. The bungalow was of brick, square and solid-looking, and was the first of the new bungalows to arise at Constantine Bay.

Our Easter holidays that year were wonderful. We camped in our nearly finished bungalow, Scottie was with us, recovering from his unhappy spell of drilling in Ulster, and we liked having him around. I was looking forward to my last term at Winton House School at Ealing, and was then going to school in Germany for a year; Sappho's most recent novel had just been published. And in July Scottie was going to take me to Wimbledon to see Suzanne Lenglen play!

Quickly and inevitably the war loomed nearer. To Sappho it was entirely unexpected, as hitherto her attention had been occupied by the threat of trouble in Ireland, and the fact that Scottie was committed to go and fight for Ulster. If the Home Rule Bill was passed, she expected civil war and had looked upon the European disturbances as hysteria. Scottie, with his army background, had no such illusions and became restless. On August 3rd he decided to go to London and consult a friend in the War Office, as he saw a chance of doing what he had always wanted to do, join the army as a doctor, even at the age of 49. Sappho went to London with him, and left us in Cornwall with a Dawson cousin.

Scottie's friend at the War Office was fairly senior and quite willing to help. It was very early days and no one knew how many doctors would be needed or how quickly, but on 4 August Scottie was offered a commission in the R.A.M.C. – 'Did he want home or active service?' He wired 'active' and again went to the War Office.

Sappho waited for him at a restaurant where they had arranged to have lunch. And she wrote:

> I waited 2 hours and then he came, happy and glorious, and much taller! He had a commission in his pocket – after all these years he was an officer in His Majesty's Army.

Scottie had to get his kit and join up at Woolwich in five days, so there was not much time to shut up the house in Southall, find a caretaker and deal with the practice, leaving his partner in charge. Also there were financial arrangements to discuss. It soon became clear that Scottie was no longer thinking much about his wife and children, or even his practice and was living in another world. He was going to be free of domesticity, free to live among men of similar background to himself – men belonging to the armed forces ... The horrors of war, the sufferings of the sick and wounded, had not yet impinged on his imagination; he felt exhilarated, happy, fulfilled – at last.

Suddenly Sappho realised that she really knew nothing about their financial situation and had not been able to consult her husband about ways and means. On his last day she collected the pass book from the bank, which she had never looked at before, since Scottie had never shown it to her or fully discussed his affairs. Now, for the first time she examined this important little book and found out that they were overdrawn £150, and that quite large and unexplained sums had from time to time been entered on the credit side, when the balance had been overdrawn. She tackled Scottie at once and showed him the pass book, but he was totally uninterested and refused to discuss the matter, and it was only then that she became aware of his completely unbusinesslike attitude. They were living beyond their income and, whenever they were overdrawn, large sums were transferred from capital to their current account. Finally, Scottie said, 'My father left me £10,000 – a lot of money – I don't think you need worry ...' And with that he went to the war, and Sappho was left to cope with the house, the practice and us three children.

With her husband in France, her two sons going back to boarding school in September – Christopher for his first term at Oundle – and only me around, Sappho once more had time on her hands. The advent of war had upset her, destroyed values, and for a few weeks she lost her bearings. But her energy and resourcefulness soon found a means of expression.

On 28 August *The Times* published her letter from Wastehills, suggesting it was time for women to take up duties they could perform easily and 'with perfect propriety', whereby the men would be set free for the necessary fighting. She suggested that some of the great Suffrage Societies should enrol a corps of such women, but she then unwisely added: 'I should be glad to hear from people in favour of forming the Women's Defence Relief Corps.'

The great Suffrage Societies did not respond, but individual women wrote from all over the country welcoming the idea and suggesting the originator should start an organisation.

Sappho immediately decided to do so, but realised she could not organise.a nation-wide Corps from Cornwall. Where were she and I to live? And what should I do, since I strongly resisted any idea of returning to school, although I was only 15. Finally we were able to share a flat temporarily with an old friend of Sappho's in Holland Park, and I went quite willingly to the Buckingham Palace Road School of Cookery for six months to learn plain cooking and household management. In 1915 I got a job as a very junior clerk in the War Trade Intelligence Department, which had offices in wooden huts put up in the drained lake in St James' Park.

When Sappho had a major Idea, which happened four times in her life, this being the first, it was in each case immediately successful in arousing considerable interest in the group for which it was intended, and the initial organisation of the Women's Defence Relief corps proceeded with speed. On 24 September, she received her first subscription of 2s 6d. On 25th a Miss Tudor called and offered to be Sappho's private secretary, unpaid. On 26th sixteen more women enrolled, and, at Miss Tudor's suggestion, Sappho wrote to eleven duchesses. Miss Tudor proved to be 'a splendidly businesslike, keen, energetic young woman'. On 27 September Sappho was invited to speak at Shepperton; on 29th Miss Tudor said she must have a committee and write to the Queen ...

The W.D.R.C. grew rapidly and, during the next two years, Sappho had a foretaste of the kind of civic entertainment she was to endure – and enjoy – over and over again in the days of the P.E.N. She was received by Mayors and Mayoresses and Chief Constables at Town Halls up and down the country – at Bolton, Wallasey and Sheffield – and became accustomed to seeing her name on posters in foot-high letters and to feeling sick with nerves. She had to learn to speak, and to review her corps, and to encourage the hundreds of women who came to meet her. And what did they see? A plump, unfashionable little woman, aged 49, who did not possess a decent suitcase and probably arrived at the Town Hall carrying her overnight belongings in a string bag. But she had bright, observant eyes, a friendly

outward-going manner and more than her fair share of dynamism.
The long distances she travelled were difficult and exhausting in
war-time England, and she sometimes collapsed and had to cancel all
engagements and go to bed for a few days.

The flat-sharing did not last long. We found a large furnished room
in Culworth Street, St John's Wood, where the landlady 'did' for us,
and where we could, if need be, get an extra room for the boys during
the holidays. In addition to organising the W.D.R.C. Sappho began
to write articles, book reviews, and even war-time cookery recipes,
which she invented, in order to help keep us and pay school bills.
Scottie's pay was quite inadequate, and Sappho was determined to
manage without further transfers of capital being entered in that
frightening pass book.

The W.D.R.C. had a successful career as a pioneer Corps until the
Women's Land Army and other officially backed organisations
gradually got under way, although that was not until the middle of
1917. But by that time Sappho had found other people willing to run
it, although she continued occasionally to address meetings on its
behalf and to manage its publicity.

Meanwhile Scottie was cheerfully and happily involved in his new
life. He was sometimes attached to a Field Dressing Station,
sometimes to an Ambulance Unit, was promoted Captain and then
Major, was wounded in one of the engagements at the Somme, had
trench fever … came home on leave.

In 1915, when he was in charge of a section of a hospital at Rouen,
Sappho had an Idea, though a minor one. She managed to persuade
the War Office to allow her to visit Rouen as a journalist and report
on hospital conditions – and she took me with her. We were supposed
to be nothing to do with my father – just 'a distant cousin of his who
happened to be a journalist' was her tale. It was a very exciting
adventure for me – my first visit abroad, and in war-time too. We were
shown round the hospital by the Colonel and other staff officers
covered with red tabs, and with my father a silent and very uneasy
member of the group. I was strictly warned NOT on any account to
speak to him, in case I inadvertently addressed him as 'Daddie', and I
kept well away from him on those tours. Sappho was quite at ease,
chatting with the Colonel and making a charming impression, but I
felt sick with fright, and I am sure Scottie did too. I imagined all sorts
of horrors overtaking us if we were found out.

We stayed at the Hotel de la Poste, and Scottie visited us to show
his 'cousins' round the lovely old town with its cobbled streets and the
many churches which chimed the hours and quarters all night and
kept us awake. The Prince of Wales, fresh-faced and young, was also

in Rouen and was staying in our hotel. The French ladies were enchanted with him – 'Comme il est beau – comme il est rose – votre Prince de Galles.' Wandering about Rouen I twice saw Prince Edward scurrying down the street and round the corner in an effort to evade the tall Guards Officers who had been detailed to look after him and see that he did not get into any danger.

Sappho's visit was a gay and impudent deception – if the War Office really was deceived – although I am sure she *did* write the report on hospitals.

When Scottie came home on leave he was rather fed up that, because we had so little money, and Sappho was working hard to supplement what we had, if we went anywhere by train she would not agree to travel first class, which he considered his right as an officer. He had to accept this, but could stand up to her sometimes, if he felt she was totally in the wrong. On one occasion he (in uniform) and Sappho and I were going somewhere in a very crowded train. We had got seats, but our carriage was full and when a woman on the platform, with a child and many packages, tried to enter, Sappho held the door handle inside and said, 'There is no room in here – try further up.' My father took her hand from the handle, saying, 'Moderation, my dear, moderation in all things.' He then opened the door, helped the woman in and gave her his seat. My mother sat with a set furious face – she hated not getting her own way – and I felt very uncomfortable. Perhaps for the first time I was made aware of my parents' different attitudes.

14

Family Disruption

Apart from the war, Sappho's main interest was still in writing and writers. Whether she was in London or in Cornwall, where we spent all our wartime holidays, whenever she heard of a writer staying within reach, she would either call on him or her, or write to them, having first read their books. Few people could resist her genuine interest and, in the disruption of a country at war, most writers were glad to renew acquaintance with one of their own kind. It was surprising how often and in what strange places they turned up.

Near us in Cornwall, at Porthcothan Bay, we found an old friend, J.D. Beresford and his wife, living in a farmhouse for the duration. Dorothy Richardson was staying with them, and I remember her as a quiet, plumpish woman with light brown hair and a good skin. She often wore a pink blouse with a black velvet bow at the throat, and she and Sappho liked each other – they were both oddities: when Dorothy married Alan Odle, an even greater oddity, Sappho liked his drawings, and they all remained friends for a number of years. She was also a great admirer of Dorothy Richardson's 'stream of consciousness' novels.

There is a charming letter from Jack Beresford, written from that farm in July, 1915, complaining about the speed with which the mild temperature and superfluity of rain turns a garden into a wilderness almost over-night.

> Picture us, rueful and a little worried, gazing at our garden ... Cornwall is proving too strong for us. The Magician sleeps in a dark corner under the lilac bush, invisible to us but mighty powerful. In the dry weather he is apt to be careless and lazy, and we are more than a match for him. But, when he is invigorated by a grateful rain, he wakes to an enormous activity. We go to bed, congratulating ourselves that we are pretty well keeping pace ... and in the morning the whole garden is lush with a new growth. And, while we throw up our hands in shuddering despair, the Magician peers through the lilac leaves and grins at us and chuckles.

During 1916 there was one major change in all our relationships, because at last Sappho discovered Scottie's affair with the young woman at Southall. At Christmas he came on a week's leave when we were all together at Wastehills and, after three days, he received a telegram from the War Office – he said – recalling him at once. Sappho was greatly disappointed: he had been especially nice during his leave. After we returned from seeing him off at Bodmin Road Station, I was in the garden when I heard a kind of explosion inside the bungalow and found Sappho locked in her room crying noisily. After a time she told me that on the writing blotter of the desk in the sitting room she had noticed some clear ink-blotted writing in Scottie's hand, so she got a mirror and was able to read the imprint of a letter to his friend at Southall, to whom he had written: 'I am hurrying back to my little lady' and signing himself 'Your only lover'. He was on his way there at that moment.

Sappho reacted tempestuously and was angry, miserable and self-pitying. Although there had been many times when the unsatisfactory nature of her marriage had been brought home to her, it had not occurred to her that Scottie might not accept this, as she had. If she, who had never been in love with him, could manage, surely he, who had persuaded her into marrying him because *he* was in love, could do likewise. She had been a good wife, and this was a shocking and terrible thing to have happened.

And I, at 17, agreed with her, although I wished she would not 'take on so'. I identified completely with her. I had never seen a great deal of my father, and hardly anything at all during the last two years, and I was very immature and inexperienced and took a strictly moral point of view.

I am quite sure now that this was not the first time Scottie had deceived his wife, although this was the most serious affair, which had already existed for some years.

Scottie wrote humble and protesting letters in response to his wife's outraged demand for a divorce. He assured her he had never *loved* anyone else, which I am sure was true, but he left the matter in her hands. They finally decided not to take any definite steps for the time being. Or rather, Sappho decided this, as Scottie was, from the beginning, appalled at the possibility of losing his anchor against his moods, miseries and depressions.

Meanwhile my father, like thousands of others, continued to play his quiet, unostentatious role in the R.A.M.C., always serving as near the front as he could get. Sappho recorded that, shortly after that unhappy leave, he was wounded a second time at the Ypres salient, got trench fever and was offered a 'cushy' job at home which he refused. Instead, he served on a hospital ship, going to Le Havre eight times, and finally returned to France, once more attached to a Field Ambulance. In view of all this it must have been difficult for Sappho to remain angry and they resumed married life for the remainder of the war and for a year or two afterwards. Scottie did not in fact give up his lady friend, but he took greater care to see that the relationship was not too obvious.

But there was another family mix-up during the war. My brother Christopher was good with tools, was always inventing things, and for that reason he was, in September 1914, sent to Oundle School, famous for its engineering shops and with Sanderson as Headmaster. But the boy was unhappy there, as he had also been at his preparatory school, and he finally wrote and told Sappho this in the summer term of 1915, when he was just 14.

In 1915 Sappho had not yet emerged from her obsessionally patriotic mood, and she began to consider that it might be a good idea for Christopher to leave school and do an engineering apprenticeship for three years, thus contributing to the war effort. Although both the headmaster and Scottie were against this, Christopher was happy and impressed that his mother had so surprisingly come to his rescue and was delighted to leave school.

During one of her visits to Coventry on behalf of the W.D.R.C. Sappho had met Mr Siddeley-Deasy, of the automobile firm, and he had agreed to take Christopher into his factory as an apprentice. He was found lodgings five miles outside Coventry and had to cycle in every morning to be there by 6 a.m. He found it impossible to get to work on time, and his landlady was a dragon, so he moved into digs in Coventry. But, mixing with men and older lads, he began to play 'slippery Sam' and, although he kept his 'lodging money' intact, he gambled all his pocket money away. He also had a couple of cycling accidents, in one of which he had slight concussion and knocked some of his teeth loose. However, he managed to finish his three-year apprenticeship in the summer of 1918.

The whole episode was a disaster, and I have never understood how Sappho could have imagined that a boy of under 15 from such a sheltered background, who had been at boarding school since he was 8, could have managed his life satisfactorily, unaided, at his age and in war-time!

On leaving Coventry, aged 17, Christopher met and was greatly influenced by Kenneth Richmond, the psychologist, and there and then my brother decided he wanted to be a psychiatrist. In spite of manifold difficulties with my father over proper medical training, Christopher never deviated from this interest, although he did not actually begin his medical training until 1937. He qualified at Bart's Hospital in 1942 when he was 41, and then specialised as a psychiatrist.

15

The To-Morrow Club

From September 1916 Sappho and I lived in a large studio in Barrow Hill Road in St John's Wood, which was later bombed and is now demolished. I was still working as a clerk at the War Trade Intelligence Department.

The studio in Barrow Hill Road, although large, was not really adequate for the two of us to live in *and* entertain, but Sappho found a way out of this problem. She was always interested in the young, especially if they were writers. Her memories of her own unhappy childhood and her efforts to free herself from her intolerable environment, as well as the hardship she suffered in those first years in London in the late 80s and early 90s, caused her to be sympathetic to those with similar troubles, and especially to any youngster who was rebelling against the narrow religious and moral doctrines of the period. The war was a releasing agent, and, after the years of grinding war effort, young people were coming out of the forces with new ideas of democratic living ... and with a desire to talk, to discuss. At that time Sappho was doing a good deal of book reviewing, so she often wrote encouraging letters to the authors of first novels and invited them to come to tea. Most young writers were flattered by such an invitation from their reviewer, and many were delighted to accept. Elizabeth Delafield, whose first novel, *Zella Sees Herself*, was published in 1917, was one of the first of these visitors; also Henry Williamson, Alec Waugh, G.B. Stern. It was just as well the fashion for cocktail parties had not yet arrived, as they would have been too expensive. Many of Sappho's contemporaries also came visiting, and both groups – the young and the middle-aged – stayed and talked – and talked ...

Early in 1917 Sappho had her second Idea, and the To-Morrow Club was born.

The To-Morrow Club was the forerunner of the P.E.N. Club and, in organising this smaller association, Sappho served an apprenticeship which prepared her for the far greater responsibility she undertook with the P.E.N. which followed four years later in 1921.

The To-Morrow Club was intended to help the writers of To-Morrow: the young would-be authors who had not yet had anything published, and beginners who had had perhaps one book, a poem or an article accepted. Sappho planned to provide a meeting place where these young people could come together, and where they could also meet already established writers by means of informal talks. She outlined her scheme to all her young friends, and they were enthusiastic. She also wrote to her contemporaries, and they were intrigued and promised their support. J.D. Beresford knew John Galsworthy and suggested Sappho wrote to him. Galsworthy replied:

1a, Adelphi Terrace, London, W.C.2 May 14th, 1917.
Dear Madam, The idea is a good one, but depends so very much on the way it is carried out that I should like to write to Mr Beresford before attempting to respond to your appeal. And this I will do at once. Yours sincerely, John Galsworthy.

The letter was addressed to 'Miss Scott'.

Evidently he was satisfied by what he learned from J.D. Beresford, because he agreed to speak at a To-Morrow Club Meeting.

And this was how these two personalities, John Galsworthy and my mother, so totally different in upbringing and way of life, first came to know and appreciate each other.

Having thus got a nucleus of support, Sappho wrote to the press, and was at once inundated with letters expressing interest. She rushed ahead with her plans ... a place to meet, a secretary ... I was just 18 and had been private secretary to the author, Stephen McKenna, for about a year, but I would have some time over to help.

At first we met in an unattractive room in the Bedford Hotel. I think it must have been the meeting place of some angling society, because part of the decor were a number of shiny stuffed specimens of large fish in glass cases – we called it the Fish Room. Soon, however, we found a big, dark, low-ceilinged, panelled room on a first floor at 65, Long Acre, formerly used by the Ibsen Club, and this was hired every Thursday evening.

Sappho appointed herself 'Fixtures Secretary' and undertook to find a subject, speaker and Chairman every week. She continued to do this for the next five or six years, until long after she was involved with the P.E.N.

The To-Morrow Club was immediately popular – in 1917 it fulfilled a need. Sappho was a good organiser and an admirable hostess, as well as an indefatigable worker, and the new venture enabled her to meet her friends in less congested conditions than in our studio. She had no inhibitions about inviting the Great to come to the Club, nor any about introducing her young friends to them, and she created a welcoming atmosphere, so that many of the speakers came several times. This new venture also gave her an excuse, if she ever needed one, to write to, and thereafter meet, anyone in whom she was interested.

No records were kept of those early To-Morrow Club meetings, which were all very informal. But by the time the war ended, eighteen months later, it was very much a going concern, the first President being J.D. Beresford, and the second Sheila Kaye-Smith.

Sappho worked hard for her new Idea, but she also enjoyed it very much, and perhaps it was her enthusiastic involvement that made so many other people enjoy it too. She amused herself occasionally at the expense of club members and guests, such as the time when Alec Waugh, recently returned from being a prisoner of war, talked about his book, *The Loom of Youth*, written when he was still at school, which had upset a good many heads of public schools. Sappho invited my brothers' headmaster, a personal friend, to be her guest at that particular meeting – she knew well what his angry reaction would be – 'So good for dear C. to have to *listen* to the young for once.' She was always a rebel against establishment, and she had welcomed Alec's book as an attack on public schools. But she was disappointed, and here is Alec's account of that evening.

> I first met Amy Dawson Scott, or Sappho, as she was called by her friends, in March 1919. She asked me to speak at the To-Morrow Club. My first novel was a story about Public Schools ... and I was an object of controversy. I imagined she would want me to speak about the Public Schools ... this was my debut in my literary world, and I took a good deal of trouble about my speech. The long, dark room was crowded, and I thought it went rather well. When it was all over, Sappho bustled up, I thought with gratitude and congratulations. Not at all. She fixed me with a steady glare. 'This is all a mistake,' she said. 'You don't care in the least what happens to the Public Schools. You have a knack of narrative. You put down the facts as you saw them, and, because you did not appreciate the implications of what you were putting down, you raised a hornet's nest. Forget it; stick to story-telling.' I was disappointed, but I have remembered what she said. For better or for worse, I have stuck to my story-telling. I have not signed manifestos about Franco or the Congo ...

I don't remember precisely when Alec and I became friends, probably in 1918, certainly before he married his first wife, Barbara Jacobs (daughter of W.W. Jacobs). Our parents were friends, and I used to visit the Waughs in North End Road, between Hampstead and Golders Green, where a group of 17- to 19-year-olds met to gossip, play word games and charades and drink – *tea*! Sometimes Evelyn, aged about 14, was there; he was already an unpleasantly unattractive though witty boy, both physically and in his personality, and I was always glad when he had returned to school and thankful he was too young to join the To-Morrow Club, to which Alec and his young wife came regularly. In fact, he has told me that he and Barbara always kept Thursday evenings free in order to come to that smoky dark room in Long Acre. For many young people interested in writing and writers it was the highlight of the week in the last dreary months of 1918 and those immediately following.

Also among the early members of the To-Morrow Club were Allen Lane, Stephen Southwold, Elizabeth Delafield, Louis Golding, Henry Williamson. And the speakers were mostly drawn from Sappho's older writer friends ... Sheila Kaye-Smith, J.D. Beresford, May Sinclair, Violet Hunt, Ford Madox Hueffer, G.B. Shaw, the Sitwells, and John Galsworthy. The first time the latter came to the Club, Sappho wrote:

> Galsworthy spoke last night, and we had a tremendous evening. Studying the shape of his head, I felt sure he was going to preach, and he did. The width of his brow just saves him, but he has that high top that takes from human intelligence, rendering it didactic, dogmatic and muddly. However, he is a nice man and the Club worshipped him, and I think he liked them.

First impressions are not always reliable and when, a few years later, Sappho wanted John Galsworthy to become President of the P.E.N. she had revised her opinion of him.

John Galsworthy was, to me at 18, akin to a god – a being apart – a Great Man – chatting genially to anyone who could get his attention. He was then 51 and enjoyed talking to young people: he took them seriously and listened to what they had to say. Sappho kept a protecting eye on him and occasionally rescued him from the Club bores – he was much too kind and unassuming to extricate himself. If really bored, she thought he might not come again.

My old friend Henry Williamson wrote of the To-Morrow Club and of Cornwall, to which Sappho introduced him:

> I, a mere vagrant ... see only the (to me) intense days of its inception in Long Acre and later Caxton Hall; in both places I was a mere literary spiv, externally, at least. And I remember, later, the beautiful sands of Constantine where I stayed with my bride, and we all, – Denis Arundell, Hermon Ould, your mother and me – walked barefoot around Trevose Head and elsewhere along the breaking blue sea. And

the dim-seen mullet, salmon, and bass on the shelly sea-floor, pursued
by seals ... and the new potatoes grown on seaweed in the sandhills,
like partridge eggs clustered in a nest ... Looking back one sees all
things *en clair*. – T.S. Eliot speaking – Swinnerton – G.B. Shaw – and
the playwright Ernest Goodwin – May Sinclair, the thrilling afternoon
when Lauritz Melchior sang and revealed a great talent. And of course,
the excellent Alec Waugh, Violet Hunt ... What a cluster of talent your
mother drew about her, then and later.

After the talk there were questions, a cup of tea and general
mingling chat. No alcohol was needed to ensure a successful evening.
The Great forgot their status and were prepared to be flattered and
pleased by the interest shown in them by the Young!

Stephen Southwold, who also wrote as Neil Bell, and was
nicknamed 'Bunty' by Sappho, was one of the not-so-young writers
who frequented the To-Morrow Club and later came to our house in
St John's Wood. He was a great friend of us all, but he did not admire
Sappho's writing. In *My Writing Life* (Alvin Redman, 1955), he wrote,
twenty years after her death, of the time he met her at the To-Morrow
Club in about 1917-18, when he was 31.

> She wrote 'powerful' novels of the 'starkadder' sort which few people
> read; and lush verse, (free in more ways than one) which few editors
> would print. I don't mean Bawdy or Obscene. Voluptuous is perhaps
> the word. Why it so rarely achieved publication was because it was
> tediously long and not very well done. Yet before her marriage she had
> won considerable praise for her books of verse, notably from Robert
> Browning and her many friends, for she was a friendly person.
>
> She was now in her middle fifties (52 actually) and was short, plain,
> plump and amorous. She had a spiteful, biting tongue and a warm and
> generous heart. Altogether an astonishing woman. She was popular
> with both men and women, and with the former, no matter how young
> in comparison with herself, she was ever hopeful of an affair ... to be
> invited was, in its small way, a cachet ...

Bunty Southwold was entitled to his opinion, but I do not think he
was much of a critic. In the same book, on p.64, he also disposes of
T.S. Eliot – 'Who has never written anything to equal the best of
Edith Sitwell, Dylan Thomas ... Masefield', adding 'I don't think
Eliot is a poet at all.' Sappho actually wrote *no* long poems after her
first two epics were published in 1889 and 1892, when she was in her
early 20's.

He also disagreed with John Galsworthy receiving the Nobel Prize
instead of Wells, as, in fact, did many others, writing 'But there have
been more fatuous choices since then, T.S. Eliot, for example ...'

Bunty's description of Sappho being 'amorous, ever hopeful of an affair' must surely have been a projection of his own feelings. All the years he knew Sappho she was emotionally obsessed by Arthur Lynch (see below pp. 86-8) and, as companions, she liked men of about her own age. But she was also warmly maternal towards the young, and I suppose this could sometimes have been misunderstood.

'A biting tongue'? Yes, on occasion. But 'spiteful'? No.

16

Noël Coward in Cornwall

We had so little money during those last years of the war that, to make ends meet and yet have a roof over our heads in Cornwall, from about 1917 Sappho used to let Wastehills to summer visitors and herself rented an old stone cottage called 'Levorna' for £12 a year. Although it was small, we could manage and even have friends to stay.

During that summer of 1918 I decided to leave my job as Stephen McKenna's secretary, which I found very boring. I wanted to join some branch of the Women's Services, but first of all I took a long holiday at Levorna, and I remember that year's group of visitors very clearly. If they stayed at Levorna, it was as paying guests; if there was no room with us they stayed at nearby farms and paid for the meals they had with us. Sappho found their company stimulating and often persuaded her friends to copy her and walk barefoot round Trevose Head or down the rocky coves.

May Sinclair came that year, and Sappho delighted in her company. She found her mind

exceedingly interesting, clear and critical, although her surface consciousness is over sensitive, over conscientious and lacks robustness.

My own memory of May is that, although she was quite strong and athletic – for her age (53) – she was also plump and unused to the Cornish cliffs; and on one occasion she got stuck on a cliff path and had to be rescued by me.

Then there was E.M. Delafield – Elizabeth – sitting happily on a stool by Levorna kitchen fire, writing a novel, whilst we played ball against the wall – from *inside*. She was the one writer friend of Sappho's whom we all liked and we thought her one of the most delightful, sympathetic and beautiful young women we had ever met – tall and dark and stately.

G.B. Stern – nicknamed Peter – came down that July, staying at a farm. She was about 28 and seemed quite old to me. She plaited her dark hair in a pigtail and added brownish make-up to her already dark and sun-tanned face, and she wore very bright, vivid clothes and a bandana handkerchief round her head to make herself look like a gipsy. She seemed to us very affected, and she was quite useless on the cliffs or in the sea. Sappho wrote of her:

> I like Peter very much, but, as Marjorie says, 'Peter has principles, but doesn't use them.' She is a dear, but quite untrustworthy where men are concerned, which is tiresome.

I don't know how she acquired the name of Peter – her real name was Gladys, which I can understand her disliking.

Peter·was fond of Sappho and found her useful. She wrote:

> Sappho was apt to arrive suddenly with timely offers of a shelter for life in her own house, a pound of Cornish butter or a holiday in Cornwall. The latter – and the butter – I accepted, and there I learned her maternal passion for lame ducks was only equalled by her passion for the soil, the wind and the harsh sea coast of North Cornwall.

Looking back there seems to have been an endless procession of literary visitors, scribbling their novels in Levorna kitchen and talking … talking … talking.

I and my brothers, still schoolboys, were not at all intellectual and were often very bored by Sappho's friends, the one exception being Elizabeth Delafield. We greatly enjoyed Sappho's company and resented her spending her time in dull talk instead of being concerned with us.

Our final visitor that summer of 1918 was Noël Coward. Although he was totally unknown then, he soon began to make a name, which caused me to remember his stay in detail, even if he had not put us all, rather unflatteringly, into one of his books.

Peter Stern had had letters from two young men who admired her novels, and she wanted to have them to stay in Cornwall. One was Geoffrey Holdsworth, who was about 28 and whom she married shortly afterwards, and the other was Noël Coward, who was 18. They had written to her from adjoining hospital beds, before being invalided out of the army, and Sappho was trying to arrange for them to stay somewhere near. Finally, it was agreed that they should come in turn to a nearby farm – not as our guests, since they were not *our* friends, but they would have some meals at Levorna.

We were *not* pleased. More of these boring literary visitors! We tried every device to persuade Sappho not to 'give in' to Peter, but she, a loyal friend, was unmoved, merely saying, 'Dear Peter has nowhere at present where she can entertain her friends … and this is important for her.'

We accepted Geoffrey, but the other strange young man, Noël
Coward, sent us a telegram, as he has recorded, saying: 'Arriving
Padstow 5.30. Tall and divinely handsome in grey', and this damned
him from the first. Sappho wanted me to drive the pony and jingle in to
Padstow to fetch him, but I refused, muttering furiously in the current
slang, 'Conceited ass.' So a boy from the village went instead. It is not
surprising that Noël felt himself to be unwelcome, which was just what
he was.

Another ingredient was added to the already uncomfortable situation when, the day before he arrived, a friend who visited us from
another part of Cornwall and who had some connection with the
theatrical world, told Sappho that this strange young man was a pansy
– or whatever the word was then. Sappho was quite unnecessarily
alarmed on behalf of Toby, then a good-looking and charming 14-year-
old. She had little knowledge of such matters, had no one to ask, and
had a horror of any kind of 'perversion'. She was in an impossible
predicament, but finally explained as much as she could to me, telling
me to keep a protecting eye on Toby. And I was pretty innocent myself.

A pity my sensible, calming father was not around – but he was still
in France. In the present healthier age of acceptance of sexual
deviation, it all now seems quite ridiculous, but this was nearly 70 years
ago ...

Undoubtedly Sappho and I both behaved badly and even boorishly
to Noël, but in 1918 it was perhaps understandable, just as it is
understandable that Noël did not forgive us.

Quite apart from the 'gossip', which we could not mention, we had
nothing in common with Noël. He was a brilliant, sophisticated boy,
already successfully involved in a stage career, and knowledgeable
about the theatrical world of London, of which we were totally
ignorant, and yet he was of *our* generation, not our mother's, or even
Peter's. Surely he should have enjoyed our ploys, not the endless
discussions with the two novelists? We rapidly recognised his wit and
brilliance and listened spellbound to the endless game of repartee that
he and Peter played – it was a marvel I have never forgotten. I can,
however, see how shattering this visit must have been for him, and his
memory of it is gloomy, whereas mine is quite cheerful. Although he
went off for long walks with Peter, who was the only one of the party
who was a verbal match for him, he also came with us sometimes. I
remember a group walk across the sand of Treyarnon Bay, when we
discussed our future careers. After the usual doctor, lawyer suggestions, we turned to him: 'What are you going to be, Noël?' 'A
success,' said he and wrote on the sand in big letters, 'Read "Cats and
Dogs" by Noël Coward.'

One evening I took him 'spratting' in Harlyn Bay. This 'sport', which consists of digging out sand-eels for bait at the edge of the sea, usually takes place at low spring tides by the light of a full moon, and Noël and I walked the 2 miles across the cornfields on a wonderful moonlight summer night. Suddenly he asked me why we had all disliked him so much ... and I told him. Nowadays we should have gone by car, and I probably should not have remembered the occasion at all. But, because the last few days had obviously been a strain, and I was by nature outspoken – and we were, after all, near the same age – I told him the truth. It must have been a relief to me to express what was worrying me.

Noël stopped short in the brilliant light of the full moon and looked at me with his mischievous faun's eyes. Then he threw back his head and laughed – and no more was said.

By the end of the holiday we had all become reasonably good friends. Noël joined the To-Morrow Club and sometimes came to Sappho's At Homes on Sundays. He was there the day that Lauritz Melchior, the famous Wagnerian tenor, sang for us. His magnificent voice rang through the big room and attracted a small crowd in the road outside. Then Noël, quite unconcerned, sat down at the piano and sang one of his own charming little songs. On another occasion I remember sitting on the stairs with him and Alec Waugh at one of Violet Hunt's literary parties at South Lodge, Campden Hill, poking irreverent fun at the VIPs below us.

Meanwhile, in the early autumn of 1918, I joined the Women's Royal Air Force as a motor cyclist 'Despatch Rider'.

17

After the War

Early in 1919 Scottie was demobilised and got a job as President of two pension boards in Chelsea, and he and Sappho bought the tail-end of the lease of a big house at the corner of Alexandra Road and Abbey Road, St John's Wood. There they re-started married life, but it must have been a difficult time for both, since neither had changed and both had had five years' freedom from domesticity.

Sappho was deeply involved in the To-Morrow Club, and the new house at once became a centre for committee meetings and social gatherings of all kinds, including tea-parties on Sundays. It was a hive of activity.

Christopher, who was working for his Matric, and I, still in the W.R.A.F. until September, 1919, were living at home, with Toby returning from Malvern College for holidays. Sappho had a full and interesting life which did not include Scottie. He alone of her circle was unable – and unwilling – to appreciate her restless pre-occupations and her delight in talking literary 'shop', which to him was uninteresting and in which he did not wish to take part.

Christopher maintained that Sappho and Scottie quarrelled a good deal, she losing her temper and being pretty unreasonable and unpleasant. As for me, I was in love for the first time and quite uninterested in my parents' lives.

About that time – 1919-20 – Scottie and Sappho agreed to a divorce, and I remember accompanying my mother to the Law Courts in 1920, where, in a few minutes, she was granted a Decree Nisi on her undefended suit. She had been married nearly twenty-five years and, in spite of everything, was much upset and wept.

Scottie bought a colliery practice in south Wales and went to live there with 'the new Mrs Scott', as my mother referred to her, although I do not think, in fact, that they ever married. As he left our house for the last time, he said to my eldest brother, 'I am leaving the woman I love and going to live with the woman who loves me.' He was then 56.

*

When Sappho's book *Wastralls*, the first of her Cornish novels, was published in 1918, she again received good reviews and recognition from friends and critics that she was a novelist to be taken seriously. Once more William Heinemann, when he accepted the book, gave her unstinted praise, writing:

> The finest novel I have read for a long time; it is too grim, however, to be a best seller.

So he would 'publish shortly', as 'it won't take much paper'.

Edward Garnett, that tall, ruggedly grey figure, also encouraged her – she belonged to the group of writers of whom Frank Swinnerton wrote in *The Georgian Literary Scene* (p.194):

> Hardly a man or woman writing novels of serious intention in the period covered by this book failed to receive from Garnett essential praise and critical support.

And Israel Zangwill thought so highly of *Wastralls* that he wrote to the *Observer* on 13 April 1919 to draw the attention of the public to 'a new writer', whom he compared to Emily Brontë and Edgar Allen Poe. He had never heard of Sappho until then.

During and immediately after the war there was great interest in and gossip about Dorothy Richardson and her 'new' style of writing. She had been sponsored by J.D. Beresford and Edward Garnett and was the subject of discussion at many a literary tea-party. Sappho, who knew her quite well, having met her in Cornwall during the war, enjoyed a mild reflected glory and joined in the chorus of admiration, although with some reservations.

In her second Cornish book, *The Headland*, Sappho tried to emulate Dorothy Richardson's style. This brought a protest from Alfred Knopf, who was considering publishing her book in America. On 17 February 1920 he wrote to Mr Heinemann:

> I have now read with some care Mrs Dawson Scott's novel and her poems ... Let me say at once that the novel is most decidedly my kind of book and while, frankly, I can't imagine it having a large sale, it is not the kind of thing I would want to let get by me ... I suppose you know the more or less notorious novels of Dorothy Richardson, which I happen to publish over here? Well, Mrs Dawson Scott seems to be suffering from an extreme case of 'Richardsonitis'. The effect on her seems to have been crudely mechanical. She appears to have gone through her manuscript and, with unflagging pertinacity, kicked out every punctuation mark she came across and stuck in its place a trio or

quartette of periods. Overdone in this way the device seems
emphatically to me to mean nothing at all, and Mrs Dawson Scott has
need of no such oddity to camouflage an inability she hasn't ...

In spite of Mr Knopf's strictures, *The Headland* received lavish praise
and encouragement, and congratulatory letters from her contemporary writer friends poured in.

This praise from her friends was exciting and consoling to Sappho,
making up perhaps for the failure of her marriage relationship and her
inability to earn enough money for her needs through her writing. She
was in return warmly interested in the literary efforts of her
contemporaries.

May Sinclair's novel, *Mary Olivier* (1919), had had bad reviews,
and, in reply to Sappho's sympathetic letter, May wrote:

July 1st, 1919 ... The reviews of 'Mary' get wusser and wusser. Virulent
sneers and jeers from Katherine Mansfield in 'The Atheneum'. Sniffs
from 'The Manchester Guardian'. The rumour of Something
Inadequate done by St John Adcock. A *very* good review from W.L.
Courtney in the Daily Telegraph. A letter from H.G. Wells – two words
exquisitely healing to hurt vanity, and a simply gorgeous letter from
Evelyn Underhill ... so I'm feeling much better.

Poor Violet Hunt, still nostalgic for Ford, who had left her, was
more concerned with her own emotional troubles than with the books
of her friends.

1919. ... You see, I can't come to-day ... and I can't come to Cornwall
after all. I am so 'moidert', as Ford says – I must get something settled
with him and stay in London ... Ford makes an entire fool of me, one
way and another.
   Lying here (as they say in novels), I feel an immense goodwill
towards my friends and even enemies. I even think kindly of poor silly
old Ford, putting solicitors on to me – lawyers' letters that are read to
me and that I mayn't answer, thank God! It's so funny how he suffers
for his frantic effort to avoid the performance of every human duty! I do
love him, you know, and wish I hadn't come to be his Duty instead of
his Pleasure.

Sappho's correspondence was not confined to her own books and
those of her friends, but with a variety of literary projects. She must
have been a godsend both to causes and to people who needed
encouragement, since, once convinced of their worth – and I think she
was easily convinced – she plunged to the rescue with all her energy
and powers of persuasion.

In the autumn of 1919 Sappho, who was friendly with Thomas Moult (currently editing a monthly called *Voices*, in which he occasionally published her poems), had obviously written to May Sinclair and tried to persuade her to allow Moult to print something of hers in *Voices*. May's reply was uncompromising:

Private. Confidential. My dear Sappho. I am embarrassed. For I have seen not only the October number of *Voices*, but the July, August and September numbers; and I have tried to read the poems of Mr Moult ... I am sure that Mr Moult is all that he seems to be, a good little man, inspired by the Love of Letters, and anxious for the honour and glory of Letters, willing to lose from £8-£10 a week for Letters, but ... Whatever he does and whoever he gets for his magazine, the poor editor's poems will sink it ...

And May refused to hand over anything she had written!

18

Letters from Warsaw

In the summer of 1920 my love affair came to an end and we parted. Sappho knew the *Times* correspondent in Warsaw and through him I got a job as Secretary to the British Passport Control Officer in Poland. A feature of Sappho's character was that she never objected to her children going off on adventures.

I was in Warsaw for nearly a year, from the end of October, 1920, and every week Sappho wrote me a long letter detailing her day-to-day activities, the people she met, the lectures she planned for the To-Morrow Club, the books and articles she was writing. These letters, often written on odd pieces of paper, were in the form of a diary. They were continued every couple of days and posted at the end of each week.

And for some reason I kept them. When typed, they amounted to nearly 30,000 words, and there were many themes running through them. Whilst quoting directly from some, I have re-written in narrative form a good deal of the story of Sappho's life during that year.

She wrote to me on 4 January 1921:

> Your father stayed here until yesterday and said he has had an awful fit of depression. I expect he has not got over the break yet. I wonder why he did not go to her? I expect it was a bit too crowded with children. [My father's friend had two children by her marriage.] So I've written briskly to cheer him up and told him he'll feel better in a few weeks.

The long period of strain had also had its effect on Sappho. The first few letters she wrote to me in Warsaw in the autumn of 1920 and early 1921 constantly referred to the low state of her health.

In the February she went to Cornwall in order to get on with *The Haunting*, the third of her Cornish books, and she wrote:

I'm beastly seedy, get a headache whatever I do – and I'm finding it so difficult to write.

And,

Last night was the worst night I've had – so much headache and sleeplessness. It's trying to work when I'm run down, and that's no wonder after the awfulness of last year – the upheavals were enough to knock anyone to pieces. But I am much happier and more cheerful and that is the beginning. Looking back I can see how I enjoyed my freedom in the war, and I shall enjoy this. I've only got to get sane and cheerful again ...

I've had a lovely day, only a very little headache, and I've nearly finished chapter 7. It was after all more cold than rainy – a black east wind – but I went down barefoot to a sea with its hair being blown backward like a veil, just to see if I could. The beach was carpeted with brightly coloured shells – no sea coal, no wood, but swathe after swathe of gay shells. Good-night, dear 'charmante and ravissante' daughter – it was me, moi, myself, what made you! Much love, Mother.

(I think this must have been a reference to something pleasant that a French writer I had met in Warsaw had written to Sappho about me.)

As the year progressed, she recovered, until in the early summer she could write:

Really, Marjorie, life is a most amusing and lively show just at present. I'm as cheerful as a cricket. It's many years since I enjoyed myself so much and, now that I'm free, I'm perfectly good-tempered. Isn't it odd that one little morose man should have made all that difference to me? I wonder if it is just the usual effect of long-continued matrimony? You've no idea how delightful it is to have Daddie's furniture all gone to him. There's space to breathe. I'm sleeping on Grandpa's old green velvet sofa. I remember it in the drawing room at Gothic Lodge, Dulwich, where I was born. On it, when I was a little girl of 7, I sat beside my father in the dark drawing room to hear that my mother drank and I was to try and find out where she hid the stuff. On it, nearly 50 years later, I sleep very comfortably.

She continued to buy small pieces of land in Cornwall, and built two more bungalows; she also bought land at Birchington, Kent, on which she built two flats. She let all these small dwellings to summer visitors in order to supplement her meagre resources.

Sappho named the Cornish bungalows 'Holt', after the small Norfolk town where her Dawson ancestors originated, and 'Lincs' after the Dawson family home on Plumstead Common. Some years later she changed the name 'Lincs' to 'Lynx', after Col. Arthur Lynch, to whom she gave the nickname of 'Lynx'. Since this bungalow is adjacent to the Golf Course, its name is a constant puzzle to present-day summer visitors!

Sappho loved masculine society and described at length her various friendships. But my own view and that of my brothers is that our Mother had no sexual relationships. I don't think she was physically attractive, although people of both sexes congregated around her, because she was interesting, vital and amusing. She enjoyed the admiration of men and being taken out to dinner – but there it ended. In her mid-fifties she was once invited by a man of her own age whom she met on a boat going to America to join him in his flat in New York, but she told my brother Christopher that she decided against this because she found it impossible to behave in a way that was so completely alien and out of keeping with her early life and upbringing.

Edgar Jepson, the novelist, was a great friend who often took her out to dinner. Once he insulted her by saying he thought she had the brain of a man – 'The last thing I want to have', retorted Sappho.

She lived a hectically full life, doing more things in one day than most people do in a week, but she was getting her health back and making up for the years of boredom at Cowes.

Although Sappho obviously enjoyed all these contacts and friendships, her emotional life was dominated from 1920 to March 1934 by her deep love for Colonel Arthur Lynch.

Arthur Lynch was an heroic figure. An Irishman who trained as a doctor in Paris and London, he was also an electrical engineer and a prolific writer of serious books such as *Roman Philosophique* written in French in 1915, *Principles of Psychology* in 1920, *O'Rourke the Great* in 1922 and twenty-five other books. He fought on the side of the Boers as Colonel of an Irish Brigade and, when the war ended, he returned to Ireland, where he was elected M.P. for West Clare and Galway in 1901. Although there was a warrant out for his arrest for High Treason, he came to London to take his seat in the House of Commons, having first notified Scotland Yard of his intention. He was arrested, tried and sentenced to death, but at President Roosevelt's request he was reprieved, served one year in prison and then continued to represent his West Clare constituency in Parliament from 1902 to 1918. According to *Who's Who*, he was a colonel in the British Army in 1918.

Sappho first became aware of Arthur Lynch in February 1920, when he returned from a lecture tour of America. She was always hoping to get an opportunity of lecturing in the States, so she arranged to meet him to discuss possibilities. His courageous career appealed to Sappho, as well as his looks – a tall, lean man with dark eyes and white hair that bushed out above his ears and earned him the nickname of 'The Lynx' or more often 'My Lynx'. 'A very wonderful individual', she wrote, 'beautiful in person, in his living for his principles and in all he had written.'

Arthur Lynch was married, had no children and never went about with his wife. He could be charming, but often was the reverse, a difficult curmudgeon of a man. He gave Sappho no encouragement that I could see, yet she came to believe that he loved her in his own queer, contrary, way, and her obsessional adoration of him dominated her life from their first meeting until his death in March 1934, a few months before her own. She referred to 'The Lynx' in most of her letters, writing candidly to me of her feelings, which embarrassed me. I did not really want to hear about The Lynx, and I was uncomfortable at having to read about this middle-aged and – to me – *old* love affair. Also, I could not believe that Arthur Lynch reciprocated in any way, and I couldn't understand how my mother could go on ringing him up and writing to him. I was young and deeply in love before I went to Warsaw, but I had myself ended the affair, because I did not think the young man loved me enough; I thought she ought to do the same.

Arthur Lynch was an extremely important part of Sappho's life from 1920 until they both died in 1934, and I have therefore quoted quite a lot from her letters to me and from her journals.

Feb. 1921. Rang up my Lynx, who was grumpy. I asked him to say definitely whether he likes or doesn't like me. All he says is 'I won't discuss it with you.' To-day is the anniversary of his first visit after his return from America ... I write about once a fortnight and ring him up once a month, and he endures it, rather as if he were being crucified ... and yet he doesn't end it ... Oh, Lord ... I ...

I rang up the Lynx. He grows more human, just a wee bit. I realise now what happened – he fell *in love* with me, he did not love me, and found he had aroused a wild, turbulent thing beyond his understanding, and he was afraid. Gradually, though, he will come to love me ... perhaps.

I have had a curious experience. I'd been rather restless and then this afternoon was so again, and I thought it must be worry about him. So I went to him [a clairvoyant journey]. Now hitherto I've been often, but after travelling a long distance I find him in a sort of fog. I can perhaps see his eyes, perhaps merely feel that he is close, but this afternoon I saw – after travelling a long way – a window, and then found myself in a room. The Lynx was in bed and, after cheering him up kindly, I walked about the room looking at his things. A very bare room [of which she made a drawing] ... I stayed quite a long time and came back much cheered. I wondered if it was pure imagination, but Mrs Mac [a medium] and Toby, who can also 'see', thought not. They said it was an ordinary psychic experience – the sort they both have. He [the Lynx] has, I am sure, come back from Russia, because I 'saw' him last night and this morning.

I wish he wouldn't only furtively visit me in dreams!

Although we sometimes had rows, and there were many occasions when I was extremely angry with Sappho, who was often quite unreasonable, yet I think we also had a rather unique mother-daughter relationship during this period.

*

While I was in Warsaw I became engaged to a young man with whom I was not in love; and, as he was conventional, we planned to get married in church when I returned to England.

I was not at all religious, but I rather fancied myself in a white dress and veil!

At the end of July I got a letter from my Ma!

Marjorie, it is no good my not talking straight to you. If you are married in church, I shan't be at your wedding. Nothing will induce me to give the lie to my life by doing so ... Only by people making the protest of not being married in church can we hope eventually to do away with the evils of a state church. I have brought you up to live for some sort of ideals ... I believe you should be free to do as you please, only I also am free, and you must not seek to drag me into doing a thing which my scruples forbid.

As it happened, as soon as I got back from Warsaw and plunged again into the excitement of London, and the foundation of the P.E.N. I broke off the engagement. (When I did marry Arthur Watts four years later, I had grown up and he and I were of one mind about white weddings.)

And from my father:

23.5.21. I am very glad you have decided as you have. You will probably guess that I don't in the least agree with your mother, and I hope that you will find you can stick to it. ... I don't believe you can help falling in love with him after marriage if not before, and I don't believe the feeling you once had *can be repeated*. I don't think that your mother's misfortune (or lack of judgment) in marrying me should deter you, for I don't believe our case would have turned out so badly if we had had one idea or taste in common. But we had *none*, and you say you have.

Well, I've not got much more to say except this: Don't be influenced too much by your mother, for though very clever, she doesn't know everything in the world.

I am trying to make a living, unfortunately this strike in England is making things pretty bad for me, for there is no money while it lasts and even afterwards the miners will work part time and have smaller wages ... Your loving father Horatio F.N. Scott.

My poor father was advising me to follow his and my mother's example, i.e. marry a man who loved me but with whom I was not in love. I am glad I didn't.

19

The Peak of the To-Morrow Club

The To-Morrow Club had become highly successful and well-known, and 1921 was a peak year. It had developed exactly as its Founder had intended and still gave her the means of meeting and entertaining her many friends – for the cost of a cup of tea. As with the Women's Defence Relief Corps, it filled a need and had been an immediate success.

The tea parties which had started as soon as we moved into the big house at Alexandra Road in 1919 and which initially I helped to arrange, had become a regular routine. They continued after I went to Poland in September 1920 and for a good many years after that. I am again indebted to Alec Waugh for his personal account:

> There were a number of literary hostesses – ladies interested in writers and writing – who kept open house. That is where Sappho Dawson Scott came in. Her house was always open on Sunday afternoons, but it was far from being a haphazard gathering. With Marjorie's assistance, she arranged a nucleus, and on Wednesday every three weeks or so, there would be a card saying 'so and so will be here on Sunday – I think you'd interest each other ...'
>
> Sappho had a way of hitting the nail upon the head. In the middle twenties there was in Margaret Irwin's work something fanciful, elusive – was 'fey' the word? At any rate Sappho fixed her with a minatory, mandatory glance: 'What you need, my dear child, is an affair with a prominent labour leader', which was Sappho's way of saying 'come down to earth'. Whether or not she followed the advice, only Peg and her maker and presumably one other person know – but she did in fact marry [soon] ... and there was undoubtedly a note of solidity in the fine series of historical novels [that followed]....
>
> Sappho was an important figure; her voice was influential in the adjustment of reputations on that literary bourse [of London]. Everyone knew about her, everyone talked about her, most of her friends liked her, they all respected her ...

During the eleven months I was away she spent at least twelve weeks out of London, mostly in Cornwall, but she managed to meet and write to me concerning 85 different people, nearly all writers, most of whom had been to her house several times. Some of these, who were great friends, she saw over and over again, either in her home or at the To-Morrow Club meetings, and there were many more with whom she was on warm and friendly terms, although she did not actually see so much of them.

She also arranged a weekly dinner for 'my starving men, and an occasional starving woman'. These had started in the very early To-Morrow Club days, when Sappho discovered that some of her young would-be writer friends – notably Henry Williamson and Hermon Ould – were often *hungry*, and these meals continued on into the twenties. She wrote:

> I provide a really good cooked meal, and then give them some tins of food to take home to tide them over until the next week.

She also took trouble, both in her home and at the To-Morrow Club, to introduce her protegées to literary agents, editors, publishers, but only if she thought her young friends' efforts were worth while. If she didn't, she told them so. While her contemporaries called her Sappho, these young people mostly addressed her as 'Mrs Sappho'. I think she must sometimes have been rather alarming, since she did not easily forgive any liberties or slights. But Hector Hawton, who later became a director of the Rationalist Press Association, did not think so. He had been a journalist apprentice on the *Western Morning News* as a very young man and had come to London in 1920 to work for the London Press Association and later the *Evening Standard*. A colleague told him about the To-Morrow Club, so he went along one evening, met Sappho and was invited to our house. He described her as being

> such a good hostess. She didn't let you just sit or stand, but brought up someone to meet you and, if that introduction did not look a happy one, she found someone else.

He was not a bit frightened of her:

> She was so kind, and I liked her. You are not frightened of someone you like.

And here is Sappho's own account of one of these 'At Homes':

> Thirteen dropped in to tea. All the usual and Peter (Stern), May Sinclair and Mary Webb – I've just read her latest, *The House in Dormer Forest*. It is beautiful. Henry Williamson was really nice and brought

me a book. Collins has just given him a contract. I had a long talk with
Louis Golding: his book, *Forward from Babylon*, is really very good – I
wept unashamedly at the boy's description of the death of his mother. I
am writing an article for America, 'Forward from Russia', showing
how Zangwill, John Cournos and Louis Golding are the result of their,
or their forebears', flight from the terror of Czardom.

Violet Hunt was as usual charming and stayed to supper ... Ford's
baby has come (born to the woman for whom he left Violet) and she
said, when I marvelled at her constancy, 'I fancy the way he kisses.'
That is the thing a person can't get over – they have a fancy for ... 'the
way he kisses'. That tiresome Ford!

Sappho had arranged a first-rate programme of talks for the
To-Morrow Club in 1921, which included in its speakers Siegfried
Sassoon, Lady Rhondda, Sheila Kaye-Smith, Lord Dunsany, John
Galsworthy, Gilbert Frankau, Edith Sitwell and Harold Monro.

It was Galsworthy again and we had a tremendous evening ... The
Sitwells came last night – all three of them – and all 6 foot high ...
Charming to talk to, but arrogant on paper.

But deeply involved as she was with the To-Morrow Club, in the
summer of 1921 she was already moving towards the foundation of the
P.E.N.

Mary Austin, representing the American *Bookman*, came to London
with an introduction to St John Adcock (editor of the *Bookman* in
London) who in turn introduced her to Sappho.

With the arrival of Mary Austin without, or with only inadequate
introductions, a small seed was dropped into Sappho's receptive and
restless imagination; her interest in international matters, so far
confined to America, had been deepened by a visit she had paid to me
in Warsaw in late May, and these were two of the ingredients stirred
into the pudding bowl of her London life, which culminated a few
weeks later in the idea of the P.E.N.

But, in that July of 1921, she was exhausted, the To-Morrow Club
season had ended, and she was off to Cornwall with my two brothers.
Several of her friends would be going down to stay at nearby farms,
including Mrs Mac, the medium, with whom Sappho intended to
have long psychic sessions.

And I was due home in two months.

20

Sappho's Literary Standing

Before describing the P.E.N. about which she wrote to me in Warsaw during August and September, I think it is worthwhile outlining Sappho's social and literary position in 1921.

During the three years from 1918 to 1921 her reputation among writers both here and abroad had consolidated, although it is difficult to understand how she found time to write not only three novels, but also poems, articles and book reviews for a wide variety of journals. Her books were also published in America, and *Wastralls* was one of the three chosen for consideration by the Femina Prize Selection Committee. Actually the prize was finally awarded to Constance Holme for *The Splendid Fairing*.

Even after the foundation of the P.E.N. and her deep involvement in the organisation of this, her most important Idea, she also edited, together with Ernest Rhys (editor of the Everyman Library), a series of collections of short stories. These were published in England by Messrs Holden and Hutchinson, and in America by D.A. Appleton. Some of the titles were *26 Mystery Stories*, *28 Humorous Stories*, *26 Adventure Stories* etc., and this all entailed a lot of correspondence, writing to the authors for their permission to publish, or to estates where the author was deceased, sending small cheques and 'thank you' letters. Most authors, however famous, were delighted to have their stories republished, although they were often dilatory in replying and had to be written to several times. One of these collections contained stories by W.W. Jacobs, E.M. Delafield, Flora Annie Steel, H. de Vere Stacpoole, A.E. Coppard, Wilkie Collins and Pushkin! Although all this was a heavy administrative chore, it kept Sappho in touch with all kinds of writers who were then invited to join the To-Morrow Club.

As she discussed her fellow novelists' work, so they discussed hers, and she began to be well-known. Many American and European writers and journalists came to London with introductions to her and were invited to tea and she and her group of novelist friends – all women – had published 21 books between 1918 and 1921! There were also the books by her very young men friends – Henry Williamson, Louis Golding, Alec Waugh … In her circle she was judged a serious writer, a woman of letters, with something of value to contribute to the literary scene. Because she liked company and modest entertaining, her house was the centre of a fairly wide group of representatives of all the different branches of writing – editors, sub-editors, publishers, newspaper proprietors or columnists, literary agents, translators, as well as the 'real' writers – novelists, poets, playwrights, historians. I am sure, if she had happened to come across a printer, she would have been greatly interested and he also would have been invited to come to tea.

There were, of course, other circles, who were not sympathetic towards her and whom she neither knew nor wanted to know, although she might admire their books. The 'Bloomsbury group' was one of these, and I think, if they came across each other at all, Sappho would have been regarded as something of a menace, with her flow of ideas – in which she would try to involve others, her forthright and uninhibited approach, her requests for short stories for her 'Collections'. She only met the Sitwells, or T.S. Eliot, for instance, when they came at her invitation to lecture to the To-Morrow Club, and I don't think she ever came across Virginia Woolf. Like everyone else, they came willingly, but I think it unlikely they would have admired her books, even if they ever read them.

And yet those Cornish novels have an historic value now far greater than when they were written, due to the catastrophic change that has come to the way of life in Cornwall. The characters, set in carefully observed backgrounds, were often thinly-disguised local people; and, although the main theme or plot was invented or based on a legend, many of the smaller, day-to-day events had really happened and were described truthfully, with only a change of name – just enough deviation to prevent positive identification. Sappho had come to know well Alice Tippett, the farm labourer's wife at the cottage at Trevose, where we stayed in 1908. Alice was able to transcribe Sappho's sentences, written in ordinary English, into Cornish phraseology. She would read a sentence, and Mrs Tippett would correct her with: 'We do say …'. Also, Alice was for many years the village midwife and had a fund of spicy tales concerning the 'goings on' in the village which were very useful to a novelist. She was observant, wise and full of human understanding, and the two women, roughly the same age, were friends for 'a pretty many years'. Yet Alice always addressed Sappho as 'ma'am' or 'Mrs Scott'.

Wastralls, the first book set in Cornwall, was dedicted to 'Alice

Tippett, to whose kind help on many a Sunday afternoon I owe the west country talk'. Sappho made a point of using local names that were fairly commonplace, fifty years ago, but are rarely heard now: Richbell, Tamsin, Loveday, Gray, Dusha, Vina (Lavinia), Sabina, Isolda (pronounced *Eye*solda), Zenobia, Doney (Sidonia), and for the men Pascoe, Leadville, Freathy, Ephraim, Tavis, Enos, Malachai ... Nowadays the old Cornish surnames are usually prefixed by Pam, Pat, Doreen, or Maureen, and Peter, Julian, Anthony, David or Roger. Sad!

And some of Alice Tippett's wonderful Cornish phraseology, expressing the West Country dialect in common use at that time, is set down in Sappho's Cornish books as a permanent record: 'I'm all behind like a cow's tail'; 'She'm pretty and wish't', meaning 'She's ill', or 'ill-wished'; A grandmother to a lively toddler: 'Come on then, me 'andsome, come on then, me lover – why, 'e's a proper dragon!' And I once asked Mrs Tippett why she always referred to a sow or mare as 'he'? And her reply was: 'They'm all "he", save an old Tom Cat, and he'm she.'

The first three Cornish novels, *Wastralls*, *The Headland* and *The Haunting* were published in quick succession in 1918, 1920 and 1921, all by Heinemann, and there was then a gap until 1925. In 1920 William Heinemann died, and she lost a dear friend, writing of him sadly:

William Heinemann has died of aortic disease – my kind friend. A diamond mind, a greatness of generosity, a man who lived for his ideals.

A collection of her poems called *Bitter Herbs* was published in 1923 and she had sent it to Heinemann in 1920. He had taken it home to read and it was found in his flat after he died.

21

P.E.N. – the Idea

Within a week of her arrival at Levorna Cottage, Constantine Bay, in August 1921, Sappho wrote to me in Warsaw and mentioned for the first time her Idea of the P.E.N.:

> August 4, 1921. Levorna, Thursday. Marjorie! I've got an IDEA! A Dining Club – men and women of repute! I'm going to write to Violet [Hunt] about it – she and I could do it – it neatly cuts out unnecessary husbands and wives. Tuesdays for the Dinners – 8 p.m. at The Florence Restaurant. They have them in America – those clubs.

And in other letters, written at weekly intervals, the Idea grows apace:

> Wednesday. To-day we walked to Porthcothan [along the Cornish cliffs] – a heavy grey sky, but lovely walking, so soft underfoot. I wrote to Adcock [St John] suggesting a dinner club for P.P.E.N. (Poet, Playwright, Editor, Novelist) people, and if he says it's a good idea, I'll worry Violet and Cynthia Stockley.

> Yesterday we drove to the moorland village of Rosenannon, St Wenn, and I got rooms for myself for the first week in September.
> My Pen Club has got its first members – John Robert Gregg, the American publisher, and Muriel Stuart. Also, Gregg will help me in any way he can and, if I get started here, he will get going in America. I'm greatly pleased and encouraged.

> Arthur John Rees is going to join the Pen Club, thinks it's a capital idea, will bring along 'real men' and be on the Committee. I'm delighted. This must be a real man-and-woman club, not me doing everything.

> I've started my international dinner club ... and the first dinner is to be at The Florence Restaurant, Piccadilly, 4/– on Tuesday, October 5th, then every Tuesday until further notice – Oh, I'll send you a paper

about it. I want Violet [Hunt] and Cynthia Stockley on the Committee, also Gregg.

If it is to be international, it must have an American who knows who's who on that side of the water, and the Greggs have had a cold welcome over here and realise how indifferent and inhospitable the English are. I have also asked Mrs Mann [Elizabeth Craig] as she is such a good advertiser and was editor of some woman's paper – and she is also very charming.

By this time I had had time to recover my breath and wrote protesting that she had enough to do already with the To-Morrow Club, her many friends and all her other interests. Also that, as I was coming home after a year abroad and was engaged to be married, I wanted a little of her time and attention.

Sappho, of course, was not deflected. She wrote:

Tuesday. I observe your encouraging attitude towards my P.E.N. Club. My family is always so encouraging – to begin with! Perhaps if I explain a little, though: Mary Austin, the biggest American publicist and journalist, was sent here to write up our authors – valuable publicity for our books in America – and there was no organisation here to receive her and put her wise to our movements in literature. If we had an International Dinner club, with centres in every capital city in the world, membership of one meaning membership of all, we should have a common meeting ground for all writers in every country. *Now* do you see? Already the idea is being talked about in the papers – I've got one Australian and three American members ...

Thursday. Well, the idea is more to draw the nations together – a United States of Europe and America in literature. Do you get me? I want centres in Paris, New York ...

Saturday. I got leave from Austin Harrison to write an Article for the English Review on the books of Violet Hunt, Fryn Tennyson Jesse, Constance Holme and Olive Salter, so have been absorbed.

I shall enjoy my lonely week at Rosenannon. I shall try to make acquaintance with the whole village! I know three families already, and there are only about a dozen.

On September 1st she was driven in a pony trap over to Rosenannon, St Wenn, so that she could absorb the moorland atmosphere needed for her current book, *They Green Stones*. This book, not published until 1925, was dedicated:

> To the members of all P.E.N. Centres, because the Idea of the P.E.N.
> came to me on the Cornish Moors, when writing it.

In spite of the above dedication, the Idea of the P.E.N. did *not* come
to Sappho in that way. It had obviously been germinating in her mind
for some time, and Stephen Southwold (nicknamed Bunty) in *My
Writing Life* records a conversation he had with Sappho in the
summer of 1921, just *before* she went to Cornwall in early August:

> Many have claimed that the P.E.N. Club was their brain child. They
> lie. It was Sappho's child, and hers alone, and I was present at its birth
> ... I remember it clearly. I had stayed on to supper after one of her
> literary teas ... Suddenly she said, interrupting what I was saying and
> with complete irrelevance – 'A Literary Club, Bunty, which will
> include everybody who's done anything. Don't you think that's what
> we need? Now, what are we going to call it? Any ideas?' I made several
> fatuous suggestions. 'I've got it,' she said, 'the P.E.N. Club. All
> capitals. P. for Poets, E. for Essayists, and N. for Novelists. And there's
> the play on 'pen'. What do you think of it?'
>
> I said I thought it was crackerjack – a Suffolk word for something of
> surpassing excellence, and she smiled and went on: 'We must have a
> president, and he must be big enough to act as a magnet to draw in all
> the rest. And there's only one man can do that just now.'
>
> 'Wells,' said I.
>
> 'Oh, my dear Bunty. Not H.G. He's the last man. Dozens wouldn't
> come in if Wells was president. Think again.'
>
> 'You don't mean Shaw?'
>
> 'You're not very bright to-night. He's more impossible than dear
> H.G.'
>
> 'You don't mean Galsworthy?'
>
> 'But I *do* mean Galsworthy. He was made for it. And everyone will
> come in like sheep following the shepherd. He hasn't an enemy. He is
> charming, delightful, a pleasant speaker, has infinite tact. And he's a
> gentleman. H.G. isn't. Nor Arnold [Bennett] – not that I thought of
> asking *him*. Hermon Ould will be secretary – he's a born secretary and
> loves work.'
>
> So was born the P.E.N. Club with John Galsworthy as President,
> Hermon Ould as Secretary ... There were 150 Foundation Members, of
> whom I was one.

Many people have included references to the P.E.N. Club and to
Sappho in their reminiscences. Those I have read have almost
invariably been inaccurate, and Bunty Southwold was the same as the
others, although his inaccuracies were only minor. I think his account
of his talk with Sappho is probably correct, in the main, although his
book was published 34 years later, but ... Hermon Ould was *not* the

first secretary of the P.E.N. – *I* was, for nearly six years, and there were 44 Foundation Members and not 150.

In her conversation with Bunty Southwold about the possible first P.E.N. President, Sappho was dead right in her differentiation between J.G., H.G., and Arnold Bennett, although she always felt more at home with the two who were not 'gentlemen', and used them, particularly Wells, when she needed their help. Galsworthy was right for the first president, and Wells undoubtedly right for the second.

On the other hand, once she had emerged from the chrysalis of her early life, and after she left Cowes in 1909, I don't think she ever again thought of herself as a 'lady'!

As for planning the P.E.N. Club before she went to the moors in September, both my brothers remembered her telling them to sit down on the lawn beside her whilst she outlined her plans for the P.E.N. And she recorded their reactions.

> With dulling, lengthening faces, they both said, 'Oh, Mother, what a silly idea.'

But she *wanted* to have thought of the P.E.N. whilst on the Moors: this fitted in in some way, and in time I think she believed she had – just as Violet Hunt 'believed' Ford had *married* her – or did she?

At Rosenannon Sappho stayed with a farm workers' family in a 4-roomed cob cottage.[1] There were about a dozen cottages at Rosenannon, and the small community usually received a couple of letters a week. After my mother's arrival the postman came daily – with a sack containing parcels of books for review and quantities of letters with queer foreign stamps. In addition to these unusual features in village life, Sappho continued to wear her customary long gowns, and she walked up the lane and on to the moorland paths without shoes!

Sappho was known as 'The Mad Lodger'.

> Sept. 1st. I have had a lovely day. I set out to walk to the top of Rosenannon Downs, and as I went I picked blackberries and mushrooms. The downs stretched to the sky, rusty-coloured, due to the mixture of furze and heather and dried fawn grass. Up and up I went, and at last I got to a tumulus at the very top, and when I looked over, what do you think I saw? I was looking due west at Black Rock, [outside the entrance to Padstow Harbour]. Below was Wadebridge, and I looked straight up to Padstow and out to sea. It was a tremendous view. The pointed tents of the china clay dumps on one side, and the sea on the other. To right of me Bodmin Beacon, to the left Castell and

[1] Built of clay, gravel and straw.

Dinas. And the village was so far below I couldn't see it ...

But soon she was back in London.

Sept. 11th. Alexandra Rd. Many people are joining the P.E.N. No, Jermyn St won't do – it must be Soho to please the people from abroad. Marjorie, I've had my fortune told, and I was 'Queen of Clubs' – isn't it appropriate?

May Sinclair had written on August 30th apropos the P.E.N. idea:

My dear Sappho – it sounds all right. But how is it going to work out? Is Mrs Wharton going to meet Mr Wells and Mr Conrad and the editors of the Times and Quarterly? Or is Miss Sadie P. Tucker of Powkeepsie going to meet members of the To-Morrow Club? Because after all, you know, Mrs Austin succeeded in meeting most of the people she wanted to meet without any 'organization', and I don't imagine that Mrs Wharton ever had much difficulty. The trouble is that your qualification is so very wide: the success of a club of this sort depends as much on the people you *keep out* as on those you let in.

Sappho wanted May's support, so when, in late September, May invited her to lunch to meet Kate Douglas Wiggin, she went, although she was extremely busy, in order to 'get round May':

I explained that I'd told her about the P.E.N. because of her position in the literary world, as her due – tho' I knew she wouldn't be interested. She promptly said she *was* interested, and it was an excellent scheme, but clubs ... So I said 'Yes' and invited her to be my guest the first night ... and she accepted! said she's bringing Mrs Belloc Lowndes ... Now America loves May, and that will help us over there, so I'm excited and pleased. I've invited Fryn [Tennyson Jesse] and Sheila [Kaye-Smith] too. It must be a galaxy that first night.

May became a faithful and devoted P.E.N. member.

Sept. 13th. So I begin my last letter to you. Apparently it is the word 'international' that makes the P.E.N. Club attractive. I have framed the rules for the International Committee in each country. Each centre must have a representative on the International Committee of every other centre – this is not a jig-saw puzzle, but a neat and simple arrangement.
    Galsworthy has joined and many, many others. A dinner of about 40 on the 5th October ...

In these letters there is only one mention of what Sappho called 'The United States of Europe and America in Literature', but I assume she spoke of this when she wrote outlining her Idea to all the friends who responded so enthusiastically, because John Galsworthy wrote:

> Dear Mrs Dawson Scott. Anything that promotes the internationality of Art is to the good. The material and roots of Art are essentially national – or shall we say individual and local, but when once a work of art is achieved, all national and local barriers should be let down. So I will come to the dinner, since you so kindly express the desire to have me there. Yours sincerely, John Galsworthy.

Although the Idea of the P.E.N. had obviously been at the back of Sappho's mind for some weeks, or even months, once it had taken a definite shape which she had expressed in writing in early August, it was only two months before this was translated into reality at the Foundation Dinner on 5 October.

22

The Foundation Dinner

Forty-four writers and journalists came to the Foundation Dinner, and they all joined the new P.E.N. Club, being known from that date as 'Foundation Members'. They had not been especially selected because they were renowned: Sappho simply invited all her friends and acquaintances who had anything to do with writing, and a fair number of these were journalists and editors. She actually wrote to nearly double as many as came, and although quite a few were unable to attend the inaugural meeting, they nearly all promised support and joined within a few months. That is why such old P.E.N. friends as Henry Williamson and Alec Waugh were never technically Foundation Members, although Rebecca West was.

Those present included:

Louis Golding
C.S. Evans
Beverley Baxter
Rebecca West
Kate Douglas Wiggin
Stephen Southwold
May Sinclair
Violet Hunt
Austin Harrison
Marjorie Dawson Scott
Hermon Ould
W.L. George
Elizabeth Craig
Netta Syrett
Ethel Colborne Mayne
Fryn Tennyson Jesse
Sheila Kaye-Smith
John Galsworthy

After dinner Sappho outlined her Idea, and all present were enthusiastic. Austin Harrison was elected Hon. Treasurer, myself

Hon. Secretary and, after at first refusing, John Galsworthy was persuaded to become President – for one year.

In fact John Galsworthy remained President for $11\frac{1}{2}$ years, until his death in January 1933.

At that Foundation Dinner the following were also elected to form the nucleus of the first Executive Committee: Austin Harrison, L. Rose McLeod, Rebecca West, Elizabeth Craig, Horace Shipp, C.S. Evans and Louis Golding.

The success of the Foundation Dinner brought the P.E.N. fully into being, the first Committee meeting taking place a week later, with Austin Harrison in the chair. 'But,' commented Sappho,

> he had not the necessary gifts, and, in despair, we went to Mr Galsworthy to ask if, besides being President, he would act as Chairman. He agreed and from that moment our difficulties disappeared.

In the 12 years from 1921-33 Sappho and John Galsworthy worked closely together for the P.E.N. They were very different in character and yet complemented each other – she gay, enthusiastic and forthright, unconventional and wayward; J.G. shy, quiet and unhurried, wise and deliberate, unswayed by emotions, though often moved. But they had certain fundamentals in common – a deep belief in internationalism, a dislike of grandeur and show, snobbishness or racial prejudice, and they both loved the under-dog. In fact, although coming from such totally different backgrounds, they were of one mind to a surprising degree. And, as they had known each other since the early days of the To-Morrow Club in 1917, each had had time to assess the other's qualities.

As President of the P.E.N. one of J.G.'s great advantages was that he had a critical and legal mind – he was, after all, a trained lawyer – and this was of immense benefit to the P.E.N. He counteracted Sappho's impulsiveness, and was a controlling influence over her sudden ideas. There were occasions when, without J.G.'s restraining voice, these might have led the P.E.N. into difficulties. She, fortunately, recognised these special qualities in J.G. The two were almost always in agreement over P.E.N. policy, whereas in minor matters, such as Thomas Hardy's funeral in Westminster Abbey, they agreed to differ. I do not remember them ever being at odds over a major problem, except Sappho's desire for a P.E.N. House or Home, and then she gave way (see below, pp. 155-7). If it was a question of P.E.N. ideals, J.G. invariably deferred to her.

*

Although Austin Harrison was not a very strong chairman, the first meeting of the new Executive Committee was a long one and a number of decisions were taken and rules made, of which I will only mention one:

> No one guest shall be allowed to attend P.E.N. dinners more than three times a year.

Sappho invented and supported this rule in order that husband/wife members would not always be obliged to take their spouses to dinners. She had not forgotten Heinemann's advice in 1898 about husbands and wives cramping each other's style. The pattern of P.E.N. meetings (in London at least) has changed so much in the last twenty years that this rule is never adhered to now, even if it still exists.

Suggestions were made regarding writers with European and American connections who could advise on whom to approach to start centres in the countries where they had influence, and a list was prepared of British writers to be invited to join. J.G. himself wrote to those he knew personally, including Joseph Conrad, Gilbert Murray, Siegfried Sassoon ...

Two weeks later, on 26 October, the Committee met again, this time with Galsworthy in the chair, as he was to be, whenever he was in England, for the next twelve years. Sappho was present much more often as she did not travel so much or so far, although she was seldom chairman.

In late October the first Ordinary, as distinct from the Foundation, Dinner was held, at which 72 people were present, among them several Canadian and American authors.

Meanwhile, many writers responded to invitations to join, including G.K. Chesterton, Cunninghame-Graham, and Joseph Conrad who wrote to John Galsworthy on November 1st, 1921:

> Dearest Jack – I was just about to sit down and write to you (about *To Let*) when your letter arrived with the P.E.N. Circular. I'll do as directed. I have also noted the Chairman's leniency in the matter of attendance at dinners. Indeed, my dearest Jack, I would very seldom find anyone I knew there – by which my natural shyness would be increased 1000 per cent and probably cause my death from acute embarrassment. (*Life & Letters of John Galsworthy*, by H.V. Marrot, 1935.)

I was also instructed to write to a carefully chosen list of distinguished foreign writers, who were admired in England, and invite them to become Honorary Members of the Founding Centre. Thomas Hardy and W.H. Hudson were asked to represent England.

The new P.E.N. Executive Committee was entirely non-political – I think the members hardly knew what each other's politics or religions were. In fact, looking back, it seems as if the Committee members were at first almost unaware of the political connotations the names of some continental writers would evoke. Their choice of Hon. Members was quite simply those writers who were most read and known in Britain.

They soon learned better.

One of the first countries to be approached about starting a Centre was France, and both Anatole France and Romain Rolland had promised their support. Edith Wharton was asked to be the Hon. Member for America. This, however, raised a difficult question – the first of many similar problems, as, owing to Romain Rolland having been approached, Edith Wharton refused the invitation to represent America. She wrote to J.G. that she considered it would be difficult to organise a Centre in France, since both Romain Rolland and Anatole France belonged to the same political party. The Committee was surprised and tried to find a way around this problem, finally deciding to invite Pierre Loti also to become an Hon. Member, and to regard Rolland as an Hon. Member of the English Centre only, not necessarily even a member of the French Centre! On 6 December, J.G. wrote to Sappho:

I enclose a letter from André Chevrillon, from which you will see that our choice of Rolland is still a stumbling block. I propose to write to Chevrillon and try to make him understand that our choice has nothing to do with the French Centre ... I have become convinced that the English Centre must only lead by example and cannot dictate what shall be the procedure of other centres in the matter of membership. We shall hit many snags if we try to and, further, we shall be going against the free spirit of friendliness which is the very base of the Idea. Let us *force* nothing on anyone, and we may succeed. We will set example by (1) inviting as Hon. Members of our Centre the foreign writers we most admire in England, and, (2) by making the members of every other centre members of ours. But there, I think we must stop.

J.G. was an expert chairman with a thorough knowledge of Committee procedure, and he was meticulous in taking no major decisions until the matter had been discussed in Committee. More often than not he was able to clarify the particular issue in such a way that the Committee was willing to follow his lead.

At the very end of his life, in August 1932, after the Hungarian

Congress, he refused to reply *officially* from the P.E.N. to a letter in the *Manchester Guardian* concerning a certain trial and possible death sentence in Hungary because 'it would take weeks to get the opinion of the Executive Committee at this time of year ...'

But he wrote personally and urgently to the Regent of Hungary, Admiral Horthy.

23

The International Committee

By January 1922, Selma Lagerlöf, Knut Hamsun, Blasco Ibañez, Romain Rolland, Maurice Maeterlinck, Anatole France, Georg Brandes, Arthur Schnitzler, A.E. (George Russell) and W.B. Yeats had all agreed to become Hon. Members of the English Centre, and their acceptance at once gave the newly formed organisation great international prestige.

The earliest centre to be formed was in Paris in the January or February 1922, and the Secretary was Benjamin Crémieux. He became a great P.E.N. figure whom we all came to know and love – thick black beard, gesticulations and capacity for non-stop oratory notwithstanding. He was a Jew who, unhappily, did not survive the war, which was a deep sorrow to all who knew him.[1]

Almost at the same time as the French Centre started, we heard that Señor Lòpez-Picó had founded a centre in Barcelona; and Louis Piérard, Editor of *Le Soir* (Brussels) wrote to say the first dinner of the Belgian P.E.N. Centre would be in April. Also in April J.G. reported on a visit he had made to Scandinavia, where plans were going ahead in Norway and Sweden.

By this time it was clear that an immense volume of work in connection with the international side was piling up, too much to be dealt with by the small Executive Committee, and Sappho suggested it was time to establish the International Committee, which she had already foreshadowed, to organise and maintain contact with the centres. She and J.G. would be on it, but other members would be writers living in England who had international contacts: such as William Archer, Edward Shanks, Rosita Forbes. The first meeting of this international committee was on 22 February 1922 at Sappho's house.

[1] Storm Jameson referred movingly to him in *Journey from the North*, vol. 2, pp.15 & 16.

That summer the young Italian poet, Lauro de Bosis, son of the poet Adolpho de Bosis, who had been a friend of and greatly influenced by d'Annunzio, came to London to find out about the P.E.N. He was about my age and a most charming, handsome and romantic young man. He was as surprised and delighted to find the formidable Secretary of the P.E.N. was a girl of 23 as I was to meet him. I showed him round London, we talked of the P.E.N. – and other things – and he returned to Italy and started the Rome Centre, which was, therefore, one of the earliest.

Lauro de Bosis won the Prize for poetry at the Olympiads in Amsterdam in 1929 for his poem 'Icarus', which was translated into French by Romain Rolland. Lauro himself translated into Italian an abridged edition of Frazer's *Golden Bough*. He wrote to me sometimes until I married in 1925, and remained secretary of the Rome Centre until his death in 1930.

In July, Marcu Beza, cultural attaché at the Roumanian Embassy in London, announced the formation of the Roumanian Centre, with some members from the Academy and some younger writers, and with the Queen as Hon. President. Queen Marie was herself a novelist, and was, incidentally, half English, being the daughter of the then Duke of Edinburgh.

Already some centres were having teething troubles: Marion Ryan, an American journalist and a founder member of the English Centre, reported that she had been present at a very successful dinner of fifty people in New York, but that the American Centre was being very exclusive and trying to keep the Club small – they appeared not to have grasped the international aims of the P.E.N. – the membership was very limited, no attempt was made to entertain foreigners, and the President, Booth Tarkington, took very little active interest. J.G. said he would write and ask what their Annual General Meeting arrangements were and gently suggest Mr Hamlin Garland as President next year.

One of the difficulties over the establishment of the American Centre was whether it was to call itself the New York Centre or the American Centre. Alexander Black was the chief organiser, but correspondence was with Maxwell Aley, who later became and for many years remained, Secretary of the New York Centre. J.G. reflected on this problem and then wrote to me:

I think we shall have to adopt a policy of recognising New York as the American Centre, with any branches that they may advise us to recognise ... it is obviously not for us to dictate or advise America how to arrange its P.E.N. Club, and I send you a draft letter on those lines.

Brian Rhys, son of Ernest Rhys, had written from France that Anatole France had agreed to be President of the French Centre. However, as it seemed from his letter that the French Centre was being organised entirely by the Left and Young Party, I was asked to write a careful letter suggesting that the Founding Centre would be very pleased to know that some of the older writers were also joining and to reiterate the non-political aims of the P.E.N.

The Committee was entirely against Brian Rhys' suggestion of a Government subsidy.

By the time the first A.G.M. was held in October 1922, about seven centres had started and several more were in the initial stages.

24

Scottie

Sappho left an immense amount of written data. She wrote easily and quickly, using a stylo pen, and, as if her journals and letters were not enough, she also wrote a full-length novel called *Any Woman*, which she had typed and bound, but which was never published. It is undoubtedly the thinly-disguised story of her own adult life in novel form, from her girlhood in London until 1930, when, in her current journal, she wrote: 'Feb. 28th. Have finished *Any Woman*.'

This novel starts before I was born, and, although the only one of her real children who plays a part in the story is her youngest son, my brother Toby, there are many incidents and descriptions which seem authentic. The character of Scottie and her gradual disillusionment with her marriage, and her own feelings and attitudes are all there; also her love for Arthur Lynch. Yet I had to bear in mind that she was first and foremost a creative writer and that, in her other published novels, she had often begun to draw a character from real life who had gradually developed a personality which finally had little to do with the original. Also that she used incidents that had actually happened and attached them to her own characters, if they fitted in with her story.

I decided that, when the events described in *Any Woman* were within my own memory or my brothers', I could accept and use them, but where I was unable to check, I would have to reject. The detailed accounts of the drinking habits and love-affairs of the husband in the novel (Alfred) I only half-accept, since Scottie did not appear like that to us, his three children, or to other members of the family to whom I have talked. Also, in her journals, she makes frequent affectionate references to him.

Arthur Lynch, or a character very like him, also plays an important part in the book, but that can be accepted because she really only describes what she made clear in her journals, her letters and in her life – her love for him and constant hope of fulfilment, which she never achieved.

My father's death was, however, described faithfully in the book.

In 1922 Scottie was a General Practitioner in a Welsh mining district, where he lived with the new 'Mrs Scott' and her children. As he had written to me in Warsaw in 1921, the miners' strike had made it very difficult for him financially, and recently Sappho had told him she could manage without the £100 a quarter which he had agreed to send her. He had replied gratefully.

Suddenly she received a telegram from 'Mrs Scott': 'Dr Scott has gone away. Has he returned to you?' This was followed by a letter to my brother Toby saying: 'Your Dad is not here. I should be glad if you would come down. Mrs Scott.'

Sappho was greatly alarmed. She suspected suicide and was momentarily glad that she had told Scottie that he need not send her any money. But she also thought that, in releasing him from what he would consider a duty, she had set him free. She remembered his depressions – would there be anything now to hold him back?

The next day Sappho and I and Toby and Scottie's unmarried sister, 'Auntie Maud', took the train to Cwm Amman in South Wales, where we were met by 'Mrs Scott', a small, rather sallow little woman of early middle age, dressed in black. She said: 'You must not blame him ... the Doctor took poison ...'

We learned the sad story. He had not been himself for a fortnight – some worry about a tax claim he could not meet. (We found out later that this had been one of those first assessments the Inland Revenue sends out that one disputes. It was for £40 and he would not have had to pay it.) Mrs Scott continued:

> I got frightened, he was so restless. Then on Tuesday he went out after dinner to see a patient at the hospital. He always hated going there – he said it was dark – he didn't come back. He went to the chemist and bought prussic acid – to poison cats. [Cats! My Father, the kindest of men ...] He went to the hospital, but didn't go in – there is a tree outside, and they saw a man lying there asleep ...

Sappho gave an account of the sequel to the above story in *Any Woman*, and as I was there I give it:

> Grief overwhelmed Reb [the wife]. She no longer saw the woman standing before her, she saw only Alfred, who had been her husband. He would have paused outside the hospital, would have looked towards 'the place that was dark', turned from it to the bitter draught. Better death than the further effort. The poison could not have tasted worse than many of the medicines that he had prescribed. She could see him slipping down in that sudden sleep. 'He is with you?' she asked. The

woman shrank. 'Oh no – no – I couldn't have him – he is in the hospital mortuary. I haven't seen him – I waited till you came.'

After all, she had not been his wife for 25 years.

'We will drive to the hospital at once.' Not for a moment longer should he be left to his lonely, perhaps remorseful dreams. For all she knew he might be able to see them, hear what was said. If so, he should be reassured. He might grieve that he had not been able, any longer, to endure.

The house of the dead had several chambers which were partitioned by glass and lighted from above. On a raised bier Alfred slept. Reb walked in quickly and the others followed. Had she thought he would be unhappy at having failed her and the children? That he would need her tender re-assurance?

He lay with his lips parted so that strong stained teeth could be seen between the moustache which was as ragged with cigarette burns as before the war; but, although he lay there she could have no doubt that he was gone and already far away. He was tremendously at peace. Her grief was blown from her, a feather in a high wind.

Although Sappho wrote that eight years later in 1930, my own feelings at the time were quite different, although this was a factual account. That visit to the mortuary was one of the most shocking events of my whole life. I was 23 and had lived through the First World War, during which I had lost friends and cousins, but I had never seen anyone dead, and to see violent death in my own father appalled me. I could hardly bear to look at his face, and it did not strike me as at peace. I was overwhelmed by imagining the misery and distress that must have brought him to this.

Contrary to the description in *Any Woman*, Sappho was not at all calm. She was hysterically upset, weeping and inconsolable. There had been an inquest – suicide while of unsound mind – and the funeral was the following day. We stayed that night in a depressing small hotel which catered especially for travelling salesmen; I shared a room with Auntie Maud, and Toby lay on a bed beside Sappho, who wept unceasingly, and whom he tried to comfort and calm.

I did not feel deeply sympathetic towards Sappho on that occasion. She had, after all, divorced my father two years previously, after years of quarrelling, and he was living with someone else. She had never appeared to give him a thought in her busy London life, and I had all those letters about her feelings for The Lynx. I thought she was hysterical and uncontrolled, but luckily Toby's love for and identification with his mother in that crisis transcended all other feelings, although he was only just 18, and he was able to support and guide her through that dreadful night and the funeral next day.

I do not know what happened to Mrs Scott. She had children and had left her husband to live with my father, and their love affair had been going on for about ten years. Had I been a little older and more experienced I would have wanted to make sure she found some way of managing, but after the horror of the funeral – held in pouring rain and mud in an ugly Welsh cemetery, with Sappho red-eyed and weeping on one side of the grave, and poor little 'Mrs Scott' on the other – alone – I hardly thought of her again. Poverty, loneliness and the needs of children had not yet impinged on my imagination.

And my father? After the war – that war he had so much enjoyed – he walked daily from St John's Wood to his Pension Board office in Chelsea, to avoid crowds. Confined spaces? Dark places? In the end he could not manage without his anchor, that strong personality to whom he had been attracted when a lonely young locum in Sutton nearly thirty years before.

Could Sappho have saved him from the final 'dark place'? She did not understand the world of psychiatry, as her eldest son came to understand it, when years after her death, aged 40 he qualified and practised as a psychiatrist.

25

The First International Congress

So much interest had been aroused internationally in that first year of the P.E.N. that by November, 1922, Sappho and J.G. thought it was time to have a meeting in London of representatives from all the newly established Centres. It was therefore decided to hold a special Dinner on 1 May 1923, to which all the Hon. Members of the English Centre plus two or three members or delegates from each Centre should be invited. The announcement of this plan encouraged half-formed centres to complete their organisations, since they all wanted to take part, and we were delighted to learn that eleven centres would be represented. Invitations were also sent to the Hon. Members *we* had elected, although usually these writers were already honoured members in their own countries.

The Dinner was to be held at the Hotel Cecil, costing 12s 6d each for men and 10s 6d for women, to include cigars, white and red wine and coffee – presumably the extra 2s for men was for the cigars. In addition to the dinner on 1st May, Mr Basil Dean had offered to entertain the whole gathering to a Gala Night at his new theatre, when two plays by Gordon Bottomley and Lascelles Abercrombie would be presented. There would also be a reception at the Suffolk Galleries, and an expedition to Stratford-upon-Avon, when Violet Hunt and Rebecca West offered to be escorts. The estimated total cost of all these festivities, including the rail fares for the delegates from Catalonia and Roumania, was £200: 164 Hon. Members, delegates and ordinary members were present.

J.G. and my mother took a great deal of personal responsibility for the arrangements, with me as dogsbody to both, and J.G. went to endless trouble to ensure the support of British writers. Bernard Shaw at first refused a request to go to Stratford, pleading a prior engagement, but our date was changed, and he and his wife Charlotte came to the lunch at the Arden Hotel. He wrote as to the visitation of foreigners:

If they are all as hopeless at languages as I am, the babel will be hideous. I have tackled Hauptmann and Bojer, and Bojer, who knows English, came off the better. Give them both my love. Never heard of Nexo – sounds like a polish in an oil shop. G.B.S.

Violet Hunt offered to have Romain Rolland to stay with her for the Congress – she spoke French – and on April 14th J.G. wrote to Sappho:

Apropos Violet Hunt and Rolland, does it occur to you that he may feel it odd to be the guest of a bachelor woman? We don't want to risk his not coming for any such reason.

In the end M. Rolland came under the protection of his sister.
On April 18th, in answer to a 'cri de coeur' from Sappho, J.G. wrote:

Poor dear Mrs Scott, I do sympathise. As to people who don't send cheques for their dinner, let them come all the same, and we will collect afterwards, if we have to sell them up.

A cheque for £20 should be sent at once to M. Beza (founder of Roumanian Centre), for the Roumanians. And Hauptmann should be written to asking *how* we shall provide their travelling expenses. The Catalans also should have their cheque – 2 return fares. Shaw will be at Stratford and will lunch with us at the Arden Hotel. Bennett will come to the reception, Drinkwater to dinner and reception, Barrie to the dinner. Squire will do anything he can, will try and bring Shanks ... I think Sutro should have an invitation ...

One small incident at the P.E.N. banquet has stayed with me: as I walked among the guests with my seating list, a very small man with a moustache smiled at me and asked, 'And where do I sit?' 'Well, who are you?' I queried. And he said gently, 'My name is Barrie.'

G.B.S. and his wife, who spoke perfect French, duly came to the lunch at Stratford, although I do not remember that they fraternised overmuch. However, encouraged by the great man coming at all, and egged on by J.G., Sappho, ever an optimist, invited Shaw to preside at a P.E.N. Dinner. He replied, on a postcard:

Galsworthy was pulling your leg. He knows I abhor literary society. As to presiding at a literary dinner – words fail me. What attraction do you find in it? You can't have really enjoyed that foolish crowd at Stratford. G. Bernard Shaw.

He was quite wrong, of course: Sappho had enjoyed the expedition very much indeed. Some years later she tried to persuade Shaw to preside at a Tolstoy Centenary dinner, but he declined, saying quite kindly that 'the P.E.N. was Galsworthy's affair, and he was not going to barge in.'

At Stratford, after the luncheon, the cosmopolitan party duly visited the Shakespeare Theatre. I had tried to book the first few rows of seats in the Dress Circle, but two were permanently taken by the novelist Marie Corelli and her companion. She quite often did not use these tickets and was asked if on this occasion the P.E.N. could have her seats, but she said 'No'. And there she sat, in the middle of that large crowd of writers from many countries, who had never heard of her, although she was, of course, well-known to a section of the reading public in this country. Miss Corelli was not a member of the P.E.N. – I doubt if, in those early days, she would have been elected – and, although I deplored the situation and felt uneasily guilty, since certainly no one was being 'friendly', I was too busy and involved guiding, rescuing and shepherding the chattering P.E.N. flock to do anything about it. In fact, my chief memory of that first Congress was of being in a constant state of sheer fright that something would go terribly wrong and that my inadequacy as a linguist in that multi-lingual crowd would let me down at some crucial point.

However, in spite of all the difficulties, this first P.E.N. Congress was a huge success, immense enthusiasm was generated, and the pattern laid down for future congresses.

Two invitations were received to hold the second Congress in New York and Paris. Although France had actually started first, it was considered that the French Centre was not yet sufficiently organised to enable it to hold a Congress, and J.G. managed to persuade the French Secretary, Crémieux, to postpone their invitation until 1925, and the American one was accepted for 1924.

26

Russia, New York and the Queen of Roumania

As soon as the International Committee was established in 1922 it began to explore the possibilities of forming a Russian Centre, but with little success.

To avoid confusion I have put several references to Russia – spread over the next few years – together. For those of us who have lived through the last sixty years, the tentative efforts made by the P.E.N. in the twenties seem rather naive, but at that time the Committee was putting out feelers through any writers it was in touch with who had some contact, however slight, with Russia.

In 1923 Stephen Graham joined the Committee and reported that Boris Pilnyak who had just been a guest at a dinner, was very keen to start a Centre in Moscow when he returned there in August. He thought the idea of the P.E.N. was splendid, that it would not be used politically and that it could be organised in conjunction with the exiled Russian writers. It was agreed to write to Ivan Bunin, Alexander Kuprin, Maxim Gorky and Dimitri Merezhkovsky and ask their views.

At a later meeting of the International Committee the following succinct paragraph appears in the Minutes:

It was explained to Mr Graham that, in view of the replies received from Messrs Bunin, Gorky and Merezhkovsky, it would be impossible for us to authorise a centre in Moscow at present.

Russia never could, and cannot still, subscribe to the P.E.N. Charter.

These replies were sent direct to J.G., so we do not know in what terms they were couched.

On 22 December 1924, J.G. wrote from Italy:

My dear Mrs Scott. I have just wired you regarding Wright and his proposal: 'Pause until Paris May meeting.' Hagberg Wright is a nice man, but I have no great faith in his practical judgement. Moreover, I think he is definitely pro-Bolshevist; his remark about the emigrés certainly suggests it. I doubt if they are dead, and I don't see why they *deserve* to be. This Russian question is ... the knottiest we have had before us. It all comes back to the question whether we can be in the least sure that we shall be dealing with literary men or disguised politicians ...

Again on the subject of Russia, when he was about to visit the Scottish Centre, J.G. wrote to Sappho on 12 October 1927:

I will give your message to Edinburgh. I wish to heaven you were going instead of me. The real trouble with Russia is this: Anyone else in any country can form a centre, and nobody will fling mud at us – at the P.E.N. as an organisation – because of it. The moment we accept a Russian Centre, we shall be tarred a little with a political complexion – all the Right will jib. I think Russia's life is one long political bite at the other nations, this must be the case – no matter how unpolitical (in name) the writers wishing to form a centre may be. My own feeling is that we should admit a Russian Centre as soon as (but not before) Russia joins the League of Nations. By doing that she would at least drop officially her attitude of open hostility to every other people; and we might take the risk of a little mud. Till then it isn't really worth it. We should have the Arcis business over again in our P.E.N. life. Until Russia can live and let live (which is all she is now asked to do) I'm afraid she's too dangerous to touch, or at least too unprofitable.

Over the years many attempts have been made by P.E.N. members in many countries, by J.G. himself, by H.G. Wells and by Sappho, to start a Centre in Russia, but all to no purpose.

*

My brother Toby had got a job in New York in 1922, and in May 1924 Sappho, as Founder, was invited to be present at the Second P.E.N. Congress. She was, of course, delighted to have the chance of seeing Toby and of visiting the States for the first time. J.G. sent a message for her to read during the Congress:

Friends! I have asked her in whose brain the P.E.N. first nested to take with her these few words of greeting ...

At the Dinner in New York on 13 May 1924, Sappho said:

Dear people. I am here to-night as the Mother of the P.E.N. Club with its 19 centres ... In Vienna a few months ago at a P.E.N. dinner a French writer met a German and said P.E.N. means 'Paix entre

Nous'. I had invented the little arrangement of letters to cover the membership – P. Poets and Playwrights, E. Editors and Essayists, N. Novelists – but the new rendering seemed to me infinitely better.

She described the International Committees which took place in her house and, having given them J.G.'s message, she went on to speak of how the Club was managed when he was abroad:

Every question of importance was referred to him, and we, the Secretary and I, have long letters from him every few days ... Without his poised grasp of P.E.N. ideas, we should never have been able to maintain our non-political ideal.

Sappho travelled the cheapest way, by steerage, as it was called then, and wrote of her journey:

The only objection to the steerage is the behaviour of the American Immigration Authorities, who insist on your being stripped to the waist with all the other third-class women passengers.

She was very modest, and this must have been an ordeal.

They did not take any notice of my being only a visitor – I had a return ticket – tho' I protested.

On her return to London she broadcast on her American visit and described the facts about travelling steerage. The next time she went to America, when she bought her third-class tourist ticket, the Tourist Office official said, 'Aren't you the lady who went steerage and broadcast about it?' He then arranged for her to have a cabin with a porthole on the Majestic on the way over, and another on the Olympic returning.

Whilst Sappho was in America I ran the P.E.N. alone, with J.G. available to advise on the telephone. Ten days before the June dinner, at which Karel Čapek, the Czech playwright, was to be the guest – his two plays, *R.U.R.* (*Rossums Universal Robots*) and *The Insect Play* were being played in London – Marcu Beza, Cultural Secretary at the Roumanian Embassy, telephoned, and said that the President of the Roumanian P.E.N., Queen Marie, was coming to London and would honour the P.E.N. by attending one of its functions. She could not come to the Dinner, but would come to lunch on the same day instead!

I was shocked and unwilling to make any such alteration, but, when I phoned J.G., he considered the problem for a few moments and finally said,

If we refuse, we shall lose our Roumanian Centre, whereas I doubt if it will matter to Čapek whether he comes to lunch or dinner – he is a very nice chap. I am sorry about the extra work for you, but I am sure we must agree to their request.

The Restaurant was, of course, gratified to be entertaining a Queen as well as the P.E.N. and agreed to provide special flowers and a larger 'top' table, and I spent a frantic week of preparations.

Queen Marie had said that about twenty members could be presented to her, and these were chosen by ballot. I was astonished to find that, whilst many people were cross at the change of time, most of them wanted to be presented, and were greatly disappointed when their names did not come out of the hat. In fact, Mr Lewis Hind, who was successful in the ballot, stood just in front of his wife, who was not even a member, and, immediately after his own presentation, pulled her forward and presented her himself!

We were all waiting for the Queen to arrive. I was on tenterhooks, J.G. looked severe and strained – he hated this sort of affair – Čapek was friendly and relaxed. There was a message: the Queen was visiting the Wembley Exhibition and would be late. She was – almost three quarters of an hour.

When she finally arrived and walked up the centre of the dining room with J.G., followed by four members of her entourage, and with the guests all standing, I felt the Wedding March should be played, although the bridegroom looked extremely embarrassed and unhappy. He knew what his P.E.N. Club was thinking.

Čapek had a smooth, boyish face and was a most unassuming personality. He had been presented with a small model of a robot, with jointed arms and legs, and, during lunch, sitting between J.G. and John Drinkwater and next but one to G.K. Chesterton, he amused himself and his neighbours by playing with his little robot, making it walk between the glasses and cutlery.

After J.G. had welcomed the guests, there was restrained applause for a Queen who was late and a tumultuous welcome for Čapek.

27

Mother and Daughter

In 1922 I had taken a full-time job as secretary to the Editor of the *Sunday Chronicle*, so some typing help had to be arranged for the P.E.N. work. But the P.E.N. continued to play a major part in my life and Sappho and I worked amicably enough together over running it.

It had its amusing side – the surprising behaviour of some members intrigued us both, and after the dinners we enjoyed gossipy post mortems on the evening's incidents.

There were invariably a few members who were difficult to place at the dinners, and the novelist Mary Webb was one, because she was always late, arriving at the same time as the dessert. People wanted to meet her, so Sappho and I, who worked out the seating arrangements the night before the dinner, took considerable care to place her suitably. I would see her advancing towards me, a small determined figure with protruding eyes (she had thyroid trouble) to ask where she was sitting. Once I said sharply, 'You are very late – again – Mrs Webb. I don't see why *you* are the *only* member who is always late.' She just looked at me with those staring blue eyes and said, 'You don't understand – I had to wash my husband's socks!'

Then there was dear, charming Stacy Aumonier. He usually drank rather too much – especially if the speeches were long and boring – and he liked to sit next to Mrs Cecil Chesterton, who had similar tastes. Together they were a riot, and soon forgot they were at a public dinner – on one such occasion Stacy joyfully crowned Mrs Cecil with a rough wreath made from the table decorations. I always placed them rather far down the room, in the hope that the honoured guest would not quite see what was going on. On that night the honoured guest was William Archer, and he *was* boring.

Stacy was married to the pianist Gertrude Peppercorn, who looked to me rather formidable, but she probably had to put up with rather a lot from the charming and irresponsible Stacy, who was not strong physically and always hard up. When asked to join the P.E.N. he wrote to J.G.:

> I am getting too old to dine with foreign poets. Besides, Tuesday is the
> night I always wash my neck – forgive your little friend.

But he joined and served on the Executive Committee, and his
presence usually transformed the meetings into amusing and gay
occasions. He was about 37 at the time and died young at 41.

At one dinner I sat next to Dennis Bradley, who wrote several books
on spiritualism and was a very good friend of Sappho's and of the
P.E.N.; on his other side was Dr Marie Stopes. They did not get
on, and I overheard this exchange. She said:

> I have read your book, and I can't think why you make people like
> Napoleon talk such nonsense.

To which he replied:

> I have read *your* book, and I can't think why you are a member of the
> P.E.N. for you can't write English.

Both turned their backs on each other, but Dr Stopes had the last
word. 'He's the tailor, you know,' she said to the man on her other
side. Dennis was the founder and head of Pope and Bradley (Tailors),
then of Bond Street.

Another guest who caused us a little embarrassment in 1929 was
Anna Seghers, the young German writer whose book, *The Revolt of the
Fishermen*, had just been awarded the Kleist Prize. She was a friend of
Rebecca West, and at first said she could not come over from
Germany. Rebecca wrote (14 November 1929):

> Dear Sappho, I am very sorry that ... [she] ... will not be able to come
> for the December dinner. She says she is too shy for dinners, has no
> evening dress and no money to buy one, and she has eleven
> grandmothers, seventeen children and 5 husbands all down with
> influenza. This at least is the impression I got when she telephoned
> from Germany. Altogether she does not seem in a propitious state to
> come over for the P.E.N. – I am coming. It was lovely seeing you the
> other day. Blessings on you. Rebecca.

Anna Seghers, however, came, and her speech was read in English
by Rebecca, who was chairman. Next month the following comment
appeared in P.E.N. News:

> It is a little ironical that the P.E.N., the first principle of which is to be
> non-political, should have had to listen with fitting attention to a
> speech that was purely political. For some reason Frau Seghers had ...

the preconception that all those present would be antagonistic to her political views. Whether they were or were not is neither here nor there ... our only interest in Anna Seghers is that of writers wishing to do honour to a fellow writer whose work had earned such generous praise from our own authors, notably Arnold Bennett, Edward Garnett, Gerald Gould and Rebecca West ... We hope that Frau Seghers enjoyed her stay in England as much as we enjoyed having her ...

During 1924 I met Arthur Watts and we were married on 14 February (St Valentine's Day) 1925 at Hampstead Town Hall.

I had been so pre-occupied with my own affairs that I had omitted to discuss with Sappho what she should wear. I usually kept an eye on her 'toilettes', but on this occasion I had overlooked this important detail and was momentarily aghast when she appeared in a bright scarlet velveteen coat dress, with puce stockings, white gloves and no hat! However, as she said, 'Darling, it doesn't really matter – everyone will be looking at *you*, not *me*.'

We honeymooned in France for some weeks, and soon after we returned I got a very cross letter from Mrs J.D. Beresford:

My dear Marjorie, your mother is impossible! A young friend of ours is a silversmith and jeweller, and we asked him to make a jewelled paper knife for you as a wedding present from us. I wrote to Sappho to ask for your address telling her about the paper knife, and I have just had a letter from her telling us not to send it, as 'you have a small house and would not have space for such knick-knacks ...'

Arthur laughed, but I was furious. Of course, Sappho was quite right – jewelled paper knives made by the protégés of friends were not likely to be welcome. But that was not really the point. I wrote a long, difficult, affectionate, excusing letter to Mrs Beresford, and begged her to send me the paper knife – my mother was quite mistaken, there was nothing I wanted more! But she didn't reply and our friendship lapsed for many years. I also 'went' for Sappho, but she was unrepentant: 'You *know* you would have hated it, and so would Arthur ... I saved you a lot of trouble ...'

I continued as P.E.N. Secretary for another two years, going to the office every morning and helping to arrange the Dinners, but inevitably I became more and more occupied with my own life and avoided sub-committees whenever possible. Also, Arthur did not really get on very well with his mother-in-law: her forthrightness did not coincide with his subtle approach to life, and her denunciation of many artists and writers whom he admired left him speechless. He was put off by *her* restless, driving personality and the constant flow of people in and out her house, whereas he enjoyed *my* cheerful optimism. '125, Alexandra Road is like a railway station,' he said, 'and I can never find the right platform.' Nevertheless he regarded her as a remarkable phenomenon, came to recognise her great qualities and kindness and could usually win her over by means of a little kindly leg-pulling and flattery. Sappho enjoyed his drawings, when they were not too subtle, and appreciated the fact that many of her friends wanted to meet him. She could never understand why he hated the robust way she introduced him, or why he almost cringed at some of the remarks it was natural for her to make. He sometimes came to a P.E.N. Dinner, and once, when Sappho had sung his praises to some member, the lady came up to him and said, 'I hear you are *the* Arthur Watts, the Punch artist.' 'Oh, no,' said Arthur firmly, 'I am his brother – the cricketer, you know.'

28

Galsworthy

In the 1920s John Galsworthy's literary reputation, both in England and abroad, was at its height, although there were groups who did not admire his work. Leonard Woolf, for example, wrote in his autobiography that:

> Galsworthy seemed to us and to all our generation a second-rate novelist, a stuffy, respectable, reactionary ...

and later Virginia recorded in her journal her thankfulness that 'that stuffed shirt' had died.

The P.E.N. however, benefited from his personal and literary popularity among the vast majority of his contemporaries, and if he asked a favour for the Club, it was likely to be granted. Even Bernard Shaw had responded amicably to J.G.'s request to join, writing in June 1924:

> Whitemailer! Very well, I will go quietly. It's your doing, though, but I will not face a recurrent irritation of a guinea a year. Here is twenty guineas for a life subscription (I am 68). If they won't accept that they can make me an honorary member and be d ... d to them.
>
> Mrs Dawson Scott had better disclaim responsibility for this, or *she* will be sacked. They will conceal their dismay to *you*. However, I am not likely to molest them. I have no objection to receiving the notices; in fact, I like to know what these institutions are doing, especially when I am in a measure responsible for their vagaries.
>
> My objection to the Club, as presented to me by Mrs D.S. has always been that literary men should never associate with one another, not only because of their cliques and hates and envies, but because their minds inbreed and produce abortions. After my first lunch at the Savage Club in 1876 or thereabouts, I swore I would avoid literary circles as plague areas: I have never regretted it. The average literary man always disliked me intensely; and I suffered him as kindly as I could; but it was useless to try to hobnob with him. Now that I am no longer a rival contemporary but a doddering old panjandrum and a

hero of letters, this does not matter so much; but I shall not change my
habits. It is on the International basis, not the prandial one that I
succumb to your decree of Compulsory Service. Ever, G.B.S.

J.G. was not naturally gregarious, but Sappho was. He was a shy
man and could not quickly and by himself generate an atmosphere of
warmth, whereas Sappho could. So much attention was automatically
given to her by the members of her circle that she had no wish or need
to demand more. She was content to be on a totally different level
from J.G. although she used him to further the aims of the P.E.N. or to
help her protégés – never herself. She introduced people to him,
explaining briefly what they wrote or what was of interest about them,
and he was able immediately to respond warmly.

With J.G. as the Great Man, whom everyone wanted to meet, and
Sappho as an ebullient and lively hostess who generated friendliness
and myself as a reasonably efficient secretary, the monthly P.E.N.
dinners were always interesting and hospitable occasions.

Alongside his preoccupation with the P.E.N., J.G. had his writing
life and his domestic life with his wife Ada, to whom he was devoted.
His nephew, Rudolf Sauter, whom he loved as a son, and Rudolf's
wife Viola, lived with the Galsworthys, and Viola ran the household.
Ada acted as J.G.'s secretary, and he dictated many of his letters to
her, which she wrote in longhand for him to sign. They all travelled
extensively every winter, but wherever he was, he was in constant
communication with either Sappho or me concerning the P.E.N. and
we always knew his movements and where to get in touch with him on
a given date.

We sent him news of the dinners, the guests, and any contretemps
that arose, me writing factually, and Sappho from the policy angle.
J.G. gave us both sensible and wise advice; he also continued to send
personal invitations to distinguished writers whom we wanted to
entertain in London.

After I ceased to be Secretary at the end of 1926, J.G.'s letters went
to Hermon Ould, as Secretary, or Sappho, and then into the office
files, but I have 48 written during the years 1921 to 1926, almost all
from distant lands, where the winter climate was warm, mostly dated
between November and March each year.

I will quote from a few of these:

March 18th, 1924. Biarritz. This is in answer to Marjorie's last letter
with the Austrian speeches. How admirable they were, and what a
good spirit in Vienna. That Centre will become, if I mistake not, the
European hub of the Club, for England is not Europe.
    About Unamuno – I am trying to stir up the Royal Society of

Literature to a protest. I am more than ever convinced that it would be a bad mistake for the P.E.N. to interfere; but England's voice ought not to be silent.

Feb. 7th 1925. You are very good to say what you do about my usefulness and about missing me, but I'm afraid it is an over expression, or should I say I hope it is?

Please give our best wishes to Marjorie; we all wish we could be at that tea-party [my wedding]. We shall think of her on Valentine's Day ...cordial greetings from us all.

April 1, 1925. Marrakesh. Dear Marjorie, I thought if I am able to go to this Paris meeting, I would go on to Prague and Vienna, where they have been asking for me.

Feb. 1st, 1926. New York. Dear Mrs D.S. We are very sorry to hear of your illness ... I'm sure an enforced rest will do you good – you are never bored – and are inclined to overdraw on your courage.

You seem to be preparing a somewhat awful fate for me in New York, but since I am lying strictly doggo all the rest of the time out here, I will put up with whatever you bring upon me ... I note all your hints concerning the line to be taken in New York ... As you say it will be a terrifying function. With some misgiving I will approach Mr Henry Pritchard about a grant [from the Carnegie Fund] ... but I'm not good at asking for anything, and you must therefore prepare for disappointment ... I hope you had a good dinner with Hermann Robbers as guest. He is now, I suppose, the leading novelist in Holland ...

Considering John and Ada Galsworthy, as I remember them, I think I should set down the impression they made on me, as a couple, especially as I have met people who never knew them and who were critical of Ada. I have been told that she was a hypochondriac, that she forced J.G. to winter abroad against his will, that she made him live a social life and so on. I have also read other references to her which seem quite unjustified.

Obviously Sappho and I, and later, Arthur, had no real knowledge of the Galsworthys' private lives – we only saw them together at P.E.N. Congresses and gatherings. But we saw a great deal of J.G. at Committees and meetings in our house, when he often stayed on to chat and was always warmly friendly; and he sometimes came to tea on a Sunday. There was never any doubt in either my or my mother's minds that the Galsworthys were a devoted couple. J.G. gave the impression of being fully himself only when he was accompanied by his wife. Unless she was with him on social occasions he usually left early.

I myself identified Ada in my mind with Irene, whom I admired (up to the Modern Comedy books) and Young Jolyon to some extent with J.G. I gather most people nowadays do not feel as I did and are full of criticism of Irene – they seem really to dislike her! To me Irene was elegant and exquisite, and I felt Ada was just that.

After our marriage Arthur and I were invited to dinner with the Galsworthys at Grove Lodge, Hampstead occasionally, and, although I was never in the least afraid of J.G. I was always slightly in awe of Ada. She was kind and charming to us both, but there was an aura about her ... we both felt just a little ill at ease, unable to relax, and on our best behaviour. Still, a slight nervousness at rather formal elegant dinners, with servants waiting at table – well, I think *one* servant – had assailed me on other occasions, and I felt this was probably due to something in my own make-up, and not the fault of my hostess.

29

London Life

First and foremost Sappho had to earn a living to enable her to pay her way and entertain modestly in London, spend some months each year in Cornwall and finally have enough money to travel to P.E.N. Congresses, although usually, as Founder, her expenses were part paid by the host centre. She managed all this, rather precariously, by letting her bungalows in Cornwall and also a house in Birchington, where she had bought a piece of land. But suddenly she came up against the three-year Average Tax scheme, which she thought outrageously unfair. In January 1928, she complained:

> Apparently a law has been passed requiring all owners of house property to pay the whole of the yearly tax in one lump ... and *now*. My Cornish cottages are shut up for the winter, and try as I might I have not been able to get any paid literary work since last September. I am a very unlucky woman. I am alone and lonely and now falls upon me this burden of taxation. And I have been told that people think I push the P.E.N. for my own purposes – to sell my books, to become known! What a world of envy, malice and all uncharitableness. 'Known' – what is *known*? I do not go to parties – except to Embassies, because they are useful to the P.E.N. I refuse invitations. I abhor the rich, the leisured, the pleasure-seeking. What can being 'known' do for such as I? Sell my books? They never sell, the papers do not even bother to review them.

But Sappho's moods of self-pity and depression never lasted long. She was very resilient and, when a friend wrote her a warm and appreciative letter, or interesting people came to see her, or a new P.E.N. Centre was formed, she usually recovered her cheerfulness, outwardly at least.

Sappho added to her resources by doing some journalism, although this was rather intermittent. In 1923 she wrote a series of articles on contemporary writers for the *Strand Magazine*, the title being: 'As I Know Them – Some Writers of To-Day.'

The articles included Wells, Shaw, Bennett, Galsworthy, May

Sinclair, Clemence Dane, Israel Zangwill, Sheila Kaye-Smith, Stacy
Aumonier. But I will only quote from two – Shaw and Stacy
Aumonier. Some of Sappho's comments – made over sixty years ago –
concerning writers long dead and (some) forgotten, are worth
recording.

Of Bernard Shaw she wrote:

> Among those whom I approached to speak at the To-Morrow Club (in
> 1918) was George Bernard Shaw. This was at the earnest request of the
> members, as, left to myself, I should not have dared. Everybody has
> heard of the amusing postcards he pens – such as the one to his agent in
> reply to a 4-page business letter. In the left-hand corner at the top was
> the word 'No!' In the right-hand corner at the bottom was a tiny 'Ha!
> Ha!' When I asked him to speak at the To-Morrow Club, I expected
> something of that sort, but to my surprise he replied that he was always
> in town of a Thursday evening and would be willing to come.
>
> Never having met Mr Shaw I stood by the door, wondering whether
> he would be flame-tipped physically as well as mentally. A slim, kindly
> man presently appeared. [Shaw was then 67.]
>
> The subtle, caustic dramatist, with his world reputation for searing
> wit, proved to be a genial, friendly sort of man, with a keen interest in
> young people and the things of to-day. With his eyes twinkling amiably
> at the crowd sitting on chairs, boxes, the window seats, the floor, he
> talked like a father to a family of promising children, or a deacon to a
> Sunday school class that he hoped to train in ways of godliness. It was
> such a different Bernard Shaw from the man who had given us the
> plays.
>
> Some well-known man took the chair, and Mr Shaw found fault with
> me on that account: 'Your banquets are too rich,' said the vegetarian.
> 'When you have induced one big man to be dished up for your
> edification, you should not ask another to take the chair. Be frugal and
> keep him for a later occasion.'

Shaw made other suggestions for altering the way Sappho ran the
To-Morrow Club, but she really was an expert in that particular field
and did not agree with him. She commented:

> As a matter of fact Mr Shaw always sees what he wants to – even if it is
> not there – and I suspect that *your* point of view is for him
> non-existent …

Until I read these articles recently, I did not know that Sappho had
first met Shaw in such relaxed circumstances, and this accounts, I
think, for his comparatively friendly attitude to her and her various
ploys during the days of the P.E.N. He understood her.

And that naughty charmer, Stacy Aumonier, who died too young, has been coming back into favour lately and not much is known about him.

Stacy Aumonier was born to manifest the qualities which enabled his Huguenot ancestors to start a new life in a strange land, when the bigotry of their own folks would have slaughtered them. They were silversmiths and settled at Spitalfields: ever since, the men of the family have worked at some decorative art. Stacy's father was a carver of architectural ornament and, having no money, premises or office, he took possession of the back kitchen.

Mrs Aumonier must have been a wonderful manager and a sweet-tempered woman to be able to keep the place tidy and in some degree of comfort, with an increasing family – Stacy had 4 elder brothers – and the stone and the tools and her man always at work in the house.

His father wanted Stacy to be a draughtsman for the firm, but stone did not satisfy him. However, he discovered he could amuse people by giving verbal sketches of well-known characters. London received Stacy with joy, and before long he was doing curtain-raisers for the Criterion Theatre. However, the theatre taught him he was not a strong man physically, and he turned to imaginative writing.

Nothing has ever been difficult for him, and his first story sold at once, both in England and America ... and disclosed that we had a new and original writer.

30

Rebecca West

Although Sappho included an article on Rebecca West in this series, there are so many references to her throughout her journals that it seems more practical to describe the friendship between these two remarkable women. Among her many friends I think Sappho was most devoted to Rebecca.

In 1918, when G.B. Stern stayed with us in Cornwall, she spoke admiringly of Rebecca's book *The Return of the Soldier*, which Sappho then read. She later wrote:

> This untidy schoolgirl who has contrived to get her sincere young opinions printed in the daily press ... gives promise of being our finest writer since Emily Brontë ...

Shortly afterwards she met Rebecca at a party at Violet Hunt's and described this first meeting:

> Never have I seen eyes so burning bright ... we sat together for a little in the window seat; and since then, whenever I have a moment's leisure, I think to myself: 'I would like to see Rebecca West.' She has one of the loveliest speaking voices I have ever heard ... its soft richness makes even speaking to her on the phone a joy.

From that date the two writers became friends, Sappho being then 53 and Rebecca 26. She was a Founder Member of the P.E.N. and on the first Executive Committee, where she remained until 1933.

From the time they first met in 1918 Rebecca was very much a part of Sappho's life, and on 8 January 1925 Sappho went to tea with her and met Anthony, whom she described as being 'a very charming little boy of about 10, with his mother's lovely brow, but not her fine width of face'. She commented:

> She [Rebecca] lives at too high a rate of vibration. When first she came in from a walk with Anthony, she looked glowing, but the colour faded and she looked grey with fatigue. She is a curiously gentle but penetrating person, and Anthony has the same qualities.

The two friends dined together from time to time, and in 1928, when Anthony was ill and in a sanatorium in Holt, Norfolk, Sappho, who had gone through the same experience with my brother Toby, was warmly sympathetic. Rebecca herself was ill at the time and wrote:

> May 17, 1928. Bless you for your letter. You are a dear kind soul and I really do feel better ... for knowing that one human being does seem to care a little what happens to me ... It was saintly of you to come and see me.
>
> About Anthony, I am hoping that Holt will do the trick sufficiently for a winter at a low altitude in Switzerland. If not I think I shall make it Arizona. I dread making Anthony into a wanderer, so I hope and pray it will be Switzerland. I did so want a nice quiet upbringing for him ...

Rebecca stayed at the Royal Links Hotel in Cromer in order to be near Anthony, and she wrote from there (undated):

> ... I am utterly tired out. Since Easter I have had all this agony of anxiety about Anthony – have dashed between here and London – have had 'flu' myself and have written about 80,000 words ...
>
> Anthony is right out of the wood physically, but in it psychically – he is bored and restless, longs for lessons, but can't get a tutor. It is a dreadful job to amuse him and so confoundedly unnatural to see him only on two-hourly visits every other day. But what is this compared with what we've escaped! I dare say your thoughts had a lot to do with it. Bless you!

And one letter (undated) when Sappho was interested and involved in spiritualism:

> Dearest Sappho, can you help me? My dearest friend on earth has died – the person whom I care for more than anyone alive except Anthony ... There is something uncertain and unhappy about her last days. Could you get me a sitting with Mrs Leonard [a medium].

Rebecca married Henry Maxwell Andrews in October 1930 and she wrote to Sappho:

> Darling Sappho, how sweet you are! The pink sugar vase is so lovely – but not so lovely as your letter. Dearest, it is just as you supposed! He was here! He is a darling, very donnish and withdrawn, very bookish, but very masculine. I think you'll like him. Bless you for everything ...

And here is the last entry in Sappho's Journal:

Nov. 1st, 1930. Went to the marriage of Cicely Isobel Fairfield (Rebecca) with Henry Maxwell Andrews, a banker. She had chosen to be married in the *depths* of the country because her cousin was the parson there.

Rebecca was a moment late. She came quickly up the aisle in honey-beige velvet and a matching close hat, carrying a big sheaf of lilies and red flowers. As she isn't a Christian or he either I wondered over this church ceremony. I think the parson must also have wondered, for he cut it as short as possible.

Lord Riddell rang up the night before to say he had heard she was marrying Lord Beaverbrook (whose name is also Henry Maxwell.) He then invited himself to the wedding. H.G. Wells said, 'You're looking very well, my dear. After it's all over, why not take a flat near me at Chiltern Court?'

June Head, her secretary, said: 'At least she is going away with someone who will buy her railway ticket. Hitherto, she has bought everyone else's.'

Sappho often made critical comments about friends or told slightly critical but amusing stories about them: she never did so about Rebecca. Although so much younger, she was to Sappho a being apart – brilliant, attractive, sincere – whose opinion she invariably sought. What she wrote about Rebecca I have quoted. What Rebecca wrote about Sappho is on pp.205-6.

31

Politics and Personalities

For about four years after she founded the P.E.N. Sappho was still responsible for running the To-Morrow Club and for providing subjects, speakers and chairmen for its weekly talks. As she got more and more involved with the bigger P.E.N. organisation, however, she was always on the look-out for someone to relieve her of responsibility for the To-Morrow Club. The difficulty was that the members firmly resisted her efforts to 'shed them'.

As Henry Williamson wrote to me a few years ago:

Your Mother *was* the To-Morrow Club: outrageous (but naive) remarks were lanced into dissidents ... it started in a Long Acre attic – splendid fun ...

The then members were very much aware of Sappho's value and did not want to lose her.

Her Sunday tea-parties continued – I and my friends were now part of them – her house was filled with people; more and more foreigners came with introductions; P.E.N. members arrived from all over the world, and she either held Committee meetings in her own house for both the P.E.N. and the To-Morrow Club, or attended them elsewhere, travelling across London by bus and train, and then probably collapsing exhausted for a couple of days. During those days, however, she would sit up in bed typing letters, articles or her books. When he was in England J.G. often arranged for his chauffeur to call for Sappho and drive her wherever she wanted to go, carefully telling her that on no account was she to tip him as he did not expect it. But this comfortable way of getting about could only happen now and then.

From her journals I have selected some of the many stories and comments she wrote down about the writers of the period, who were either her close friends, or visitors from abroad whom she entertained to tea.

Sappho was a schemer, and one never knew quite what she would

be up to next. For example, when Thomas Hardy, who was the Hon.
Member of the English Centre, died in January 1928, Sappho wanted
H.G. Wells to succeed him, because, she wrote:

> Wells is well-known abroad and highly esteemed ... Mr Galsworthy,
> urged by me through Hermon, wrote and invited him. The Committee
> was then told Wells had accepted. They were surprised, and looked up
> the Executive Minutes on the date the matter had been discussed.
> Their recommendation had been Shaw or Bridges, and Wells had not
> been mentioned! Yet somehow Wells had been asked and had
> accepted. Nobody could make out what had happened! Yet it was a
> 'fait accompli'.

It was a 'fait accompli' because Sappho regarded Shaw as an
Irishman and awkward, and she did not think Robert Bridges had the
international status to be suitable. Wells, she believed, was both in
tune with the P.E.N. and likely to take an interest in it and she
envisaged him as a future President, so she took a hand in the
proceedings. And evidently Hermon Ould was also 'in' on this little
deception of the Committee.

On another occasion Sappho decided that Violet Hunt had been on
the Committee far too long and, as she would *not* go, she must be
pushed. Even although Sappho was very fond of Violet, she was
determined the P.E.N. Committee should not be in the hands of old
ladies – except, of course, herself! So she persuaded Rosalind Wade, a
young novelist in her twenties, who had published one book, to stand
for the Committee. She was elected and Violet was dropped, and
neither knew quite how it happened. But Rosalind has since told me
that Violet never forgave *her*, who had had nothing to do with the
manoeuvre!

Being slightly delinquent herself, Sappho was delighted to connive
at others behaving in a like manner. In 1928 she had been mainly
responsible for the organisation of two very successful Centenary
Dinners given for Ibsen and Tolstoy, so she was asked by J.T. Grein to
be on the Committee of the Old Playgoers Club.

> I am not even a member of the Club. The simple and lawless way in
> which people run things is a continual source of amusement. *They*
> wished to have me because I know how to arrange dinners, and *I*
> wished to be on for my own purposes – and so I am on.

Although in all major matters J.G. could keep a wise and
controlling hand on Sappho, I wonder if he was aware of a quality in
her which might be called a 'ruthless deviation from accepted codes of

behaviour'? He was, however, also a novelist, an observer of human qualities and frailties, so perhaps he knew, but did not get involved except in matters of major importance or when she specifically asked for his advice. He *could* stand up to her when he really disagreed with her, as over her proposed P.E.N. House (see pp. 155-7) and her protest concerning the Hardy Memorial (see pp. 157-8).

Her international contacts continued to widen:

5 Feb. 1925. Ivan Bunin came to tea. A most charming, slight, grey man. He dined with May Sinclair and Stacy Aumonier on the 2nd, and the latter·was so drunk he had to go home in the middle of dinner. Then next day at the P.E.N. dinner, the Chairman was A.E.W. Mason, who was also drunk and stumbled in his speech; so probably Bunin thinks we live up to our national reputation.

Bunin told me the French eat mostly vegetables and bread, very little meat – the opposite to Russian feeding. I suggested vegetables were good for the health. 'Of cows,' said he.

And of Ernst Toller:

Dec. 1925. Yesterday Marjorie and I dined with Horace Shipp and Ernst Toller at the Bullfrogs Club, so that the latter might see a Night Club, and Toller said to Horace: 'You were a Conscientious Objector in prison?' He went on: 'I was put into prison for the first time when I was 18 – for 5 months then, and later 5 years. However, I was allowed to write my books there ... I have written nine books and 6 or 7 plays.' He wanted to see every side of London life – spent some hours in Whitechapel and then went to Lady Swaythling's bun-fight. Asked if he could see a smart dancing club such as the Embassy and so on. A dear little man with a strong abrupt square forehead and black curly hair. So gentle.

Everybody wants Toller's visa extended. The Home Office rang up Marjorie, and the kind, weary voice of the head of the Aliens Dept said Toller might stay as long as ever he liked, if *only* someone would send in his passport: that he was besieged with applications about it from private persons and public bodies – had had about 30! A few minutes later the official rang again: he had three more applications, including one from the German Ambassador *containing the passport*.

At the dinner for Toller and W.B. Yeats, Jerome K. Jerome took the chair and made a delightfully human and amusing speech, Toller a deeply friendly one and Yeats an affected long, dull rigmarole. You would never have guessed that he was once a charming man and a humorous speaker.

This was in about 1925, when Yeats, who was the same age as

Sappho, was 60.

Sappho and I went to tea with Jerome K. Jerome after that dinner, in his huge bare studio – 28 feet long – in Belsize Park. It was dominated by a portrait of him by de Laszlo. Sappho and Arthur, to whom I had just become engaged, thought it very bad. As she said:

> The old man looks like a kindly tolerant bishop; the portrait makes him look like a handsome intolerant cleric.

In March 1925, Stefan Zeromski, who founded the Polish Centre, died, and Sappho wrote:

> He was our Hon. Member for Poland, the Grand Old Man of Polish literature, and he left the P.E.N. a library of several thousand books, and a valuable collection of letters which is to go to the Centre at once. His daughter has a life interest in his money and then that comes. It will give the P.E.N. in Warsaw status. Rarely have I been more thrilled. That old man whom I never met, who was so far away from me and, in his languge and faith, so remote – he had taken my idea to heart, and this was the proof.

But from California later that month J.G. wrote more realistically that he was afraid the Zeromski money would be long in coming to the Polish P.E.N. He thought it was quite on the cards that there might not be a Poland even, by the time it arrived.

Jacob Epstein was invited to be a Guest of Honour at a dinner and Sappho noted wrathfully:

> He is a genius, he is also unwashed to an odoriferous extent. He accepted, then went to Paris.

Dr Lion Feuchtwanger, author of *Jew Suss*, was a guest on 6 December 1927, with Rebecca West in the chair, and Sappho wrote:

> Feuchtwanger was received by the English with tumultuous joy. 180 came to the P.E.N. and he got 200 letters a day and was mobbed by people wanting him to sign his book. He was overwhelmed and not being at all strong his health gave way. I gave an At Home for him on Dec. 4th and the day after the dinner he dined with Rebecca, tho' he was too ill to do it – 'the most fascinating woman in London'.
>
> None of us really think highly of the book, except as vividly written history. That is, with the exception of Arnold Bennett, who sat next to him at the P.E.N. dinner.

In 1928, just before the P.E.N. Ibsen Centenary Dinner, Sappho was invited to dine at the Norwegian Embassy, where she sat next to Sir Johnstone Forbes Robertson:

The most amusing dinner! Individuals, not husband and wife, had been asked, and therefore it was concentrated brilliance ... Wells, Shaw, Gosse, Drinkwater, Desmond McCarthy, Milton Rosmer, J.T. Grein, St John Ervine, Mrs Patrick Campbell ... and some Norwegians, were present. Shaw proposed the 'health' of Ibsen and drank it in orangeade, after the Minister murmured 'in memory of'. They all told amusing stories, and Gosse said he wrote an article on Ibsen for the Saturday Review in the early days. They accepted it, set it up and paid for it. Then they had consulted the authorities – and could not find that such a man existed. 'Oh,' said Shaw, 'that's your reputation as a humorist.' Shaw said his name in Irish is Skaugh: 'The Shaws were always younger sons and that's why we are all so impecunious.'

Of all the enchanting, loving-natured gentle people, give me Sir Johnstone Forbes Robertson. Said Sir J: 'It seems only a fortnight ago that I was the youngest at every gathering, and now I'm the oldest.' Shaw was saying that Ibsen was a far greater playwright than Shakespeare. Said Sir J: 'He shouldn't say that, but being Irish, I suppose he must have his joke.' Sir Johnstone told of George Meredith going to a play in which Kate Rorke was acting. His comment was: 'I enjoyed the play, but couldn't quite catch Rorke's Drift.'

I believe Sir Johnston is between 70 and 80, and he is as young, and his mind is as supple as if he were forty.

A month later Sir Edmund Gosse died:

Sir Edmund Gosse is dead. I met him first in the 90s at a dinner given by Heinemann when Whistler was present. I met him again last March at the Norwegian Minister's dinner in honour of Ibsen, and he was old but still astonishingly young-looking. He left the P.E.N. because the Secretary forgot to put 'Sir' on the envelope. Or, at any rate, he wrote to rebuke us for the error and shortly after resigned. However, he could not keep from interfering with what he had left. When we invited James Joyce as a Guest of Honour, Gosse wrote to Galsworthy to protest against a writer of such filth being honoured. So much for his critical faculty. But he wrote one good book, *Father and Son*, and some fairly good verse.

32

Health and Committees

In addition to her annual participation in P.E.N. Congresses, Sappho's life in London was incredibly full. She constantly overtaxed her strength, and would not accept any suggestion that there was a limit to what her body could stand. On many occasions, although she felt and looked ill, she obstinately refused to 'give in' until she had fulfilled her immediate engagements.

In December 1925 Sappho had accepted an invitation from an old friend to drive her down the Tyne Valley by the Roman Wall, and then through the Lake District, starting on December 27th.

Just before Christmas she got gastric flu, but, since she had about two weeks of engagements ahead of her, she still set off for Bournemouth on December 21st to spend Christmas with her father. At Waterloo Station she felt dreadfully ill – she actually suffered an intestinal haemorrhage, although she did not know this at the time. She continued to Bournemouth, and on Boxing Day somehow got to Newcastle by 11.30 p.m., but she finally had to admit that the whole visit was a ghastly expedition.

On returning to London she attended the P.E.N. Dinner on 5 January at which André Maurois was the guest:

> A most charming little Jew; and the chairman was W.B. Maxwell, the handsomest and most delightful writer I have ever met – a perfectly lovely man. I was ill, but talked with him for a little while, and we spoke of his mother, Miss Braddon. I said, 'Not many men put their love for their mothers first.' 'Oh, I think most do,' said he. 'Perhaps, though, they don't admit it.'

Having done the things she intended – and felt obliged – to do, Sappho then really collapsed and called on Dr Robert Briffault to come to the rescue.

> He was wonderful – stopped the pain which had been incessant since December 21st, sent me to bed, put me on gruel, and I at once began to mend. I was alone, but Marjorie came and then got her woman to come

and look after me ... I had a quiet fortnight in bed as a result of my folly. Everyone – May Sinclair, Arthur Lynch, Perceval Yetts – very kind. Above all, Robert Briffault – clear-sighted, wise, tender, encouraging – what a doctor!

She had been friends with Robert Briffault for some time: he had stayed with her in Cornwall the previous summer when he was worn out after working five years on his great book, *The Mothers*, and she had helped him with the proofs. She considered it one of the finest books she had ever read, and that summer she wrote that she was almost happy (never quite, on account of The Lynx) 'with Briffault's mind at hand and Rebecca (West) next door'. Rebecca was staying in the second of Sappho's two bungalows.

But her physical breakdowns were only occasional, and, in between, the committee meetings and work continued.

John Galsworthy was an amazingly good chairman. He never missed a point and was always concentrated and patient, carefully considering every aspect put forward. At one meeting in our house he had wondered if it would be possible to get a P.E.N. Congress to uphold the idea that, in the event of future wars, the P.E.N. would not cease its activities during hostilities, but would, on the contrary, do all in its power to maintain the interchange of ideas through art of all kinds. From this tentative suggestion a resolution concerning literature and art in time of war was put forward by the English, French, German and Belgian delegates at the Brussels Congress in 1927 (see p. 146). It was often referred to at later Congresses, notably at Dubrovnik in 1933 (p. 183) and in Edinburgh, by implication, in 1934 (p. 193).

At both these Congresses, after Galsworthy's death in 1933, H.G. Wells presided and battled with the Nazi threat.

Sometimes the committees at Alexandra Road ended early enough to turn into social occasions, with talk, tea and tales, such as the one J.G. told of Colette. He had been at the Institut Français to hear her lecture, but the lady was ill with flu and did not arrive. 'Madame Colette,' said the chairman, 'est dans son lit ...' roars of joy from the audience. 'Avec,' continued the poor chairman, but the rest was drowned in laughter.

When Honorary Members from abroad were in London, they were often invited to attend the international committees and, at one particularly long and sticky meeting Robert Frost and Arthur Lynch were present, the latter to put forward some suggestions about the formation of a centre in Greece. Lynch left early, saying to Sappho:

Do they never thaw? If I were asked whether I would be hanged or spend a week with Galsworthy, I don't know which I'd choose.

Sappho also found that particular committee 'dull and icy'. She attributed the cause partly to the fact that many of the representatives were strangers to each other, but also because she felt J.G. certainly did not like Lynch and perhaps not Robert Frost, who was there to represent America. The latter stayed on after the meeting, drank van der Hum and related how he had run away from his people and worked at many trades. Finally a relative dragged him out of his poverty, gave him a small farm, and he began to get his poetry known. 'He was a great old boy,' wrote Sappho, 'friendly and sympathetic and loving America.'

Actually Frost was ten years younger than Sappho – he must have been about 50 then and lived to be 88.

In addition to these international committees, Sappho was also responsible for a number of schemes and sub-committees. It was a busy life for anyone who lived within or on the fringe of Sappho's ever-widening circle.

After February 1925, when I married, she lived alone, except for her one little maid.

33

The Lighter Side of Congresses

Nowadays everyone is accustomed to international conferences, but in the twenties there were not so many, so they were of greater interest. It is worth just glancing at a few P.E.N. gatherings – Paris 1925, Berlin 1926, Brussels 1927 and Oslo 1928.

1. Paris, 1925

Sappho went to Paris on 20 May 1925, and I arrived the next day with John Galsworthy. J.G. was lecturing at the Sorbonne, but H.G. Wells, who was on the same train, refused to stop over to attend the Congress, even for one day.

Sappho soon discovered that the French Centre, at the suggestion of Jules Romains, intended to recommend that the International Council should have its headquarters in Paris. J.G. was not present that first day, having a temperature, and Sappho was greatly alarmed. However, I telephoned him at his hotel and outlined the situation, and he came to the rescue. He talked to the French secretary, Crémieux, and Romains, and the idea was dropped. An ambitious man, still young, Romains would not insist on his scheme at that point in his career, against the opinion of a writer of Galsworthy's international stature.

In her account of the Congress, Sappho wrote:

> If the idea had been carried, it would have been the end of the P.E.N., for the French Centre is *at present* only a côterie and not representative.

This was only the first of many problems the P.E.N. had with Jules Romains. Although he became both President of the French Centre, and International President in 1936, and was highly thought of as a writer, he was also an ambitious, egotistical and thoroughly awkward little man. He always consorted with the Great at P.E.N. affairs, his eyes looking through or beyond less important writers; even at this Paris Congress he entirely ignored Sappho, who had recently entertained him at her house in London and had taken trouble to see that he was well looked after and met interesting people.

Sappho therefore had some reason to be annoyed with the Great Man, and recorded crossly:

> Maxwell Aley (Sec. of the New York Centre) told me that last year the American Centre gave Romains the money for his expenses, but he left his Hotel bill unpaid. We saw Romains' play 'Knock', which was superbly acted, but was a play without any quality of heart or warm emotion. The same might be said of Karel Capek's plays; but they are really only impersonal. 'Knock' is hard, a piece of stone.

I, also, had taken a box at a theatre and arranged for Vita Sackville West, then on the Executive Committee, to accompany Romains and another well-known writer – I've forgotten who – to a play. I made up the number to four.

Although she was only seven or eight years older than me, I was scared of Miss Sackville West, feeling that nothing I could ever say would be adequate – in fact, although usually of a cheerful and social temperament, I was on that occasion speechless with nerves. However, this did not really matter since we were in a box. At the end of the play, as we rose to leave, Vita, looking magnificently handsome in a long, splendid and colourful silk gown, said: '*Lam*entable, absolutely *lam*entable,' as she swept out. I don't know whether she was referring to the play or to the actors, and I did not dare ask her. She took the distinguished guest (Jules Romains) with her by car or taxi, and I went thankfully home by bus.

However, the problem of the venue of the International Council having been solved, the Congress was a success. Eight members of the new German Centre came to Paris, and as it was the first occasion since the war that the Germans were being welcomed at an international gathering as equals, there had been some anxiety as to their reception. But all was peace, their Secretary, Dr Karl Federn, took the chair at a session, and the Congress accepted an invitation to meet in Berlin the next year. J.G. made a deliberately neutral spech on the subject of the charm of the French language, which he understood only moderately well, and referred to a recent dinner in London when he had sat next to Henri Barbusse. He said:

> We had arranged beforehand to produce one of those strictly neutral dialogues proper to the P.E.N. What happened? Henri Barbusse talked French all the time, so beautifully that I could do nothing but admire and make out a word or two here and there – French people speak French with a great deal more French accent than they used to do in

my youth. I have listened to *real* orators, like Romains and Barbusse, and I have followed time after time one eloquent voice speaking that older, measured French in words of at most three syllables, with a power and resonance which never failed to allay our worst passions and rouse our best interests – the voice of Benjamin Crémieux, who, at Committee after Committee, has saved us from wrack and ruin ...

He also referred to Sappho: 'On her part the P.E.N. has been an "inspiration de génie".'

Taking part in that Congress were Luigi Pirandello, Miguel de Unamuno (whom the P.E.N. had battled to get released from prison), Heinrich Mann, Gertrude Atherton and James Joyce.

2. The German Congress, 1926, and the Lynx again

At the Berlin Congress in 1926, Sappho was mainly preoccupied with the Lynx. Underlying all her activities her devotion to Arthur Lynch remained constant, and she pulled strings so that his expenses could be paid as a delegate. She always hoped he would attend the congresses, so that she could be near him for a week or so. Sometimes she expressed her feelings for him in writing, not often in her current journal, but on odd pieces of paper that somehow survived. Finding the right words to describe her unhappiness was a comfort to her, and she could not bear to destroy these phrases. I think they were seldom if ever sent to the person who evoked them.

For example, writing of that Berlin Congress:

We were to have been in this town together. The pleasure to me of these few days at the end of a journey was to have been that you would share our committees and our welcome and our expeditions. As you were not in England, I travelled hoping – a warm and rosy hope – that you would come from some other part of Europe. I felt that at any moment I might see you coming towards me through the crowd; that I might look up suddenly and meet your glance, as has happened before. In this hope I lived through the days. If I saw a grey head, it must be yours; a broad slender figure moving swiftly – but it was never you, and gradually the mercury sank and the darkness fell.

She then commented on the importance to Germany of this fourth Congress:

Our coming, the coming of the representatives of 15 nations, was important to Germany. She had suffered from the inability of the League of Nations to include her. Also, this was the first time since the war that there has been an international gathering of any sort in Berlin. Again, this was the first visit of the *French* as honoured guests.

Because of these things the Ober-Burgermeister, Dr Bus, received us in the Rathaus and gave us a 'fest'. He said: 'Many have shared her ideals, perhaps some have even had the same idea, yet she alone has had the courage and energy to shape it into an organisation.'

Later I went to have my voice preserved by the German State: it makes a record that will last indefinitely. Mr Galsworthy also went for the same purpose, and his wife went with him. He read a page from the *Forsyte Saga*, and their charming ways together made me envious. He spoke into the box and looked for her approval and admiration, and she thought of nothing but him. When my turn came I said: 'Even as individuals become families and families become communities, and communities become nations, so eventually must the nations draw together in peace.'

In the end some kind fellow proposed the health of the Mother of the P.E.N.

3. The Brussels Congress, 1927

Brussels will always remain historically important for the P.E.N. as the Congress that passed Galsworthy's resolution calling for 'Freedom of Literature in time of war', and that 'Individual centres ... should not be used ... as weapons of propaganda ... etc.'

The resolution, although slightly altered, had originated in Sappho's drawing room and had, therefore, a special meaning for her.

4. Oslo, 1928

June 9th. Sailed for Oslo. Am broadcasting a Travel Talk on my return and writing a travel article for the Children's Broadcasting Annual. Norway gives me my steamer and rail tickets free, but not my food. That enables me to attend the Congress ... I could not otherwise have afforded to, as I have not yet sold my book.

The news had reached London that the Madrid Centre excluded women from membership, and at Oslo Sappho put forward a resolution 'that women shall hold the same position as men in the P.E.N. ...' This was seconded by the German delegate, Theodore Däubler, and passed unanimously.

The King received us nation by nation. Barbra Ring had asked him to and he had asked 'Why?' 'Because kings are rare nowadays and therefore it is really something to meet one.' He has a queer back to his head, as if birth forceps had flattened it, and he was in a room filled with a clutter of furniture, books, silverware etc. But his talk was well-informed, as he spoke of the pros and cons of National Theatres. He was entirely unassuming and said he had been a sailor, 'until I came up here to be King'. He was almost painfully thin. The Banquet had only 2-minute speeches, but Martin Andersen Nexø, a very lively troll-faced duck, spoke 2 minutes in each language, making a thoroughly naughty and indiscreet speech which annoyed the Danes.

That year, after returning from Oslo in June, Sappho spent her first summer in a large bell tent lent her by her farm friends Alice and Jim Tippett, which was pitched on a piece of waste grass adjacent to their bungalow above Constantine Bay. There she stayed comfortably from 30 July to 10 September, and the following July broadcast on 'living in a tent'.

34

Vienna and Prague

Sappho wrote so fully about Henry Nevinson when he went to Vienna as a delegate for the English Centre, that her account is worth a chapter on its own.

> When the P.E.N. executive said to itself, 'Let us ask Nevinson to represent us at the Vienna Congress', it was said with unanimity, for who so English as H.W. Nevinson? Who could show the brother overseas as simply, as conclusively, how we worked and for what we stood? But would he agree? Would the war correspondent who had known Vienna, city of ghosts, in other days, be willing to deputise for the Founding Centre of a federation that hoped to prove that the P.E.N. was mightier than the sword?
>
> He hesitated, he was lost.

Arthur Lynch was also one of the British writers who went, so Sappho was happy. But she knew better than to rely on that awkward charmer to help and care for her on the journey. She was dubious as to her talents as a traveller, as Hermon Ould, the P.E.N. Secretary, who was her usual companion and guide, was in Jugoslavia and would come from there to Vienna. She was 64, but she asked Henry Nevinson, aged 73, if she might travel with him, and she wrote in *P.E.N. News* of his reception of this suggestion and the ensuing journey:

> I cannot say that my request was received with enthusiasm. 'As far as Dover,' he said. Nevertheless, once we were off, he allowed that we – 10 of us – belonged. He even unbent a little and taught us how to live in comfort when all comfort had been denied. He extracted succulent meals from the concrete of railway platforms; when we moved on the face of the waters, if chairs were to be found, the 10 would be scurrying after them long after Mr Nevinson was established and – I think – asleep in his. A magician! He was perhaps the oldest of us, yet when we returned half-rested from the 'schlaf-wagen' (which met us at Koln and left us heartlessly at Wurzburg) he was still sitting, as he had sat all night, upright in his corner and with not one silver hair out of place.

He proved a marvellous traveller. He never lost anything, and he never grumbled. Nothing upset or annoyed him. He was entirely competent. If I am ever ship-wrecked on a desert island, may I have the unwilling Mr Nevinson for my fellow castaway.

In Vienna he was put on a Committee that met at 9 a.m. – and so often these committees occur on the morning after the night before – but the opera which would prevent Mr Nevinson from keeping an appointment has yet to be written.

On the few occasions when I was allowed to walk or drive with him, I gathered information as bees collect honey. He knew where Beethoven had lived, where Schubert had written this or that. He could compare the Vienna of the old times with that of to-day, could tell you who had lived in which palace, and dissipate your ignorance as to baroque.

The above account was printed in *P.E.N. News* in September 1929, but Sappho added to it in her journal with less discretion:

Saw many baroque churches and disliked them heartily ... but there were buildings and squares that are delightful. A big Banquet in the Kaiser Burg, jolly, but too many speeches. In the end I said I was 'glad the children could speak so well and knew so many languages – they were *dear* children, they were *my* children, but the old Mutter thought they always talked too much.' I spoke in German, having got a little of that language back, and they were very nice to me.

Another night the Burgomeister gave a wonderful affair at the Rathaus ... C.M. Grieve got very drunk and apostrophized everyone as 'dear old bugger' and broke a bottle. About 1000 people were entertained and when, at 4.30 a.m. they went to take leave of their host, were told he had fallen asleep and could not be disturbed. On the last evening, after a Heurigen Fest, Henry Seidal Canby suggested we should seize the opportunity to thank Grete von Urbanitzky for all the trouble she had taken, and he made a charming little speech. Another of the English contingent said 'Let's sing "For She's a Jolly Good Fellow",' and the dozen or so English stood up and, to the open-mouthed amazement of the Europeans, sang it!

I fancy we were all entirely unmusical.

Going up to tell Nevinson that Ivan Mestrovič was there, I discovered our delegate was quite drunk. He was kind and pleasant as ever, but begged Hermon not to leave him behind. Hermon cared for him.

The Galsworthys were present at that Vienna Congress in 1929, and at the banquet J.G. spoke in German:

... this beautiful and gracious town, which has prepared a welcome for us that none of us will forget. Vienna is, I think, the School where all should go to learn the art of living ...

Let us now say: We approach the day when the P.E.N. Club will be established in every country in the world ... We were a dream, we have become true. We are like a tree which grows in rain and sunshine ... The birds of the air sit on our branches singing 42 different songs without misunderstanding each other [A reference to the forty-two existing Centres] ...

Unfortunately the misunderstandings not foreseen by J.G. inevitably arose from the thirties onwards, although the P.E.N. strove to find a path through them.

From Vienna Sappho and Arthur Lynch went on to Prague for a couple of days and were entertained by Karel Čapek. Sappho also had lunch with President Masaryk at Lany, where she came to admire the Bohemian President as 'the supreme example of his type, the simple, good man'. He had instructed his librarian to investigate the P.E.N. and what it stood for and had then said: 'Join this movement, it is a good thing.'

President Masaryk was an Hon. Member of the English Centre in 1930.

Sappho and Lynch had only a couple of days and, although they travelled together, they could not have had much time to relax. But in her autobiographical (unpublished) novel *Any Woman*, she tells the story of middle-aged Reb's love 'for Lance de Lacey', who is obviously Lynch. In the novel they go to a Sokol Meeting together in Prague – for a whole week – where Reb is the one to be received officially, and Lance has literary affairs to attend to. The two days that she actually spent with Arthur Lynch in Prague are built up into the relationship for which she longed, although even here there is no suggestion of real intimacy. But her passionate feelings for him are all written down, also Lance's acceptance of her adoration, his enjoyment of her society, and his reliance on her care of him and his belongings – luggage, coats, tickets. Lynch was incredibly absent-minded, and, although Sappho herself was not a very competent traveller, she was competence itself compared with him. His total rejection of a closer relationship is also made clear.

[Reb's thoughts]. Never a touch he thought she could notice, but when they drove to and fro in the big car which Authority had placed at her service, he leaned against her – he yielded, pretending to be unaware of her proximity. She was puzzled and once asked if he disapproved of physical relationships. 'No,' he said, 'but it depends on the case. There may be duties to others.' In answer to another question, he added, 'There are those who will not be content with a little.'

Arthur Lynch was not, I am sure, religious, and although his parents had been catholics, he had not been sent to a catholic school. Why did he keep this rigid barrier between them? In 1929 he was 68 and she was 64, and they had been friends for eight or nine years. He knew exactly what she felt for him, he could easily have stopped seeing her, made it clear he was bored. But he never did. On the contrary, when she was in London, they had tea together every so often in some small tea room, he occasionally came to her house, he sent her his books to read – which she then worked feverishly to get reviewed. At P.E.N. dinners, to which he came from time to time, they always sat next to each other – by her arrangement, of course, but obviously with his acquiescence. David Carver, the late Secretary of the P.E.N., told me that he sometimes found them, after some committee meeting had dispersed, sitting very close together on a settee talking.

My brother Christopher told me of one occasion when Sappho went off to meet Lynch, dressed in her best and very gay and happy and came back a couple of hours later in tears, because he had not turned up.

Just occasionally Lynch became human, such as at a dinner given by the To-Morrow Club in 1927 to all its past lecturers. Sappho was there and wrote:

Clemence Dane presided, and it was one of the happiest days of my life, for I sat next My Dear [Lynch] who thought my gown, which was of black velvet, embroidered with feathers and from Paris, was 'wonderful', and my wood-pussy [fur] cloak the most beautiful evening cloak he had seen in London. I purred and was happy.

35

A Ball – and Two Plays

I had been P.E.N. Secretary for five years, and I was expecting my first baby in January 1927, so it was time I stopped being so busy on matters outside my home. Sappho had anticipated this situation, and Hermon Ould, a Founder Member, currently on the Executive Committee and already a devoted worker for P.E.N., was the obvious choice. He had the same liberal and international interests that fitted in with her own and Galsworthy's views – and he was willing to take over. In the summer of 1926 we became joint secretaries for the rest of that year.

As usual the P.E.N. was in need of funds to entertain its guests from abroad, so I offered to organise a Ball in the late autumn, as my farewell effort.

The P.E.N. Ball duly took place on 26 November at the Hyde Park Hotel and was fancy dress. A hundred and five authors had donated signed copies of their books, and for the best costumes representing well-known characters in fiction there were prizes of autographed books by famous authors. The judges were Clemence Dane, Sheila Kaye-Smith, John Drinkwater, Jerome K. Jerome, who came as a cardinal, and Margaret Kennedy. The prizes were presented by G.K. Chesterton, dressed as Dr Johnson.

There was also a large bran pie containing all the donated books which were not being presented as prizes; Edith Evans or Margaret Bannerman gave the holders of lucky numbers a book. It was a real headache to decide which books went into the bran pie and which were deemed to have been written by such famous authors that they could be presented as individual prizes!

J.G. was abroad and thus safely out of all this, which greatly disappointed Una, Lady Troubridge, who had come dressed as 'A White Monkey'. My old friend, the late Ernest Raymond, who went as Sherlock Holmes and remembered it all clearly, told me that the first prize-winners were Edmund Dulac and Margaret Irwin.

The Ball was a great success from the publicity angle and raised

£100 clear for the Entertainment Fund. This does not seem much in these days, but over sixty years ago it was worth much more. I presented the balance sheet on 3 January 1927 and then retired into private life, my daughter Marjorie-Ann arriving on 28 January.

Encouraged by my efforts, Sappho organised two money-making efforts in 1927 and '29. For the first, in 1927, Leon M. Lion lent Wyndham's Theatre for a matinée, and Shaw was sufficiently tamed to allow Part 1 of *Back to Methuselah* to be played, with Edith Evans as the serpent and Gwen Ffrangçon-Davies as Eve. The Duchess of Hamilton presided over a Claridge's tea-party to publicise the affair, at which Rebecca West spoke and said, 'There isn't probably a person in London who hasn't called Sappho a pest.' But she added, 'As you get to know her, you realise she is a lovable pest.'

Sappho bought flowers, 'graduated in value', for three of the actresses, and two bay-leaf wreaths for Shaw and Edith Evans. Shaw put his on and wore it all the last part of the afternoon. He said: 'It isn't bay, it is myrtle, which means a lover – I like that better.' And Edith Evans wrote:

Dear Mrs Dawson Scott – I hardly know how to thank you for the laurel wreath. I certainly felt it was a great honour to be singled out in company with G.B.S. and given the classic emblem of fame! I have hung it up in my room and get a little thrill every time I look at it.

Sappho's next venture, in April 1929, did not, however, meet with Shaw's approval. She and Hermon Ould were by this time great friends and she was prepared to believe that he was a first class playwright who had somehow been overlooked by the critics and theatrical impresarios – and Sappho never hesitated to push her friends. Another theatre was lent to the P.E.N., and Hermon's play *The Moon Rides High* was put on. Sappho wrote to ask Shaw for his support – and to come to the performance – and received this reply:

4, Whitehall Court, S.W.1. 19th Jan. 1929. Dear Mrs Dawson Scott. My presence at a theatrical performance does not make a farthing difference in the receipts; and I cannot engage myself for the 12th April, as I may not be in London on that day.

I do not understand how the Committee of the Club can justify the proposed use of Club funds to give Mr Ould's play a chance of being seen, as you put it. Surely no auditor would pass the accounts if they included expenditure for such a purpose. And what about all the other members who have plays which have not had a chance to be seen? It may be that our constitution empowers the committee to enter upon theatrical speculations for the benefit of the Club. But you had better make sure; for the possibilities of financial disaster and internal trouble through charges of invidious selection of plays etc. are boundless.

Faithfully,

G.B.S.

P.S. I have to raise these questions because literature has always been to you a fairyland into which law does not enter; and I therefore have to regard you as 'capable de tout'.

The more friendly postscript was added to the typed letter in his own handwriting, and shows that Shaw had a human understanding of Sappho.

In spite of this criticism, the matinée was quite successful and made a little money. Club Funds, of course, were *not* used.

James Agate rang up to know if he should come and criticise the play, saying: 'I don't want to, if I can help it, for I hate the P.E.N.' Sappho and Hermon wondered why?

Sappho quoted one of Shaw's postcards dated 30 March 1929, which must have been shown her by its recipient, and I don't know who that was, but she copied it into her journal:

Ayot St Lawrence. The P.E.N. Club was formed to gratify the craze of the distinguished novelist Mrs Dawson Scott for literary society. No other reason for its existence has ever been alleged or discovered; but it has resulted in innumerable dinners, luncheons and receptions for literary guests taking place all over Europe; and nothing will ever now extinguish it.

I joined because John Galsworthy said I must. He, presumably, joined because Mrs Dawson Scott said he must. That is how the Club is recruited. I avoid it as I would the plague. G.B.S.

Sappho merely commented:

Shaw is the representative of the P.E.N. on the European Council and is a life member. Perhaps he was being funny.

P.E.N. Members had been invited to send in encouraging messages to the Play Committee on postcards, and, among many received, the one that stands out was from D.H. Lawrence:

All my good wishes ... Even if I am the black sheep among members, yet I feel that, wherever I go, P.E.N. would accept me and be kind to me if I'd let them – all over the face of the earth – which is somehow comforting.

36

Minor Disagreements with Galsworthy

1. A P.E.N. House or Home

In 1926 Sappho had another Idea – to establish in London a P.E.N. House or Home, such as the French Centre already had in Paris. She had become great friends with Marion Cran, a writer on gardens and a gardening enthusiast, who had founded the Garden Club, which had premises at 9, Chesterfield Gardens, W.1. This was a residential club, which had also a large dining room, where the P.E.N. often held its dinners at a cost of 7s 6d a head.

Sappho and Mrs Cran together worked out a scheme whereby the P.E.N. and the Garden Club would join forces and buy a large house where P.E.N. visitors could stay, where all members could use the public rooms and where the dinners could be held. Sappho wrote to J.G. and outlined the plan. He was, however, uncompromisingly against the idea and wrote on 20 July 1926, from Grove Lodge, Hampstead:

Dear Mrs Dawson Scott, as you probably surmised, I am entirely against the P.E.N., as it now exists, being connected with a P.E.N. house, as you conceive it, except in so far as present members might wish to become members of the P.E.N. house, just as they might wish to become members of the Athenaeum, the Saville, the Garrick, the Authors Club ... or any of the other clubs whose names I don't remember. And *I could not myself take any part whatever in the formation or management* of your (projected) P.E.N. house; that would have to be, so far as I am concerned, an entirely outside venture of Mrs Cran's, for which she would solicit members from the writing profession at large. If, on the other hand, the P.E.N. Club as a whole, at the A.G.M., declared in favour of being identified with the P.E.N. house, in other words of becoming a material Club, like, say, the Athenaeum, it will be quite simple for me to stand aside, and you would select a fresh President in sympathy with that idea. This proposition in fact revives rather acutely the consideration whether the time has not really come for me to step aside and give place to some worthy successor. There I leave the matter for the moment.

Sappho wrote again – although there is no letter from her extant, but I have J.G.'s reply, dated 24 July:

My dear Mrs Dawson Scott ... I find it hard to put into exact words my feeling against the P.E.N. having a permanent clubhouse of its own. My instinct is against it. If the P.E.N. is not an idea, it is nothing. Tie it to bricks and mortar and the fattening comforts of a clubhouse, and it will shrink and may perish. If Mrs Marion Cran promoted a 'Writers' Residential Club' or 'Writers' Hostel' or what not – entirely apart from the P.E.N. – and produced a fine article, I certainly see no reason why we should not lodge our foreign guests there, or let it be known as a suitable place for foreign writers to stay at. And obviously members of the P.E.N. could reside there if they wished. What I am against is (1) the use of the word P.E.N. in connection with it, (2) the P.E.N. Club taking any part in its promotion, (3) the P.E.N. Club assuming any liability (that's a good word) for its maintenance. I feel too that as Founder of the P.E.N. you would not be well-advised to join Mrs Cran in promoting such a club. Is it going to be easy for Mrs Cran to find a house that would house residentially more than a very few writers or that would seat dinners of a hundred, if the P.E.N. wished to dine there?

Sappho went to America that summer, but on her return she tried once more; she was finally defeated by J.G.'s last letter on the subject:

Nov. 8th 1926. We are very glad you are back, but so sorry to hear you are back unwell ... You evidently do not feel with me what a great difference there is between being dwellers in tents and dwellers in houses; nor I think, do you realise in the least what a commercial concern we should be turned into, if we attempted to acquire a house large enough to enable us to hold dinners for over 100. My position remains the same. If the Club wishes to turn itself into just another West-End Club, with the premises and capital-raising necessary, then it must find a new President and I shall become simply a member and well-wisher. This is a quite feasible proposition, and you might take the Club's opinion on it by correspondence and, indeed, vote, though it would require several hundreds or thousands of members recruited and several (Annual) General Meetings to get the 'capital' side of the thing arranged. Whether *you* would survive the work and worry entailed, I don't know. Another thing: at present our idealism is impeccable. Become a West End Club, and the question, 'Who's making a good thing out of this?' is in the wind at once. J.G.

I think J.G. was absolutely right, and that it was lucky for the P.E.N. – and for Sappho – that he stood his ground so firmly. She did not live to see her dream to some extent realised when Henrietta

Leslie died and left the lease of Glebe House to P.E.N. in 1947. In the meantime the Club continued to increase its centres and grow in renown and prestige with only office headquarters. In 1966, when David Carver was Secretary, the idea of larger and grander premises than Glebe House provided was raised again, and for years there were Project sub-committees and money-raising efforts to achieve this aim. It was also the main subject for discussion at a number of Annual General Meetings, just as J.G. had predicted. They never came to anything and the scheme was abandoned; and in 1975 the P.E.N. was faced with losing Glebe House, as the lease came to an end. It now shares premises with the Sketch Club at 7, Dilke Street, SW3.

2. Thomas Hardy's Funeral

When Thomas Hardy died, Sappho was outraged that, although he had stated in his will that he wanted to lie with his own people, 'Authority' decided he should be buried in Westminster Abbey. 'A few years ago,' she wrote indignantly,

> Chesterton said he was the village atheist sitting with the village idiot; 'Jude the Obscure' was called 'Jude the Obscene', and all England cursed him as anti-Christian. Now they ghoulishly operate on the dead and put his heart in one place and his ashes in another. Phaugh.

She wrote to J.G. about this, asking his views and urging him to protest, and in his usual moderate and unemotional way J.G. replied:

> Jan. 19th, 1928. I don't think I have any views about the Hardy Memorial, except that I *personally* should be prepared to support a proposed institution of a Thomas Hardy Chair of Literature in a Wessex University ... I don't think you need distress yourself about the Abbey burial. I would agree with you about the over-riding of wills, if I did not feel personally convinced that Hardy was really glad of the idea. I fancy the Will is not recent, and that his views were ascertained much more recently. Generally speaking I think you are wrong about the Abbey; it is after all a very harmless way of marking national appreciation, and it is just as well for literature that it should not be left out.

As a convinced atheist, Sappho obviously could not agree with such moderate views, and she was moved to write in her journal that day in January 1928:

> If anyone writes a biography of me, prevents me from being burned and my ashes cast into the sea, sends flowers, speaks religious mummery over my dead body, I curse them and, if I can, I'll haunt them and

destroy them. My earnest command is that no memory of me shall be left in the country that has felt no interest in my art and has not allowed me to earn by it a living. 'Their works shall praise them' is the only memorial worthy of an artist.

That was written over fifty years ago, and I feel, as J.G. did about Hardy, that she would long since have changed her mind and withdrawn her objections. After all, during all these years there has been no memory of her – except by 'her works' i.e. the P.E.N.

37

Hermon Ould and the Young P.E N.

When I gave up being the P.E.N. Secretary in December 1926 I was followed by Hermon Ould who, as International Secretary, remained 'in charge' of the P.E.N. after both John Galsworthy and Sappho died in 1933 and 1934 until his own death in 1951.

Hermon Ould was a warm and sympathetic personality and was much loved by P.E.N. members all over the world. He is still remembered by many more people than now remember Sappho.

For six years he served an apprenticeship with Sappho and J.G. to support and advise him, and this enabled him, from 1934, to bear the full weight of the organisation, since never again could there be the steady continuity which had existed for twelve years between the Founder, the first President and the Secretary, first myself and then Hermon.

In 1928 Hermon made a separate name for himself in the P.E.N. by founding 'The Young P.E.N.', with the support of both Sappho and J.G.

In April 1928 Sappho wrote in her journal:

Hermon has a scheme for forming a Young P.E.N. ... an excellent scheme ... so like mine of the To-Morrow Club, the difference being that the Y.P. is international.

J.G. then wrote to the press that the Young P.E.N. would:

consist of young writers and literary aspirants never more than 29 years old, not as yet eligible for the P.E.N. itself, and many of whom will not so far have had any work published.

It will exist to foster creative talent, bring young writers together and give them a chance to meet young literary folk of other countries ...

Well over a hundred young people sent in their names at once and an inaugural meeting was planned for 4 October, just seven years after the P.E.N. itself was founded.

The Young P.E.N. flourished, organising informal meetings and dances, poetry and manuscript readings, and being entertained to tea by older members. And in November 1929 there was news of the first, and, as it transpired, the only Young P.E.N. branch abroad – in Jugoslavia.

The first President of the Young P.E.N. was E.M. Forster, followed by Lady Rhondda, Bertrand Russell and lastly, in 1933, by Ernest Raymond, who continued in office at least until 1939 and wrote at length about it in his autobiography.

Like so many organisations, it did not survive the 1939 war – the Young People who had belonged had, perforce, other things to do.

The Young P.E.N. brought Sappho the friendship of many young writers whom she encouraged and with whom she corresponded. Leo Walmsley, Sian O'Faolain and H.E. Bates were amongst these, and some of the latter's letters to her are still extant:

The Granary, Little Chart, Nr Ashford, Kent. Jan 20, 1932. Dear Mrs Dawson Scott. I am delighted, and honoured, too, by your letter. One doesn't often get a letter of such warmth and generosity – and from another writer too.

Well, I simply wallowed in your generous praise. I've had nothing like it for ages, and the fact of your liking Esther throws me into [word undecipherable – perhaps 'ditherations'?] because this is the story Edward Garnett liked so much, and the story all other critics have attacked. You should have seen Queen Rebecca West tear me to pieces for it.

But the proof was for you to keep and show [it] to Ernest Rhys ... I do make a living in a way, thanks to my novels and my generous publishers and limited editions of a weekly article, and the fact that I began so young and am pretty prolific. At twenty six I've got a bibliographical list as long as a nettle-root – three novels and three books of [word indecipherable] and lots of oddments. But it's a squeeze and I slave myself ill from time to time. I am looking forward to seeing you ...

38

Psychic Experiences

Sappho had been, ever since she was a child, interested in telepathy, in dreams, in tales of unusual happenings, all of which gradually developed into an increasing pre-occupation with everything connected with psychic phenomena. She always spoke of herself as psychic, and often described her experiences in this field very vividly, and we took them for granted. If telepathy is accepted as being valid, then Sappho was telepathic. There were many occasions when she knew she would hear from a certain person within a day or two and watched for the postman. Sure enough the letter came. And she wrote:

> I have before noticed that there is a psychic affinity between Toby and me. What is so puzzling is – why is there none between Nellie (her sister) and me, or Marjorie or Christopher or Scottie, while there is between Tony, Edward Knoblauch, Netta Syrett and other stray persons? Why should I be able, when playing cards with Scottie, to see again and again the cards in Dummy's hand, while I never can when playing in a room full of people?

She was intensely interested in the whole subject of what is now called Extra-Sensory Perception, and particularly with the possibility of communication with the dead.

She knew that she had some special sensitivity that most people did not have, although I do not think that at first she related this to an 'after-life'. But incidents were accepted as fact and not dismissed as coincidence.

Until 1924 I was interested in Sappho's stories of peculiar incidents and listened sympathetically to anything she told me. But my interest was only on the surface, and that summer, during a visit to Zennor in North Cornwall, I was involved in happenings which put an end even to that shallow interest.

Sappho's Cornish novels were always well reviewed in the *Western Morning News* and other local papers, and she had many Cornish friends who still remembered her poet cousin, Henry Dawson Lowry. One of these was C.V. Thomas, a solicitor in Camborne, who owned a tiny cottage on the moors above Zennor. It was completely isolated, set among granite stones and heather, three quarters of a mile from the next building, a farm.

Mr Thomas unwisely described the cottage to Sappho, who immediately wanted to rent it. Hastily, but in vain, he spoke of its defects – only rain water in a butt infested with mosquitoes – drinking water must be fetched from the farm. There was a huge open fireplace where furze was burned, which you must personally collect! There was only a lin-hay or lean-to kitchen with an oil cooking stove; the postman came as far as the farm only; there were no shops or means of transport – you must walk either five miles to St Ives or six to Penzance for provisions ... It was useless. The more inconvenient and lonely, and the wilder the surroundings, the more it delighted Mother, and C.V. Thomas finally gave in.

I had had my appendix out that spring and was getting strong rather slowly; Sappho thought that a few weeks on this magnificent coast, leading a simple life, would be just the thing for me. The P.E.N. Club, now three years old, had adjourned for the summer, and she was free to visit a part of Cornwall she didn't know.

We went by train to Penzance and hired a car to Zennor, where it left us standing in front of The Tinners' Arms, surrounded by suitcases and packages and a crate of groceries. We enquired where Mr Thomas' cottage was, and someone pointed to a broad dip which went up and up between the hills. About half-way up was a farm, but no sign of any other building. 'Mr Thomas' cottage is just over the top – you can't see it from here.' 'How do we get there?' asked Sappho. Silence and a blank look. 'Well, how does Mr Thomas get there?' queried Sappho. 'Oh, he do walk,' said our informant, with a puzzled look at all our traps. But my parent was undaunted. 'How do the people who live in that farm get anything they need and bring their milk churns down?' 'Oh, farmer, 'ee do borrow the dung cart from the farm at Churchtown.' And to my horror Sappho said, 'That will do splendidly – where is the dung cart?'

Finally the dung cart – quite dry, really – was found, and a boy to lead the horse, and our belongings were put in on some newspaper kindly provided by The Tinners' Arms, Sappho helped into the cart, and we set off, with me walking behind. I was still of the age to feel embarrassed by Sappho's unconventional behaviour, especially as quite a few villagers had collected to watch this queer lady – obviously a mad foreigner – drive off.

We struggled up the stony track, lurching, slipping from side to side, but every lurch and stumble was worth suffering for what awaited us at the top. We looked down the hill to Zennor, with its grey farm buildings and golden lichen-encrusted roofs, and the small church with its Mermaid legend. The land levelled to a gentle slope of tiny fields surrounded by dry stone walls of granite and slate, on down to the blue sea, below steep cliffs, which stretched northward to St Ives and south to Gurnard's Head, Cape Cornwall and Land's End. To the east the rough moor gradually gave way to fields, and on either side were the rocky hills of Carn Zennor and Carn Galva. And all this wild expanse was dotted with rough granite blocks, with cromlechs, nine maidens, the Logan Rock and Men-an-Tol. The small hamlets had magic names such as Towednack, Nancledra, Boswednack, Madron and Amalebrea – and bracken and gorse and heather grew over all.

At last we reached the cottage, white-washed over stone walls 2-3 ft thick, small, deep-set windows – just a few – a big low kitchen with a huge open fireplace, and a wooden ladder-staircase up to the two bedrooms, one leading out of the other. And outside was The Water Butt!

Our friends Hermon Ould and archaeologist Leonard Woolley arrived the next day, and every few days I and one of the men walked the five or six miles to St Ives or Penzance to buy food, which we brought home on our backs in rucksacks. I quickly gained strength, and it was a very happy holiday.

In addition to the fresh sea air, magnificent views and compulsory long walks, I remember that summer especially because of the 'table-turning' sessions, or seances.

On the road below us, just above Zennor, was the Eagle's Nest, the house where the naturalist W.H. Hudson had lived. Many famous people have stayed in Zennor, which is, even now, totally unspoiled. In 1916-17 D.H. Lawrence had rented a cottage there, and he and Frieda were indiscreet enough to sing German songs at night! So they were officially asked to leave. And during the second war I once met Haile Selassie, in a black cloak, walking down the flinty road which wound between yellow gorse, grey stones and hills, to the Eagle's Nest, where he was staying.[1]

In 1924 the house belonged to W.E. Arnold-Foster, whom I had known when I was a junior clerk in the War Trade Intelligence Dept. during the war. His nickname in the office was 'The Weaf', from his initials and I was amazed when one evening he came unexpectedly to

[1] Only recently I learned that one of his daughters was at a boarding school in the area – perhaps in Penzance! But at that time his presence on that country road was a complete mystery.

call on us at that lonely cottage, Noon Veor.

Sappho was in one of her spiritualistic-cum-psychic moods and was planning to hold a table-turning session with Hermon Ould and Leonard Woolley, who was also interested, and myself, still willing to be included. The Weaf arrived just as we were about to begin.

In her book *Moments of Knowing*, (p.60) Ann Bridge has described this episode, as it was told her by Will Arnold-Foster, and has given a fuller account than I could have done from memory alone, but with which I agree:

> Will (Arnold-Forster) ... was living at the Eagle's Nest at Zennor. Some friends ... had lent their farm [cottage] on the moors to friends of theirs, and had asked him to be civil to them. So one evening ... he walked over ... to call on these strangers. He found them gathered round a table, bare except for a circle of letters and a glass, all set for a session of table-pushing; they invited him to join them. Will ... rather disliked the whole idea. He refused to touch the tumbler, but ... let himself be persuaded to act as 'recorder' – to sit with a pad and pencil and jot down in succession the letters indicated by the glass.
>
> They got off to a brisk start. 'Yes', proclaimed the glass at once, on being asked if anyone was there? and 'yes' again, when asked if it had a message for anyone. Who for? 'For Ruth.' Will began to pay a little more attention, while the others were discussing who 'Ruth' might be – they could not think of any Ruth they knew very well – but *he* remembered Ruth Mallory, widow of the Everest climber, whom he then knew only slightly. He asked his hostess to enquire who the message was from? 'George' came back at once. 'George who?' Will persisted. The answer was 'George Mallory'.[2]
>
> Now everyone was at once deeply interested. The tragedy of Everest was fairly recent, and the idea of being in touch with Mallory himself was almost frightening; though it must be remembered that none of the people whose fingers were actually on the tumbler knew that his wife's name was Ruth. Will, who did know this, never touched the glass at any point; he merely sat by the table, writing down the letters as they were touched. From this point onwards, though, he told me that he asked most of the questions – certainly it was he who asked what the message for Ruth was.
>
> 'Tell her she must do something about Frank,' came the reply. Will was completely stumped by this. None of George's three children was called Frank; puzzled, half-incredulous, but anxious to do the right thing by Ruth, if this really was a message from George, he asked what Ruth was to do about Frank?
>
> 'He's unhappy – she must do something about him,' was all the reply he got. Will wrote to Ruth Mallory.

[2] Will Arnold-Foster later married Ruth Mallory.

It seemed the 'message' was genuine. Briefly, as one of a number of half-starving children in Vienna, 'Franz' had been evacuated to England just after the war and had stayed with Ruth's family for three or four years. He was known as Frank, but as conditions in Vienna improved, he went back to his mother, and news of him since had been scanty. On hearing from Will Arnold-Forster, Ruth had enquiries made in Vienna and found that, in fact, the child was neglected and unhappy and in great need. She arranged for him to return to England, where he remained and did well. This ends Ann Bridge's account of the seances at the cottage of Noon Veor, but I remember the tense excitement that arose among us when that first message was tapped out.

At further seances we did not get much success. Hermon Ould asked for news of a German friend of his in Berlin, with whom he had lost touch, and there came a message that he was ill, had no money and was near to starvation. In the flickering firelight and glow from the big open fireplace, with, sometimes, a bright moon lighting the dark sky, and often a wind howling round the moorland cottge even although it was August, there was an eerie and rather frightening atmosphere.

I was actually going to Berlin almost immediately – in September – to initiate a P.E.N. centre, and I agreed to look for Hermon's friend and report. I was quite excited to be able to do this.

If I had found that the messages about the chap being ill, etc. were true, I should probably have become a firm believer in seances, but they were not. The young man had *not* been ill and was *not* starving. He had a wife and children and, although poor, he made enough money to support them. When I gave Sappho and Hermon this information, they said the messages must have come from 'poltergeists' or 'elementals'. Maybe. But I was cured. Which does not in the least mean that I reject all psychic phenomena, only, after that, I never had any wish to investigate further.

This was in 1924, and Sappho's interests in all aspects of the occult and psychic world steadily deepened in the next years: she experimented with mediums, automatic writing, the ouija board, attended seances and took part in a series of sittings for 'clairvoyant development' at the British College of Psychic Science. She had for a long time been able to achieve 'clairvoyant journeys', as when she visited – in spirit – Arthur Lynch's room (see above, p. 87).

As a result of taking part in regular seances, Sappho believed she was receiving messages from four people no longer living, one of these being Scottie. Her book *From Four Who Are Dead* was published by Arrowsmith in 1926.

She had begun to receive the messages or scripts that were to become the book in late 1924, when I was engaged to Arthur, and, as I spent most evenings with him at his house in Holly Place, Hampstead, I often came home late. Nowadays parents would know better than to question their 25-year-old daughter's evening occupations, but fifty years ago Sappho did not like the situation and protested, which caused rows between us. Then one morning she assured me: 'It's all right – I have talked to your father, and he says I'm not to worry.' As my father had been dead for over two years, I was very cross and expressed myself forcibly – and she said no more. And that is why, regrettably, I have so few personal memories of Sappho's pre-occupation with psychic matters.

J.G. also did not show any interest in the subject. Sappho tried to get him to read, and give an opinion on, one of Dennis Bradley's books concerning spiritualism, but J.G. wrote on 8 March 1926, from Palm Springs, California, 'I saw Bradley's book, but I have turned very much agin the whole thing. This for your private ear.'

However, Sappho's enthusiasm had engendered an interest in the subject within her immediate circle, and May Sinclair, who had been quite closely involved with her friend's experiments for some years, wrote the preface to *From Four Who Are Dead*. Her final sentence reads:

This script is in many ways remarkable. It is the only reasonable account of the life beyond death that I have yet seen.

Others who shared her interest in varying degrees and were sometimes present at seances in which she took part included in addition to Dennis Bradley, Shaw Desmond, Rebecca West, Constance Holme, Lind-af-Hageby, H. de Vere Stacpoole.

Sappho's second book on psychic matters, *Is this Wilson?* was, she believed, a series of messages which she received early in 1928 from Woodrow Wilson, the deceased President of the United States. It was published by Dutton early in January 1929.

39

The Survival League

In 1929, in addition to travelling to the States, Vienna and Prague, Sappho had her last important Idea. On October 13th, 8 years after founding the P.E.N., she founded the Survival League.

During her journeys abroad and through her social and literary contacts, she had met many people who had themselves had curious and unexplained experiences and who already half believed in an 'after-life'.

> Met Sir E. Marshall Hall ... he is the fairest, most secretive looking man I've seen for some time. He said if I started a Survival Organisation, he would join.

The idea of the Survival League was not a sudden one. It happened in the same way as the To-Morrow Club and the P.E.N. Club. The ground had been dug and prepared: it was waiting for some use to be made of it, and all at once Sappho knew what she was going to do. She returned from a visit to America (in connection with her *Is this Wilson?* book) in March 1929 and described her thoughts on the subject three months later:

> During the 3 months after my return, the Survival League began to take definite shape. It beame an affirmation of Survival. People had investigated and experimented for long enough, and I wanted them to accept Survival as a definite fact and find out about it. I also wished to unite the many societies who believe in that and other things. An easy link between large numbers of people would be their common belief that man survived. To that belief they added dogmas of hoary age, but they did not accept the modern view that death made very little difference to the individual: it was as if a person had walked from his friends into another room of the same house ... I wished for this union, but not for uniformity. I wished for all the experimenters and thinkers to come together and tell the world of their belief in the one fact of survival.

She consulted Dennis Bradley and took the Queen's Hall for Sunday evening, 13th October. She had lived in a tent all August in order to acquire the money to hire the hall.

The Queen's Hall meeting was a success since, as 2,400 people bought tickets, it paid its way. Among those present were Oliver Baldwin, M.P., the Rev. Fielding-Ould, Estelle Stead, Hannan Swaffer, and many of Sappho's writer friends – M.P. Willcocks, Anna Wickham, Constance Holme, H. de Vere Stacpoole, Lind-af-Hagby, Shaw Desmond ... There were also a large number of organisations represented.

About the Queen's Hall meeting Sappho wrote:

> There were 13 or 14 speakers, and Mr Bradley insisted on my speaking too, which I was sorry to have to do. It was not difficult, however, as we had Marconi microphones ...
> For 2 hours the audience sat spellbound, listening to the evidence as given by ordinary men and women of many professions and creeds in proof of survival ... evidence obtained personally, obtained without the aid of mediums. Present on the platform and speaking were business men, clergymen, a lawyer, Member of Parliament, poet, chemist, ironmonger, lecturer, novelist ... There were Roman Catholics, Church of England, Theosophists, Spiritualists, Agnostics. That made the meeting impressive.

Sappho must have given the meeting considerable thought previously, for at the Queen's Hall gathering an Executive Committee of ten was formed, with Dennis Bradley as Chairman, and a large Council. She wrote at the bottom of the two lists of names: 'I am, what I began by being, the Organiser.' She had, however, learnt one lesson – to try and arrange an exit for herself, so that she would not again be responsible for running two big organisations at the same time, as with the To-Morrow Club and the P.E.N. In the guidelines written down for the Survival League was the sentence:

> As soon as funds permit [the subscription was 5s a year] a paid secretary shall be employed and the Founder released from the necessity to act as an officer of the League.

This was a nice idea, but did not, of course, work out, and she remained closely involved – in fact the Organiser – until she died five years later.

Unfortunately Sappho ceased to keep a journal soon after the birth of the Survival League, and it has been difficult to find out what happened to this 'Idea', since everyone who attended the inaugural meeting has died, except Maurice Barbanell, who became the editor of *Psychic News*. And he said: 'It is a long time ago, and I don't remember.'

In the library of the British Museum, however, I found two little books entitled *The Guide to Psychic Knowledge*, edited by C.A. Dawson Scott in 1932, which I did not know existed. The heading in No 1 was 'Questions from People on This Side of Death. Answers from People on That Side of Death.' Sappho had written the foreword, explaining that:

> The following questions were propounded at a gathering of about 15 people, most of whom were writers, musicians, pictorial artists and M.P.s. The answers came through Mrs Garrett (Medium) who was in a deep trance ... and were given by an entity who called himself McKenzie.

> Examples of the questions asked by the group are:

> What does it feel like to die? Does it resemble going to sleep? Are people on your side aware of us? Why is it difficult for us to perceive you?

Copies of this booklet could be obtained from the Survival League, McKenzie House (named after Stewart McKenzie) at 125, Alexandra Road, N.W.8. price 7d.

I found also *The Survival Magazine*, but this did not mention the Survival League until in No. 35, Vol. 4, of December 1932, it is stated for the first time: 'This Magazine is the official organ of the Survival League, edited by Clifford Potter, from Erlestoke Park, Wilts.' In this number there is an article by Sappho, which shows that three years after its foundation the Survival League was still very much alive, as was her interest in it.

Arthur Lynch died in March 1934, and I wondered if Sappho tried to communicate with him. My sister-in-law, not then married to my brother Christopher, tells me that she was persuaded by Sappho to take notes at some of her spiritualistic meetings, and that, certainly on one occasion, perhaps more, Sappho did make efforts to get in touch with the Lynx, asking if he were 'there'? But she thinks the sessions were inconclusive, as she remembers nothing more, not being herself interested.

When I tried to reconstruct the years 1930-34, a period when I was very much engrossed in my own domestic affairs, I was puzzled as to how Sappho continued to live such a busy life. I had plenty of data about the P.E.N. but, after 1929, it seemed as if she had almost ceased to write seriously. In that year she brought out two more collections of short stories (with Ernest Rhys), a frivolous novel, *Oh, Foolish Kitty*, and the psychic book *Is This Wilson?* She also completed *Any Woman*, the semi-autobiographical book that was never published. There was then nothing creative until 1933, when her last novel, *The House in the Hollow*, came out.

There was, of course, the mysterious typed manuscript, or part of a manuscript, called *The Child*, chapter one of which is on the first two pages of this book, but from which 100 pages are missing. Before this came to light I had thought that, during the five years after the launching of the Survival League in October 1929, Sappho was so deeply involved in Spiritualism and the League that, except for her continuing work for the P.E.N. she used her remaining time and energy to further this great interest.

However, among the copies of letters sent me by the University of Texas, who now own the P.E.N. Archives, I found two letters, to Hermon Ould, and his dated replies, which show that in September, 1934, she had nearly completed her last novel, *The Child* (see p. 198).

40

Domestic Life

In 1929 Sappho had a private worry about where she was going to live. Her house at Alexandra Road, acquired cheaply in 1919 because it was the 'tail end of a lease', was coming to the end of its tail, and she had literally to consider her next move. She would not be living alone, as Toby intended to come back from America and make his home with her, and she would still need one big room for her tea-party entertaining.

In October she had launched the Survival League, and Toby arrived. On Christmas Day 1929 she wrote:

> Have bought 62, Clifton Hill, St John's Wood, for £3,000. It was advertised in an estate agents' window for £3,700, and I offered £3,000. It was in the hands of the Public Trustee, who considered my offer for a week and then took it. I had £50 in the bank and felt very much dismayed. Next day, going to the P.E.N. office, I saw that the estate agents next door were offering 90 per cent loans on freehold premises, and they agreed to lend me £2,700. The Bank lent me £300 on my present house. So, by spending nothing, I obtain a house that Toby will turn into flats for me. 'L'audace!' The property is at the moment worth £5,000. It will eventually be worth £10,000. I complete Jan. 31st, 1930.

Her expectation that the house would some day be worth £10,000 was definitely an under-statement!

She also sold the 'tail end' of the house at 125, Alexandra Road for £800, having bought it ten years previously for £600. I hope the ghost of William Edward Dawson was able to appreciate his grand-daughter's flair for property deals.

The new house, as well as being very big, had the extra attraction of a huge ground floor studio, and several basement rooms, wine cellar, pantry and passages, which could be converted into bathroom and kitchen. My brother Toby duly converted the rest of the house into flats – he had inherited a sound understanding of such matters – and he and Sappho moved there in 1932. After Sappho's death in 1934, he continued to live there and only years later, when he married, did his wife get rid of the chicken wire that covered the French windows of the studio. Sappho liked fresh air – she did not object to draughts – and winter and summer she had her bed close to those wide-open windows. The wire was to prevent the cats that roamed the St John's Wood gardens seeking warmth and friendship at night.

Sappho's deepest feelings, except for the Lynx, had always been for her children; December 11th is my birthday, and this charming letter to me has survived:

> Dec. 11th. 1928. Dear Darling Daughter. How shocking of me to have forgotten the day that cost me more pain than has all the rest of your pleasant life!
>
> I feel so conscience stricken that I am sending you this note to wish you many happy years and all of them full of love and the delights of life. Your very loving Mother.

Sappho was, in modern terms, much too possessive and dominating. But, since she thought all women should marry, she was glad that I had accomplished this and that I was happy. However, she liked hearing distinguished writers like W.B. Maxwell say they had always loved their mothers best! I did not agree with this, and if the subject cropped up, said so.

Arthur's attitudes were so different from Sappho's that inevitably I learned to avoid arguments, especially as I knew it was useless to try and get her to alter her point of view. It was not really surprising that she was extremely critical of my more relaxed relationship with my own children; she was not a good grandmother and I was never able to leave my children alone in her care – on one of the few occasions when I did, I came back to find my 2½-year-old daughter in tears and Sappho with the set cross look which I remembered very well from my own childhood; the two of them had had some little disagreement over going up or down stairs at a given moment!

In 1926 Arthur and I bought a house at St Issey, a few miles from Constantine Bay, where we lived for three or four months every summer. I was able therefore to see quite a lot of Sappho, while she sojourned in her tent, and she was able to keep an eye on the tenants in her two bungalows, Holt and Lynx. She asked only a low rent for these – they were not very well furnished – in the 'off' season, so that they were often taken for the early summer months by impecunious artists or writers, many of whom were her friends. In 1930 Rupert Croft Cooke, whom she did not know, heard there was one free that summer and called on her in London about taking it. In his book *The Last of Spring* he described his meeting with Sappho: 'A forceful

woman, decisive and grimly affable, obviously a born organiser.'
When he told her he hoped to write his second novel in Cornwall, she
said:

> Then you must have Holt. That's the bungalow for a novel. J.D.
> Beresford wrote one there last summer. May Sinclair had it two years
> ago, G.B. Stern has written in it. Dorothy Richardson is living next
> door – yes, Holt would be right for you ...
>
> I was given details of trains, how to get on with the Cornish,
> directions as to neighbouring walks, and on not disturbing Dorothy
> Richardson. I was criticised sharply for not belonging to the P.E.N.
> and commended for having achieved publication of a first novel.

There is quite lot more, and his last reference to Sappho was:

> Yet ... that stay in Cornwall was a glorious time, and I remember it
> with gratitude now. My relations with Mrs Dawson Scott ended with
> acerbity, something to do with a broken inkpot, I seem to remember,
> but my life, and the lives of a good many others, would have been
> poorer without her and her bungalows and her talk of 'peasants' and
> her championship of writers.

Even if Hector Hawton, as a boy of 18, had not been scared of
Sappho, there is no doubt she could appear rather formidable, as she
got older, to people meeting her for the first time. Noel Streatfeild
wrote of her:

> I only met Mrs Dawson Scott once, soon after I had published my first
> novel, and I admit I was terrified of her. Mr Galsworthy had suggested
> I should join the P.E.N. and Mrs D.S. disapproved. 'What is one
> novel?' she asked. 'You are a very lucky young woman to be meeting all
> these distinguished people.'
>
> Sometimes when I look around me at our present P.E.N. gatherings,
> I think perhaps we could do with a Mrs Dawson Scott, to keep us in our
> places.

Sappho continued to make a little money by journalism whenever
the opportunity arose. In October 1931 she wrote to Hermon Ould
from her tent:

> Could you send me the names of few of the most important foreign
> guests we've entertained and suggest an anecdote or two? An agency
> has asked me to send in an article suitable for John o'London's. Slept
> out last night, slept deeply and well, and now lie in the sun. A toi. S.S.
> [Sappho Scott]

And Hermon replied:

8.10.31. I am blessed if I can think of any anecdote that would redound to our credit. You probably won't want to mention the fact that when the Chairman [A.P. Herbert] proposed the health of the King, the Founder *sat down* very firmly, or that when we entertained Vicki Baum we put 30 of our guests in the basement, much to their annoyance, and that a certain famous author [Sir Edmund Gosse] objected to our entertaining James Joyce, or that the Secretary has 'done time' [Ould had been imprisoned as a Conscientious Objector during the war] or that G.B.S. disapproves of us ...

With Toby to make a home for at the new house in Clifton Hill, with her writing and the Survival League, with occasional contact with her grandchildren and more often with me, with Cornwall and her bungalows, with her many friends and constant new ones, and finally with her now routine work for the P.E.N., the years from 1930-34 were full.

41

The Peak of P.E.N.

For another couple of years after the Vienna Congress in 1929 the P.E.N. continued on its enthusiastic and liberal way. The accounts of its activities through the late twenties and up until 1931 give a vivid picture of international friendships, warmth, idealism and an exchange of literary interests and ideas – a kaleidoscope of movement and colour, as the writers of the day, great and not so great, crossed and recrossed Europe and the Atlantic, met each other at the annual congresses, made friends and argued, visited the centres during the following months and met again at the next Congress. There were discussions and disagreements and it was difficult to steer a course of political non-alignment; but Sappho and J.G., supported by Hermon Ould, formed a strong and determined triumvirate and, for a little longer, kept a steady course. The 47 centres wrote to London to say how delighted they had been to entertain Thomas Mann (who became the Hon. Member for England in 1929), Ernst Toller, Jules Romains, Scholem Asch, Will Irwin, Gerhart Hauptmann, Vicki Baum, Rabindranath Tagore, Johannes V. Jensen, Emil Ludwig, Henri Barbusse, Aldous Huxley, Ford Madox Ford, James Joyce ...

Those were peak years for the P.E.N., fulfilling the aims of its Founder. But a great deal of its success was due to John Galsworthy, who was revered and acclaimed wherever he went, however unwilling he was to be 'in the limelight'. I am sure that, in spite of his quiet humility, he enjoyed the warm affection with which he was greeted by his fellow writers all over the western world.

By chance recently, in Vol. 1 of Graham Greene's *Collected Works of Ford Madox Ford*, I came across a short piece called 'The Apotheosis of John Galsworthy'. It is undated, but likely to have been written not long before J.G. died, as it refers to his being awarded the Nobel Prize, and speaks of him giving an address in Paris[1] to his 'beloved P.E.N.'.

[1] Actually Ford is a bit muddled as to dates, as J.G. was never in Paris *after* he was awarded the Nobel Prize. He was already too ill to travel.

The occasion was probably an ordinary meeting of the French P.E.N. at which J.G. was, as International President, the guest and speaker, and I was impressed by Ford's masterly assessment of J.G.'s character:

> He presided in Paris at the dinner of the International P.E.N. which is the highest honour that the members of his craft could find for him; and, in the end, the Nobel Prize Committee honoured itself by selecting him for one of its laureates. It seemed, all this, appropriate and inevitable, for, in honouring him, the world honoured one of its noblest philanthropists.
> ... And singularly, as he emerged above the shadow of all those hard French writers, there re-emerged at any rate for me the sense of his frailty, of his being something that must be shielded from the harder earnestnesses of the world ... I don't know that he was conscious on that last triumph of the really bad nature of the hard men who surrounded him.

Apparently the subject of J.G.'s speech was to praise Turgenev as a *French writer*, which was an unpopular stance to take in Paris, and Ford continued:

> I have never seen an audience so confounded ... they simply could not believe their ears ... as for me, I was so overwhelmed ... that I ran out of that place ... and into the salon of the author of 'Vascoe' ... and the news had got there before me ... before the triumphant Galsworthy had finished ... for that was the real triumph of his radiant personality, that not one of the fierce beasts quivering under his lash so much as raised a protest. No other man in the world could have brought that off!

Over seventy years after the occasion when, as a schoolgirl, I first met – and detested – Ford, in my Mother's drawing room in 1913, on reading the above I suddenly felt linked to him in a warm, personal way.

And yet, with all the aura surrounding him, when J.G. died not long after having evoked that tribute, in January 1933, his name was hardly mentioned for nearly 30 years, until the *Forsyte Saga* was presented on television.

In 1930 Sappho greatly enjoyed the Congress in Poland, because, as well as the Galsworthys and other close friends, she was accompanied by her two loves, Arthur Lynch and Toby, and Toby's presence ensured that both she and the Lynx would be looked after efficiently – quite apart from the Congress arrangements.

At these Congresses Sappho took a lively interest in all the proceedings. She attended all the business sessions, usually sitting next to the Chairman of the day and occasionally joining in the discussion. By this time she was known at her wish to many of the delegates as 'the Mother of the P.E.N.' and this gave her a rather special status in the organisation. She was delighted when Johan Bojer sent her his book, *The Last of the Vikings* and wrote in it, 'To Mrs Dawson Scott, the Mother of us all, from her son Johan Bojer.'

Ernst Toller also wrote to her in 1933, when he was unable to keep an appointment:

> You may be convinced I am really sorry not to spend Friday evening with my Pen Mother-in-law.

When she lent Theodor Däubler one of her books, he wrote on 16 July 1928:

> Dear Young Mother ... I would like to impress on you how pleased I am to have met our young P.E.N. Mother, we are all very proud of her – especially me. Not only our opinions, but also our intellectual interests coincide ...

The Congress in Holland in June, 1931, was the ninth, and it was 10 years since the Foundation Dinner. On 5 October that year the P.E.N. celebrated its Tenth Anniversary with a special dinner at which J.G. and Sappho spoke to 200 guests, including representatives from 24 of the 32 centres.

J.G.'s speech ended thus:

> We never drink toasts, so we must drink one to-night, and I would ask you all to stand and lift your glasses to the friendly fellowship of the P.E.N. coupled with the name of our gallant Foundress, Catharine Amy Dawson Scott.

There seems, as yet, to have been little, if any, understanding of the troubles that lay in the very near future, although by 1931 the shadows were beginning to lengthen for the P.E.N. as for the whole western world. An appeal to all Governments re the treatment of political and religious prisoners, agreed at the Dutch Congress in 1931, had been printed in the world's press and received massive publicity.

No one knew that J.G.'s lethal illness had already begun as early as 1930 and that he was not completely fit even in 1931. In April 1932 he presided at the P.E.N. Centenary Dinner in honour of Goethe, and also at the Congress in Hungary from 10 May to 20 May.

His nephew, Rudolf Sauter, noted in his book *Galsworthy the Man*:

One day in June (1932) he startled us all by suddenly remarking 'You had better look at me well, now, because it's the last time you'll ever see me quite well again.'

Yet he completed his novel *Over the River* in August on the eve of his 65th birthday.

The Congress in Budapest, where the iniquitous Admiral Horthy received the delegates in the royal palace, was a disillusioning affair; politics were interposed from all sides with disturbing persistence. The entertainment, which was lavish, had official backing, but delegates were well aware of the poverty and suppression that was all around them behind the festive front.

Edwin and Willa Muir were the Scottish delegates and in her autobiography, *Belonging* (Hogarth Press 1968), Willa Muir writes at some length about that Congress. She says of the Hungarian resentment at the Treaty of Trianon:

> They choked with wrath whenever Roumanians or Slovaks were mentioned. Much worse ... was the general malaise among the various delegations. The French were detested because it was said they took it for granted that they alone were capable of providing leaders in discussion and in settling details of procedure. The Austrian delegation included men whose work we liked, such as Felix Salten, but he was going about with a worried face ... Of the others, the most ubiquitous was a stocky, tweed-clad lesbian with a 'von' in her name [Grete von Urbanitzky], said to be an agent of Prince Starhemberg, who was constantly engaged in excited conference with some of the Germans. The atmosphere of Nazi intrigue and political conspiracy between Austrians and Germans was so thick that no one could miss it, and the smaller countries' delegations were resentful and apprehensive.
>
> Every day Hermon Ould joined us for lunch in a quiet square ... where we could escape from the Congress ill-will. Then Ernst Toller, whom we personally liked, begged to join us ... This was the last straw for both of us, since Toller daily brought some new story of oppression in Hungary itself.

Although J.G. and the Admiral exchanged fairly neutral speeches, a resolution was passed on the suppression of literature, and J.G., before declaring he Congress open, saw fit to make the following statement:

What the P.E.N. is

I hope you will forgive me when I say that the time has come to speak a few quite definite words about what our P.E.N. Association does and does not stand for.

The founding Centre, you will readily believe, knows exactly with what ideals the P.E.N. was founded, and to what ideals it must remain faithful, if it is to continue to exist.

1. The P.E.N. stands for Literature in the sense of Art (not of journalism, not of propaganda) and for the diffusion of Literature as Art from country to country.
2. The P.E.N. stands for hospitable friendliness between writers in their own countries, and with the writers of all other countries.
3. The P.E.N. stands for the principle that its members shall do and write nothing to promote war.
4. The P.E.N. stands for humane conduct.
5. Such words as nationalist, internationalist, democratic, aristocratic, imperialistic, anti-imperialistic, bourgeois revolutionary, or any other words with definite political significance should not be used in connection with the P.E.N.; for the P.E.N. has nothing whatever to do with State or Party Politics, and cannot be used to serve State or Party interests or conflicts.

Did he know that this was his last Congress? Did he feel that this had to be said whilst he yet had time? In view of his comment to his family during the next month, June, I am sure he did. He had begun to fear that he was not going to recover.

The Congress was as profoundly disturbed by the situation in which it found itself as were Edwin and Willa Muir. With difficulty the proceedings remained under control – just. The following year at Dubrovnik the explosion came, but by that time H.G. Wells was International President.

J.G. presided at the AGM in October and was again re-elected President for the following year, although he once more warned the members that it was time they considered a successor: he had been their President for eleven years. But his audience remembered that this was not the first time he had said this and they hoped that, when the next AGM came round, he would once more be persuaded to remain in office. They knew him, they loved him, and they did not want a change.

42

The Death of John Galsworthy

The last time the P.E.N. saw its President was on 1 November 1932, when he presided at a dinner for Henri Barbusse. Barbusse had been refused entry to England on political grounds, but, as a result of Hermon Ould's application to the Home Office, he was finally granted permission to come.

That month J.G. was awarded the Nobel Prize for Literature and wrote his speech of acceptance of the honour. But his health was deteriorating more rapidly by then, and he was unable to go to Norway for the ceremony, or to attend a meeting of the International Committee in Paris in about the middle of November. Sappho and Hermon Ould went alone.

As soon as J.G. knew he was to receive the Nobel Prize, he told Hermon Ould and Sappho that he intended to give the money to the P.E.N. As a result, she began to formulate ideas as to how best to use this money. She was well aware that the prestige of the P.E.N. was nothing like so high in England as it was in Europe, and her thinking culminated in a schedule of ideas which she sent to J.G. early in December to his home in Bury. She and Hermon Ould knew, I am sure, that his health was failing, although she said nothing to me, and the seriousness of his illness was still not generally known. But there is a letter from her to Hermon, undated, in the P.E.N. Archives at Austin, Texas, which I think must have been written about this time, or perhaps a little earlier. She wrote:

> Hermon, we've got to realise this. Galsworthy's mind is getting more timid and shrinking, and he'll shrink away from us. It's no good leaving things to chance. Let's make an effort to improve our Committee ...

On 10 December, in answer to the list of ideas she had sent him earlier that month, in which she suggested a meeting, J.G. wrote to her for the last time:

Bury House. I am very doubtful whether I will be in or near London this side of Christmas, or indeed before March. If I can't, it might possibly suit you and Hermon to come down to talk things over, but that cannot be at present. The suggestions you make are worthy of thought. Always yours, John Galsworthy.

On 14 December he came to London to see specialists, and from then on there was no longer any hope of recovery from what in the end was diagnosed as a cerebral tumour.

Meanwhile, in the Press, only 'para-typhoid' was mentioned, and I thought, 'Well, that's not so serious, is it, as real typhoid?' And I waited for more encouraging news.

Grove Lodge, Hampstead, was only a few minutes from where we lived in Holly Place, and just before Christmas I walked round with my two children to leave a Christmas card and ask Minnie, the house-parlourmaid and wife of Arthur, J.G.'s chauffeur, how he was. I was surprised and alarmed when the tears came into her eyes as she said, 'Not very well.' 'But,' I said anxiously, 'he *is* going to get better, isn't he?' And Minnie replied, the tears now running down her cheeks, 'Oh, we hope so, Mrs Watts – indeed, we do hope so.' And I went home weeping too.

Arthur and I were ski-ing in Austria when, on 31 January, we heard that J.G. had died. It was a great sadness for me, a major loss, although, by that time, I was immersed in my own domestic life and only saw J.G. now and then. Yet I felt personally bereft and wondered how my mother and the P.E.N. and above all his wife could manage without him. I did not realise how quickly those who are left adjust to the new situation and find other, different, but often equally competent people to take the place of those who have gone.

Some months later I passed Ada Galsworthy in Heath Street, Hampstead. She was in deep black, and I couldn't stop myself crying out 'Oh, Mrs Galsworthy – I'm so sorry – so sorry ...' But she put her hand up to her face, saying, 'Don't, don't ...' and hurried past me.

I did not then know how unbearable it is to be spoken to by *anyone* about one's personal and intolerable grief.

At Mrs Galsworthy's request, the scheduled dinner took place on February 4th with Rebecca West in the Chair and David Low, the cartoonist, as guest. Henry Nevinson, then aged 77, who was regarded affectionately as the doyen of the P.E.N., spoke for the members:

He was a source of strength and inspiration that never failed ... he could be counted on not merely to make appropriate and generous gestures, but to undertake the drudgery of drafting resolutions, compiling lists, signing numerous letters or any other routine tasks that came within his conception of a President's duties. He would speak to us in that quiet voice – and here I should like to recall his sympathy, in spite of his hatred of violence, with the suffragettes, at a time when they were hounded and spat upon, not only by the unreasoning mob, but also by cultivated and respectable people like ourselves ... He had extraordinary foresight, and he foresaw the great revolution which was coming upon that upper middle-class to which he belonged, the revolution impinging upon their wealth and their apparent but false stability. That revolution is around us now ...

Sappho spoke also:

For eleven years he has worked with the secretary and myself, and I have learned from that association what are the gifts necessary for a president. He should have enthusiasm for the ideals of the association; he should have ideas for its development, initiative, wisdom, tolerance. He should be willing to undertake work which he dislikes, in fact he should be the servant of his ideals.

Nobody but Mr Ould and myself know how willing Mr Galsworthy was to give all the help in his power, how astute he was in the interests of the P.E.N., how everlastingly kind. I remember a thousand little things, and I cry unhappily 'We shall never see his like again.'

A man belongs to his generation. Mr Galsworthy belongs to mine. Therefore his personal loss will appear to the older members of the P.E.N. greater than it can be to the young people who will take his place in this worldwide federation of writers. But our first President will be an example, a shining light, to all who follow.

43

H.G. Wells as President

Meanwhile, the seeds Sappho had sown in 1928, when Hardy had died and she had 'arranged' that H.G. Wells should take his place as Hon. Member for England, bore fruit. Wells was the obvious choice to succeed J.G., and he accepted and came to the April Dinner, when E.V. Knox (Evoe), Editor of *Punch* since 1932, was the guest.

Wells was at his best. He referred warmly to J.G., was witty and friendly and promised to serve the club to the best of his ability. He then said:

> The tradition of the internationalism of the P.E.N. Club is enormous and vital, and so far as we can I hope we shall keep it alive. We are going to have great trouble in the near future. We are the Mother Society, and the P.E.N. Club, wherever it is, must be the club of free rights ... I think I have the sense of the society when I say that it is only free pens throughout the world that can maintain at any sacrifice the traditions of the great republic of literature which is so much greater than any political organisation.

But the pattern had changed. Up till now, no decision was taken by the secretary, in between Committee meetings, without consultation with J.G. or Sappho or both, either by letter or phone. Wells was not so available and, in any case, he had no intimate knowledge of the difficulties which continually arose in the day-to-day administration of such a large organisation. Inevitably Sappho and Hermon worked more closely together, and Ellis Roberts was elected the working chairman of the Committee. Nevertheless H.G. Wells took his new position seriously and spent considerable time in preparation for his first – and very difficult – appearance at the Eleventh Congress, to be held in Jugoslavia on 25 May 1933 where he would without doubt be elected International President to replace Galsworthy.

Wells was a very different President – less legalistic and tactful, more vigorous and aggressive. The following are a few extracts from his opening speech:

We of the P.E.N. ... are trying to evoke ... a mental community throughout the world ... almost all the present political boundaries are becoming misfits; we can only adapt ourselves to these new conditions by a complete revolution in our political and economic ideas ... we have to march ... the real issue is 'where are we going? Are we to march to world union and world peace, or are we to be marched back to perpetual separation and endless war?'

For the first time – although it had nearly happened the year before in Hungary – the Congress was so deeply divided that it was clearly going to be impossible to reach a compromise. A few of the delegates were determined Nazi sympathisers, whilst the great majority were equally anti-Hitler. Wells had the unenviable task of keeping politics out of the discussions, of pacifying the more excitable delegates who were burning to attack the Hitler regime, and of ensuring that the German delegates had a fair hearing.

Dr Henry Seidal Canby (U.S.A.) put forward a resolution whose preamble was as follows:

Whereas there are again abroad in the world aspects of Chauvinism, which debase the spirit of man, causing him to persecute his fellow-men, robbing him of generosity, of nobility and understanding; and whereas it is the duty of the artist to guard the spirit in its freedom, so that mankind shall not be prey to ignorance, to malice and to fear, we, the members of the American Centre of the P.E.N. call upon all other centres to affirm once more those principles upon which the structure of this society was raised.

He then drew attention to the Resolution passed at Brussels in 1927 (see p. 146) and concluded:

We likewise call upon the International Congress to take *definite steps to prevent the individual centres of the P.E.N.* founded for the purpose of fostering goodwill and understanding between the races and nations, from being used as weapons of propaganda in the defence of persecution inflicted in the name of Chauvinism, racial prejudice and political ill-will.

The passing of this resolution would enable the Congress to ask the Germans to give an account of their position, but a group of delegates led by Jules Romains got together and produced a more general resolution, although it did refer to the destruction of books. The German delegates then informed the Chairman (H.G.) that they would support this notion *on condition that there was no discussion*.

Wells refused to bargain – if delegates wished to discuss the subject they were at liberty to do so. Jules Romains paid a tribute to the 'courtesy and amenable conduct of his German Colleagues' – he felt it 'would be disastrous if, after so much good feeling had been demonstrated, it should prove impossible to come to a unanimous agreement.' Jules Romains was never universally popular in the P.E.N. after that, and blotted his copy-book on several later occasions, especially during the 1939 war. (See Storm Jameson's *Journey from the North.*)

The Chairman remained adamant. He declared that the P.E.N. existed largely to advocate freedom of expression and that, if those who had come from all over the world with the intention of discussing the extremely critical situation in Germany were prevented from doing so, the P.E.N. would be stultifying itself.

One of the English delegates then put the following questions:

1. Had the German Centre protested against the ill-treatment of German intellectuals and the burning of books?
2. Was it true that the Berlin Centre had issued a notice to its members depriving those of Communist or 'similar' views of membership, thereby violating the first rule of the P.E.N. that it should stand aside from politics?

Ernst Toller wished to speak, and the German delegate, Fritz Otto Busch protested; when Wells supported Toller's right to do so, the German delegates walked out. Uproar followed and impassioned speeches were made, and some of the Austrian, Swiss and Dutch delegates temporarily withdrew, but most of these later returned. Toller's remarks were strongly supported by some of the Austrians, notably Franz Theodor Czokar, later to become President of their centre from 1947 to 1968.

As the *Manchester Guardian* reported:

It is ironical that a meeting of writers pledged to stand aside from politics should have been the occasion of one of the stormiest of political demonstrations ... It is the prevailing opinion that this year the P.E.N. has entered upon a new phase. The gracious, astute, steadying presidency of John Galsworthy has given place to the highly stimulating presidency of Mr H.G. Wells.

Sappho was thankful to have someone of Wells' literary stature and tough calibre at the helm – a writer who could command the respect – if not perhaps the love that had been extended to his predecessor – of all his fellow writers – a determined personality, prepared to do battle for his principles.

She must have been quietly amused if she remembered *in what way* Wells had become President!

Arthur Lynch being a delegate, she was personally content, and my brother Christopher, now on good terms with her, was there too. Together with Hermon Ould, they went on the various expeditions and had meals together in a group. She often sat beside Wells when he presided, and was very much at the centre of the Congress, but she knew that he could be relied upon to keep control over all those warring and quarrelling delegates, whom she regarded in some sense as her 'children'. And she was able to enjoy the less urgent and searing moments in her contacts with her kindly hosts. She wrote:

> Hermon Ould asked what of all I had seen and done in that 'rocky land of strangers' which, altho' it consists of several countries, can be spoken of as Jugo-Slavia, had most impressed me … and I tried to think. At once a number of pictures arose. I saw Curčin, Mestrovič, Andrassy, Vidacovič, Hassanovič, Joey, Vlado – most of them complete with wife and children; I saw parties with kindly burgomasters, drives through tremendous gorges and along a smiling sea-coast; I lived through exciting moments when Mr Wells said, 'Your President is obstinate and he will have things done in an orderly fashion', but in the end the memory that lies most warmly in my heart is that of three women, who at different times were my hostesses.
>
> In three different houses to which I was taken for a meal, my hostess said: 'You look tired. If you like, you shall have my room to rest in for an hour.' And how I slept! How much better I felt when I awoke in those strange rooms. How grateful I still am for the kind thought that made further effort possible and even pleasurable. Mrs Katič, Mrs Wenderlovič, Mrs Burda – I think of them as a symbol of the country and of the hospitality we received, of the careful thought that arranged every detail, and also, that spontaneous realisation of the needs of a guest, which is the last and most human touch.[1]

---

[1] It has not proved possible to identify all Sappho's Jugoslavian hosts.

44

Summer 1933 and the Expulsion of Germany

In July Sappho escaped as usual to Cornwall to relax and gain strength for another strenuous winter.

She chose to live in a tent partly because she enjoyed doing so – her domestic arrangements were simplified and she could devote her whole time to whatever she was involved in at the moment, but also because it was so inexpensive – she had no overheads!

As before, her bell tent was pitched on a grass patch near her old Cornish friends, Jim and Alice Tippett, and at meal-times they brought her some of whatever they were eating on a tray. There was a lane or track going past her tent, with no hedge between and a field beyond that. She wrote of one of these respites:

> Have enjoyed being here very much and am much stronger in consequence. At night I had my tent flap open and heard the sea. Sometimes I strolled out through the dewy grass. The peace of night and sleep ...
>
> Tent life is not complicated by the innumerable bits of life that share one's shelter, altho' the sow-pigs [woodlice] are rather destructive; a hat of mine went the way of all hats owing to their strange hunger, and earwigs nestle to me rather more than I wish. A grasshopper bounded on to my tray and off again on his affairs, and spiders, abnormally legged, hurried from the shocking sight of my undress.

Sappho did not live an isolated life in her tent. Old and new friends and tenants staying in her bungalows learned she was there and came to call. They usually found her sitting cross-legged on a camp bed, inside or outside the tent, according to the weather, typing. She was something of a landmark in the neighbourhood, respected and loved by the older local people with whose lives she had been involved for twenty-five years, and even now remembered by some who were then young. One present-day grandmother has told me of the shock she got when, aged about 7, she and a little friend (boy), were playing hide and seek around the tent one evening and suddenly came upon

Sappho standing at her tent-opening 'starkers', enjoying the evening air and her 'privacy'. They all remember her for the same reason ...

> Mrs Scott? Of course I remember her – didn't wear shoes and wore those long dresses ... always wanted to know how we talked ... [in the Cornish dialect].

That summer of 1933 Sappho was depressed for longer periods than was usual for one of her normally cheerful temperament. Arthur Lynch's health began to cause anxiety after Dubrovnik, and by the September he was seriously ill in hospital. She was also more and more aware that her writing, her books, were mostly unrecognised, although her novel *The House in the Hollow* was published that year.

She must still have derived considerable satisfaction from the P.E.N. of which she was the centre and in which she held a unique position. Ernest Raymond, in vol. 2 of his autobiography (p.41), gives a good description of how she appeared to many of the members:

> All who remember Catharine Amy Dawson Scott's resistless but amiable onrush through a room (or through life) know that she gave her whole life and strength to causes that seemed right to her; but only those who sometimes sat and talked with her in quiet know how big her heart was, and how much of her driving force drew from quick maternal impatience ... She belonged to a fine type whose inconsistencies seem necessary for the advancement of mankind. Essentially autocratic, she loved freedom and democracy, and worked for them autocratically; loving toleration, she would fight for it with an impatience that touched intolerance; and, knowing that peace was the only habit for sane people, she enjoyed the battle for it. She instanced splendidly the truth that, despite all its sorrows, life and liveliness are one. A fine, strenuous life, and one of which her children, whether born of her body or her spirit, whether in her home or in the International P.E.N. can be proud.

Did she miss that long partnership with J.G.? That communication with him over something that was so dear to them both? Glad as she was that Wells was President, the situation was not the same; she had more responsibility for the everyday details of the organisation, and she could no longer write long letters to J.G. all over the world and be certain of receiving a calm, measured reply, coupled with advice that she was willing to take. Although he took the P.E.N. seriously and was deeply involved in any really important problem, it was a point of honour with Sappho and Hermon not to bother Wells with minor matters.

On the credit side, she and I still got on very well and were real friends. We avoided the subjects on which we did not agree, such as the way I brought up my children and Spiritualism; and I enjoyed the times when I deserted my family and spent a companionable evening with Sappho. Once that summer I said something thoughtless about it being sad to be old and not able to enjoy life – I was not, in fact, thinking of her, who did not seem old – and she suddenly turned on me:

> The young do not understand – they think that just because one's body becomes feeble, one is incapable any longer of enjoying the lovely things of life – the sea and the rock pools – the colour – the night sky ...

Mostly we visited Sappho in her tent, but twice, when we organised a village fête and regatta in aid of the St Issey Silver Prize Band, we persuaded her to leave *her* tent and come over and tell fortunes in a tent at *our* fête. She could easily become a very realistic-looking gipsy, with a gay head scarf added to her usual long dress, bare feet and rather flamboyant jewellery. She was a huge success, foretelling the future from the lines on people's hands and from tea-leaves in a cup. All the other attractions cost 6d, but Sappho charged, at our suggestion, 2s 6d, and there was a long queue. Surprisingly, some of the young people whose fortunes she told have since assured me that many of her prognoses came true.

Worried and sad about the Lynx, and apprehensive about the impending International Committee meeting which would discuss the German P.E.N. Centre, Sappho returned to London in mid-September 1933 to help Hermon prepare for the Annual General Meeting on 3 October, at which H.G. Wells presided.

The dinner for the members of the International Committee was on 7 November 1933, with Wells presiding, and the Committee was to meet the following day. The members that year were:

H.G. Wells, Chairman (England)   Will Irwin (U.S.A.)
Mrs Dawson Scott (Founder)   Edwin Muir (Scotland)
Benjamin Crémieux (France)   Edgar von Schmidt-Pauli (Germany)
Vaclav Hyka (Czechoslovakia)   Josip Torbarina (Jugoslavia)
Hermon Ould (Gen. Secretary)

No one seemed anxious to offer hospitality to the German representative, Dr Schmidt-Pauli, so Arthur and I decided to do so. We lived in a small Georgian house at No. 1, Holly Place, Hampstead – very inconvenient, but delightful all the same, and to make room for our visitor in Arthur's dressing-room, which we used as a guest room occasionally, I cleared his shirts etc. from two drawers and made a little hanging space in his cupboard. Dr Schmidt-Pauli arrived in a taxi, and from our first floor sitting room window we watched with fascinated horror as suitcase after suitcase was unloaded and carried up the narrow path to the front door and into our minute passage-hall which we had some difficulty in getting even a pram through. As we went down to the front door to greet our guest my anxious eyes met Arthur's and I said hastily, 'Just leave everything here for the moment – Arthur, will you take Dr Schmidt-Pauli upstairs and give him a drink? I'll be down in a minute.' I then flew further upstairs and took all Arthur's hanging garments – he hadn't many suits anyhow – out of the cupboard and piled them, with the contents of the rest of his chest of drawers, on to our bed in the next room – and carefully shut the door. I would deal with that confused mass of wearing apparel later!

Dr Schmidt-Pauli was a tall, good-looking, intelligent and cultured man who spoke perfect English, having been to Cambridge. I think he wore a monocle, but I'm not sure – perhaps it was gold pince-nez! In any case a monocle would have looked right on him. His visit to London to attend the P.E.N. International Committee on behalf of the German P.E.N. was evidently important in his eyes, or maybe in the eyes of those who sent him. He brought clothes for every conceivable occasion – a dinner jacket and tails, dark suit, tweed suit, and even morning coat. He also brought the overcoats to match – how could he possibly wear a *tweed* overcoat with a morning coat? There was also a hat box with the appropriate hats. I think on one day, he visited friends in the country, where he could wear his magnificent tweed suit.

The next day was the dinner for members of the International Committee. Also present were Robert Neumann, a great P.E.N. figure in those days, and Ernst Toller, so known and loved here. As I was dressing for the dinner, Dr Schmidt-Pauli knocked on my door and asked my advice. Should he wear his Iron Cross? I said I thought *not*, on the whole.

He was considerably put out that no arrangements had been made for him to speak at the dinner, while Crémieux, the French Secretary, spoke eloquently for fifteen minutes on the Ideals of the P.E.N. It was a function charged with emotion and tension, and I remember feeling embarrassed and uneasy in expectation of some kind of explosion. However, the evening passed without incident.

Sappho, later, gave me an account of what happened at the International Committee, which took place on the following day.

Dr Schmidt-Pauli made a statement and answered questions ... He was asked whether the German Centre had in fact sent out a communication to its members, in Clause 3 of which it was stated that those who supported Communist or similar views must regard themselves as relieved of their rights and duties as members of the German Centre. He agreed that this was so, and that the German P.E.N. held to this decision. When asked to define the words 'similar views', he stated that several shades of liberal opinion would come within the meaning of that term ... It was pointed out to him that the P.E.N. was an organisation pledged to stand aside from politics, and had no right of interference in the political opinions of its members. Also discussed was an obscene pamphlet about Jews, which had been sponsored and circulated by the German Centre.

The following resolution was thereupon proposed by the Founder, seconded by Will Irwin[1] (U.S.A.) and carried with one dissentient, namely Dr Schmidt-Pauli:

> That in the opinion of this Committee, Clause 3 of the communication to members of the German Centre dated March 16th, 1933, is incompatible with the general constitution of the P.E.N.

Dr Schmidt-Pauli made the following statement:

> After the statement of the International Committee, I do not see for the moment any possibility of successful cooperation between the German group and the International P.E.N. If the President and Committee of the German Centre agree, I must say now that the German Group can no longer work with the International Federation. We German writers will continue as before to work for the peace of the world, but in what we consider the right and successful way.

And from that date the German P.E.N. Centre ceased to exist until after the 1939 war.

Dr Schmidt-Pauli was a charming guest, and Arthur and I avoided P.E.N. politics.

The year ended with the December dinner, at which Sappho presided, with W.B. Yeats and Lion Feuchtwanger as guests. After mentioning the thriving Indian Centre and the formation of a Cairo Centre, she referred to a centre which the P.E.N. had valued highly – Germany. 'To me,' she said,

> the P.E.N. is a nursery, in which the children of many different mothers meet in order to learn to work and play together in friendliness and, above all, with *understanding*. When a child grows overbearing, shows

---

[1] This must have been quite an occasion for Will Irwin, who was in Belgium the day the war started, representing the American Journal *Colliers*. He was still there three weeks later to describe the carnage which followed the German advance. See *The Guns of August*, by Barbara Tuchman.

temper and conceit, it is put outside the P.E.N. door ... As you all
know, this child who has been put outside the P.E.N. door is Germany.
We are all deeply attached to this P.E.N. child and hope ... we may
soon welcome it back.

45

Sappho's Last Year

At the November International Committee it had been suggested that a Centre composed of those writers who had left Germany for various reasons might be formed, and in March 1934 the Group had its first meeting, the members being:

George Bernhard	Heinrich Mann
Bernard von Brentano	Klaus Mann
Lion Feuchtwanger	Balder Olden
Bruno Frank	Ernst Toller
Max Herrmann-Neisse	Arnold Zweig
Emil Ludwig	

President: Heinrich Mann   Secretary: Rudolf Olden

Arthur Lynch died that spring, and Sappho wrote:

His life has been a romance of many-coloured adventure. He had a mind of great vitality and versatility and a truly remarkable memory ... Arthur Lynch died after long suffering ... at St Mary's Hospital, where he had studied medicine. But I cannot believe that his soul is 'with the saints'. I feel that death to him is a fresh and delightful adventure in which, accompanied by old friends and new, he has gladly embarked.

Sappho believed implicitly in a Life after Death, and she 'knew' that she would be with Arthur Lynch again and was comforted. I once asked what she would do about Scottie, but I got no satisfactory answer!

The Congress in 1934 was in Scotland in June. Incredibly, as it seems now, Arthur and I employed both a children's Nannie and a cook-general – and a daily woman! So I decided to go to Scotland before our annual migration to St Issey in Cornwall. Sappho and the Dennis Bradleys, Hermon Ould and I went to Edinburgh by the night train, and I noted at the time in my *own* journal:

We enjoyed it all very much, altho' Mother seemed feeble, and the
P.E.N. people, accustomed to her positive manner and apparent
strength, did not realise that she had aged and needed caring for. So
she did too much and got very exhausted.

So often at Congresses there are innumerable stand-up buffets and
sandwich meals, but never a simple sit-down hot lunch or dinner; and
strangers in a big town do not know where to go for an inexpensive
meal. Sappho did not know Edinburgh well, was, as always,
extremely hard up, and had not the strength to go searching for little
restaurants. I was not staying anywhere near and, being released from
domesticity for a few days, was enjoying myself on my own. Luckily
Dennis Bradley and his wife *were* in the same hotel, realised her
predicament, and gave her some good meals and looked after her.

The Congress was again deeply involved with the ever-increasing
persecution of liberal/left-wing, or Jewish writers in Europe. The first
meeting was opened by Professor Grierson, followed by H.G. Wells,
who emphatically drew attention to the original idea of the P.E.N:

> To correspond, meet, entertain each other ... an admirable and genial
> idea which has worked great things in creating *international personal
> friendship*

and he spoke of writers he had met in Dubrovnik, including Signor
Marinetti and Ernst Toller. He regretted that Schmidt-Pauli

> good fellow and obstinate fighter, had had to be sacrificed on the altar
> of his instructions from Berlin ... There is no doubt about the
> friendship side of these gatherings. But is that all? I wish it could be.
> But suppose we find ... that a door has been barred to some guest we
> should have rejoiced to entertain? ... Can we hold our banquet and
> disregard ... the maltreated bodies lying on the threshhold? I submit
> we cannot ignore these things. When Politics assaults Literature and
> the liberty of human thought and expression, we have to take notice of
> Politics. If not, what will the P.E.N. Club become? A tourist agency –
> an organisation for introducing respectable writers to useful scenery ...

Mr Wells then referred to the new problems facing the P.E.N.
which troubled him considerably – the Vienna Centre, the Italian
Centre, the non-existent Russian P.E.N. and the relationship between
the English P.E.N. and the Foreign Office. (This was a reference to
the refusal of the Lord Chamberlain to license a play bearing on the
German situation, at the request, it was said, of the F.O.)

The problems Mr Wells raised, were fully discussed, and Signor
Marinetti, named by Wells as 'that great writer', was questioned as to

whether the Italian P.E.N. was a 'comprehensive' or an 'exclusive' club.

There could be no happy ending to a gathering faced with such problems, and H.G.'s last words were:

> The defence of liberty of expression and that defence alone, defines a task big enough for all of your efforts as a society. On that basis we may hope to be united and effective throughout the world. That is what I have come to this Conference to say. Have I your agreement?

During the Congress the President had mentioned the problem of Russia. He hoped to go to Moscow the following month and said:

> There has been a considerable change in the spirit and tone of Soviet Russia recently; Russia is looking West again, so that such a liaison is much more possible than it was a year or so ago. But here again, I think we must stick to the fundamental principles of the P.E.N. If there is to be a Russian P.E.N. it must be freely and fully open ... to Russian writers of every colour, white, black, pink, as well as red. It must be independent in its organisation and it must have something more than a formal relationship to Russians in exile ...

In the end Mr Wells was unable to go to Moscow in the August, but he sent a message from the P.E.N. which he reported to the A.G.M. on 2 October. Later that year there was also a letter from Signor Marinetti:

> Illustre Amico, Vi prego di scusare il ritardo involuntario di questa mia risposta. Dato che oggi non esiste nel mondo scrittore italiano che manifesti una azione contro L'Italia Fascista, il Pen Club Italiano, che io ho l'onore di rappresentare come Presidente, è lieto di dichiarasi aperto a tutti gli scrittori italiani senza distinzione.

> (Tr. Dear Friend, Please excuse my unintentional delay in replying. Since there is no Italian writer in the world today who has taken any action against Fascist Italy, the Italian P.E.N. Club, which I have the honour to represent as President, is happy to declare itself open to *all* Italian writers.)

This was greatly welcomed, but unfortunately the following note was printed in P.E.N. News in November (1934):

> In Italy an article which has become notorious, written by Signor Marinetti, seems to indicate that the application of P.E.N. principles by prominent members of the Italian Centre has temporarily ceased.

In July 1934, following the Scottish Congress, Sappho went down to
her tent in Cornwall for the last time. As well as our house on a tidal
creek at St Issey, I still owned the small bungalow at Constantine Bay
that I had built in 1923, which was usually let to summer visitors, and
sometimes, in between lets, I would go over to the coast for a few days
for the children to enjoy the sand and rocks. Arthur returned to
London earlier that year, so in September I went to Constantine with
my 5-year-old son Simon, so that we could see something of my
mother. She was 69 on 31 August and, before Arthur left, we
celebrated her birthday by driving to Lands End and around for a
couple of days. Sappho loved being driven, and rarely had the chance.

We went to Penzance and then to Penberth Cove.

A charming spot, entire village owned by rich people, therefore quite
unspoiled! Stayed with the village carpenter and his wife, and we
walked on to the cliffs to see the Rocking Stone. A magnificent storm
came up over the sea – wonderful colour and cloud effects. Mother
enjoyed it, in spite of Arthur being rather morose. ('Mothers' have a
bad effect on him – he's just the same with his own mother ...)

Nevertheless, the trip was quite a happy occasion.

Even in the summer the North Cornish coast is sometimes lashed
by gales, and one night Sappho's tent collapsed on her, and Jim
Tippett was wakened by a plaintive cry in the night: 'Jim! Oh, Jim!
come and help me ...' as she struggled to extricate herself from ropes,
canvas and general debris. He came to the rescue, and when Simon
and I walked up the road to visit Sappho the next morning, she was
quite cheerful and gave us a humorous account of the night's
adventure.

Once a day she would walk down to the sea – potter along the
ridges of seaweed and shells left by the tide, sometimes with me and
Simon, who at that time was a quiet and accommodating little boy.
But she was often, and happily, alone, although 'happily' is the wrong
word, because she was deeply sad over the death of The Lynx. She
could not talk about this to me, because I could not bring myself to
subscribe to her belief tht she would find him again on the 'Other
Side'.

On really warm days she would find a secluded cove and, in an
old-fashioned black-skirted bathing dress, would sit in one of the
deeper rock pools for a while, or paddle through the shallower ones,
collecting bits of sea coal, which would later burn green on my fire,
pink and green seaweeds, cowries and bits of coloured glass worn
smooth by the action of the sea. Up till now Sappho had always
seemed able to regain her strength and vitality after living this simple,

uncomplicated life in the fresh air for a month or so.

It seemed to me that she had become more eccentric during the last couple of years; was more easily annoyed and more unreasonable, and was more than ever determined to have her own way – in fact, her obstinacy was almost pathological. The only person who could stand up to her and cajole her into doing anything she had made up her mind against was my brother Toby. For the rest, her face took on a stubborn, set look – just as she must have looked when, as a little girl, she defied and argued with 'grown-ups'. Perhaps this was more obvious within her family than among her friends.

Roland and Olga Woosnam Mills were two of these and Roland, at the time an aspiring young writer, kept a detailed diary of the summer he spent at Constantine Bay in 1934, which included an account of how he first came across Sappho.

From Roland's diary:

Wed. 29th August [1934] To-day has been a good day ... To begin with I have met Mrs Dawson Scott. She lives in a tent, writes books on a typewriter on a camp bed and tells your fortune, at least she told mine, altho' I had really come to ask whether one of her cottages was to let. I stood in the 'flapway', explaining that I wrote books which were not published, that my name was Woosnam Mills, that both parts [of the name] were Welsh ...

In return she told me that Rebecca West, Ida Wylie, Sheila Kaye-Smith and Noël Coward had lived in her bungalows; that Rebecca West had told her to write the story of the first 18 years of her life (which she was currently doing), that she is Founder of the P.E.N., that she can tell fortunes – and that she always goes into the water [sea] on Christmas Day.[1]

Finally I sat on her bed on a horse-hair blanket while she told my fortune by my palms. My future told, I retreated from the tent.

To the young Roland of fifty years ago Sappho was a unique experience, the kind of odd character that intrigues a budding author – Roland later published ten books. He took Olga to have her fortune told, and several times during September they came across Sappho pottering across the Bay or wandering down the lane to the sea. He developed an affection for her, nicknaming her 'My Genial Toad', and wrote:

Sept. 18th: On a hummock by the roadside we came on a queer dumpy figure reading a sixpenny thriller – Mrs D.S.!

She invited me to her tent that evening to meet Christopher (her son), and after supper I wandered across the fields to see her. There

[1] Not true.

were 4 of us, the genial, chubby and affectionate authoress and Chris and his future wife. They sat on boxes, I sat on 2 biscuit tins covered with a pillow, and Mrs D.S. presided, her plump hand shaking sweets from a tin and cigarettes from a packet for our consumption.

That last summer in Cornwall Sappho would not eat ordinary nourishing food, subsisting mainly on bread and butter, tea and salads made with a lot of nasturtium leaves, wild spinach and nuts. And yet, when she occasionally came to me for lunch, she obviously enjoyed a good cooked meal. I tried to persuade her to eat more substantial and varied food, or have lunch with me every day, but she refused, assuring me rather crossly that she knew better than I could what suited her. Having accepted all my life that when my mother made up her mind, no one could make her change it, I did not insist.

Two of Sappho's last letters to Hermon have survived, obviously written in August or September, 1934:

The Tent, Constantine. Dear Hermon, I do hope the rain will cease and let me get some more sun before the end of the summer. The novel goes on. I'm about 85,000 so may be considered to be on the last lap.

13.9.34. My dear Hermon ... I've now given up all my psychic work and hope for a very quiet winter. 'The Child' will be about 90,000. I'm such a slow writer.

The larks sang me to sleep last night at past nine! They woke me this morning at six. Busy birds.

Don't you think it would be a good thing to invite Korda to a P.E.N. dinner this autumn? and Rebecca to take the chair, as she knows him well ... Love to you and David, Sappho.

Hermon followed her suggestion, and Alexander Korda came to the P.E.N. dinner on 4 December.

Sappho's last letter to Hermon from her Tent, undated, concerned the forthcoming A.G.M.:

I wonder if you have got Storm Jameson and 2 people to propose and second her (for the Executive) and the same for Maugham? How about Nevinson, Baroness Budberg or Marie Belloc Lowndes for Storm? She *really has* done things that are international ... I wonder if H.G. brought Russia back in his pocket?

Will you ring me up on Friday morning, 28th (Sept.) and I shall know then if I can come to the dinner ...

Anyway, keep
Monday free
To eat with me
And fix where each sinner
Shall sit at the dinner.
       S.S. (Sappho Scott) Tent.

Sappho went to the AGM on 2 October, and Margaret Storm Jameson and Somerset Maugham were duly elected to the Committee.

Wells spoke of Russia. Although he had not been able to go, he had sent a personal message to the Soviet Writers' Congress, a carefully worded appeal to all Russian writers to join the P.E.N. There had, however, been no response.

A couple of days after the dinner, whilst I was still in Cornwall, I received a telegram: 'Am ill. Duodenal ulcer. Please come. Mother.'

I ran up the road to ask a doctor friend if this was serious, and he looked doubtful.

So Simon and I returned to London the same day by train, to find Sappho in hospital gravely ill.

46

Illness and Death

She was at first in a public ward where the sister in charge was strict –
a dragon – and Sappho had to do what she was told, i.e. lie still, have
no visitors (except her children for short visits) and only regular small
sips of milk and water. At that time, in any case, she was too ill to
protest and had no wish to live. When she had 'passed on', she 'knew'
she would be with the Lynx. But, as she began to regain strength,
Toby persuaded her that she was still needed – that he, emphatically
– wanted her to live. When next I went to see her, she announced
cheerfully:

> Marjorie, I'm going to get better. Toby wants me to, so I've decided,
> after all, to live for another ten years.

She began at once to make plans: she had always wanted to go to
the Scilly Isles, which she believed to be like Cornwall, only more so.
Now she would go – it would be warm and sunny there.

She also wanted to be moved into a private room, and we,
mistakenly, agreed. We did not realise that her condition remained
very precarious, that it was still touch and go. She was moved on 18
October and on the 20th she wrote to her sister at Bournemouth a
letter which gives a vivid if painful account of her illness:

> They've moved me round here and it's nice and they are letting me eat
> more. McIntosh [her doctor friend] came yesterday, my first visitor,
> and he seems to think it's a clear case of duodenal and that after the
> X-Ray they'll operate. He says it's not a bad operation and is the best
> treatment, as it obviates all chances of recurrence.
> So he is confabbing with Toby.
> I think it might amuse you to hear of some of the contretemps. In the
> midst of everything Ernest Davies [an old friend] rang up and couldn't
> understand why he couldn't speak to me. As Kate, [her maid] said, 'It
> sounded so queer that Mrs Scott couldn't come to the phone because
> she was having a haemorrhage!' So he *arrived* – to see what had
> happened. Well – he saw.

Then, a bit later, when Toby was expecting the ambulance, Rebecca rang up to fix the day I was to go and see *her* at the hospital – she'd been operated on for stone in the kidney the Sunday before. Poor Toby said, 'If you go on arranging I shall burst into tears. I'm sitting here expecting the arrival of the ambulance to take my mother to hospital.'

The night before I'd been talking to Perceval Yetts about *his* illness. He'd had a haemorrhage into the spinal cord. But my haemorrhage – well, as Kate said, 'I know it couldn't be, but it seemed to be at least 5 pints.' So now I'm asking Yetts how he managed to get all this into his spinal cord. So neat and tidy of him! So different from me!

Hospital ways are funny, too. At my last ward we were washed at 5 a.m. and had breakfast at 6. I found I didn't mind. I was too ill to care what they did to me or when they did it and night and day were much the same ... very long and wearisome ... the only pleasant breaks being my tiny 2 hour feeds – 3oz milk/1 water.

The drugs used were so strong that I was not allowed to use Eau de Cologne, or scented soap, or have a scented flower near me, as it affected the drugs.

It's good of you to send me the mags – I'm allowed to read now. One of the children comes to see me every day and I'm glad. They've been extremely good to me.

I was very bothered, after the first 7 days, by *hunger*, and I used to watch the other patients eating, as that was next best to having things myself. Then I used to think over all the men who might be induced to take me out to dinner – and anyway I made them all send me grapes. Yours, Amy.

Unhappily, in the private ward, the sister in charge was not as formidable as the first one. Sappho, who had immense persuasive powers, got her own way too much – she had a lot of visitors, she wrote letters, she was not obliged to keep very quiet and, although she was in bed, her mental life went on as before, as Hermon Ould made clear in the tribute he wrote about her in P.E.N. News that month.

Early in November she had a relapse and a blood transfusion, and she died on 4 November, two days before the Dinner for the International Executive Committee.

As when John Galsworthy had died nearly two years previously, the dinner arranged for 6 November took place with Wells in the Chair.

Luckily for the P.E.N. it had in Hermon Ould a devoted and experienced Secretary, able to hold the P.E.N. together through the increasingly anxious years up to 1939 and then through the war itself. In addition he was supported loyally by the P.E.N. Presidents. Wells remained for another two years, followed by J.B. Priestley, Henry Nevinson and then Margaret Storm Jameson from 1938-44 – throughout the war years.

Sappho's most important Idea had been left in good hands.

This book now comes to a natural end with some quotations from what her contemporaries in the writing world wrote about her, beginning with Hermon Ould:

P.E.N. News, November, 1934:

On the 18th of October she was pronounced out of danger, and the next day wrote a letter to me which is so characteristic of her that I quote it:

I came off the danger list yesterday and tho' still very feeble, am beginning 'to want to know' – the Committee etc. Could you come along one afternoon? O Hermon, those haemorrhages – and the consequent hunger and thirst!

The worst of her suffering past, she was not going to lose any time in picking up the threads. I never knew anyone so avid of information, so eager to know. For an hour I sat with her retailing the news of the day and trying to prevent her from spending her newly-regained strength in excited commentary. She wanted to know about the assassination of the King of Jugoslavia (and what did Dr Curčin think about it?) the chaos in Spain and its probable effect on the P.E.N. Congress in Barcelona next year; the mooted formation of a Turkish Centre, initiated by 'dear Piérard', the International Executive Committee, at which she looked forward to seeing 'darling Crémieux' ... And I was expected to supply information about the Scilly Isles, where she planned to spend next summer, recuperating after this 'tiresome' illness. Two days later I tried to visit her again, but she was in too much pain to see me ...

My mind is full of the sayings and doings of Sappho; her uncannily acute instincts about people – and her perverse detestation of things which the rest of the world agrees to admire; her generous mother sympathy – and an occasional steely hardness which was devastating; her assertions that she 'didn't really like people very much' – and her self-sacrificing devotion to innumerable friends whose troubles she made her own. Nobody who was in close touch with her can believe that the vital personality has been snuffed out. She was a wanderer by nature, proud of her gypsy ancestry, and I like to think of her rolling up the tent in which she spent the summer, ready to stake her claim in the next world.

There were so many tributes, first from members of the English P.E.N. and then from the Centres, that a selection was printed each month in the following four issues of *P.E.N. News*. Written by writers, who know how to make the best use of words, each message was unique and revealing as to the personality of the woman they mourned. I have chosen a few which seem to me to portray most of the facets of my mother's personality, including a couple that express recognition of the difficulties of her temperament. She was a 'character', and her friends knew what to expect.

Benjamin Crémieux: Il semble que cette année 1934 veuille brutalement éliminer toutes les forces qui s'opposaient encore à la violence et à la barbarie, partout grandissantes, partout menaçantes ... voici que disparait à son tour Mistress Dawson Scott, fondatrice et animatrice de la Fédération P.E.N. C'était une Anglaise typique, sûre de ses préférences et de ses haines ... On comprend que la grande guerre ait profondement marqué cette intelligence et ce coeur, et que Mistress Dawson Scott ait conçu l'admirable idée de grouper les représentants de l'esprit de tous les pays, alliés ou ex-ennemis, pour s'employer en faveur d'une compréhension mutuelle. Son initiative a réussi au-delà de ses espérances, mais pour les P.E.N. aussi, les années présentes sont rudes et les mois qui viennent le seront davantage encore. Après Galsworthy, voici Mrs Dawson Scott, qui nous abandonne au moment le plus critique du combat. Que son example, sa foi nous soutiennent ... Aux heures difficiles, tâchons tourner notre pensée vers celle qu'avec un peu d'humeur et beaucoup d'affection, nous appelions la mère des P.E.N. Clubs.

Bradda Field: Mrs Dawson Scott had the essential attributes for leadership. Vital, courageous, self-confident, she could turn visions into realities; she could gain affection and keep it. Possessing an uncanny insight into character, she never demanded more from others than they were able to give. She was not afraid to express an unwelcome opinion, nor did she shrink from accepting criticism. Tolerant and charitable, the advice she offered was invariably sound ...

Louis Golding: I think it was the heavenly large-heartedness of Mrs Dawson Scott that I always found most poignant. On the first occasion I met her, she had just read my first novel, in which I described the death of my mother. 'So you're the young man,' said Sappho. 'Do you know you made me burst into tears ... *in a bus*, with that chapter on the death of your mother?' It was in a bus I learned of Sappho's death ... and it was touch and go whether or not I, too, should burst into tears ...

Constance Holme: ... In my opinion our Founder was one of the great women of the world, for she vitalised everything she touched. Her outstanding characteristics were her courage and kindness ... But she had many other gifts. She was a fine and sensitive artist – poet, novelist and playwright – and she was a most unselfish and loving friend. To know her was an education, a happiness, and an incentive to live.

G.B. Stern: ... There was about her an indestructible quality of sturdy optimism; remarkable, considering that life seemed to spend most of its time knocking her down and forgetting to help her up again. I must recall that she was 'very good to me', and when I badly needed it, and generous with warm encouragement over my work ... In Cornwall we used to walk along the cliffs chanting the names of the coves – Wine Cove, Pepper Cove, Fox Cove, Crystal Cove – Sappho's bare feet planted as carelessly on the spikes and thistles as on the velvet tufts of sea-thrift. Her books rarely met with recognition, though three or four of them were excellent; savage, salty and uncompromising ...

Karel Čapek: The Mother of the P.E.N. Club is dead ... so was she called on all Congresses of P.E.N. Clubs at which she never failed to partake. Not everybody that called her so knew the books full of commonsense and goodness of heart of Mrs Catharine Dawson Scott, English poetess and novel writer, yet everybody liked to meet this kind, beaming lady ... Because hers was the idea to create a friendly international organization of writers that should solidify the solidarity of spirit notwithstanding the difference of lands and languages. Other more important names were necessary in order to make this good-hearted idea grow into one of the important institutions necessary to bring nearer together the states and nations. The other, the more important, were in foreground, whereas Mrs Dawson Scott in the background seemed to caress with her kind eyes and gentle smile all the representatives of white, yellow and dark nations. To-day writers all over the world will remember the kind lady with respect and love, for she was not only the mother of an idea but also the motherly friend of the writers of all the world.

Ernst Toller: Als nach dem Krieg die Propaganda-Maschinen der kriegführenden Länder aufgehört hatten zu arbeiten, blieben von dem ganzen Lügenwust nur die Verzerrung des Intellekts, des Herzens und eine Mauer von Hass zurüeck. Eine tapfere Frau, Mrs Dawson Scott unternahm zu jener Zeit den kühnen Versuch, die Mauer des Hasses zu durchbrechen und die Schriftsteller der 'feindlichen' Lander an die Brüderlichkeit des Intellekts, und an den gemeinsamen Weg aller Schriftsteller zu erinnern. Unermüdlich hat diese Frau gearbeitet. Was sie sich vornahm ist ihr gelungen. Nur wer sich an die Atmosphäre nach dem Krieg erinnern kann, vermag die Verdienste dieser tapferen Frau zu würdigen. Dabei war sie bescheiden, überliess Wort und Entscheidung den Fachleuten. Brauchte man ihre Hilfe fur Bedürftige, war sie immer herzlich und hilfsbereit. Wir werden sie nie vergessen.

(Tr. When after the war the propaganda machines of the countries involved stopped working, there was left behind, from all the lies, confusion of intellect and heart and a wall of hate. A brave woman, Mrs

Dawson Scott, made a courageous attempt to break through·this wall of hate and to remind the writers of the enemy countries of the brotherhood of the intellect and the mutual way of life. Tirelessly has she worked: what she undertook she achieved. Only those who can remember the atmosphere after the war can appreciate what she achieved. But she was modest and left the talk and decision-making to the experts. To those who needed help she was always helpful and friendly. We will not forget her.)

Marie Belloc Lowndes: To anyone who knew and loved Mrs Dawson Scott ... it seems difficult to think of her as the powerful, sombre-natured human being who wrote certain remarkable novels which I hope will revive some day. 'The Story of Anna Beames' was published in 1906, yet I remember it far more vividly than I do certain clever novels which I have read recently ... It was far in advance of its time ... but Mrs Dawson Scott was in a true sense the precursor of that special kind of creative work ... She never talked of them [her books], and many people who knew her and deeply appreciated her qualities, were unaware that in their dear, kind, sympathetic friend was hidden a novelist of rare insight and distinction.

Before I end with Rebecca West's tribute, I will quote from the testimony of one of her great friends who believed, as Sappho did, in a Life after Death:

H. Dennis Bradley: At the October P.E.N. Dinner she sat next to me ... vivacious and alive as ever, but it seemed to me that she was physically tired ... and three days later she was stricken. I never saw her again, but she wrote me three letters ... 'Isn't it queer what makes a human being in extremity select another to cling to. Why did I in that red horror suddenly remember you? There are so many queer psychic things about a death's door illness ... and there was a time after the last attack when my body knew it was going to die.'

I don't think Sappho was sorry to go ... It has made life worth while to have known her and to have loved her ...

And lastly Rebecca: I loved and still love Mrs Dawson Scott so dearly that I hardly remember the achievements on which the newspapers dwelt ... I liked so much the way that when she was old in years you could see that she must have been the prettiest young girl ... smiling and fresh. She had to the end the air of that young girl, as she might have been the day before going to the village fair: full of brisk plans, full of the tenderest hopes of lovely things that were going to happen. I never knew anybody – and this is the thing that above all makes me love her – who was so little daunted by the failure of the village fair to come up to expectations. At the end of her life, with abundant experience of its harshness, of the stupidity and cruelty of human beings, of the malice of circumstance, it had still never occurred to her to doubt that there was an explanation, by the light of which all this unkind chaos would show as merciful order, and that she would stumble on this explanation any day ... I would like to thank her, though I know she never wanted any thanks for anything she gave, for all she did for me in the years of friendship, the constant bounty of affection.

Appendix

I. SAPPHO'S PUBLISHED WORKS

Poetry

Sappho, Kegan Paul 1889
Idylls of Womanhood, Heinemann 1892
Beyond, Glaisher 1912
Bitter Herbs, Heinemann 1923

Novels

The Story of Anna Beames, Heinemann 1906
The Burden, Heinemann 1908
Treasure Trove, Heinemann 1909
The Agony Column, Chapman and Hall 1909
Madcap Jane, Chapman and Hall 1910
Mrs Noakes, an Ordinary Woman, Chapman and Hall 1911
The Caddis Worm, Hurst and Blackett 1914
Against the Grain, Heinemann 1919
Oh! Foolish Kitty, Selwyn and Blount 1928

Cornish novels

Wastralls, Heinemann 1918
The Headland, Heinemann 1920
The Haunting, Heinemann 1921
They Green Stones, Heinemann 1925
The Vampire, Robert Holden 1925
Blown by the Wind, Heinemann 1926
The House in the Hollow, Ernest Benn 1933

Spiritualism

From Four Who Are Dead, Arrowsmith 1926
Is this Wilson?, Duttons 1929

Travel

Nooks and Corners of Cornwall, Glaisher 1911

*

Between 1924 and 1929 Sappho was the co-editor, with Ernest Rhys, of a series of collections of short stories.

II. INTERNATIONAL PRESIDENTS OF P.E.N.

John Galsworthy	1921-33
H.G. Wells	1933-36
Jules Romains	1936-41

International Presidential Committee (formed during war years):

Hu Shih	1941-47
Denis Saurat	1941-47
H.G. Wells	1941-46
Hermon Ould	1941-47
Thornton Wilder	1941-47
with	
E.M. Forster	1946-47
François Mauriac	1946-47
Ignazio Silone	1946-47

Maurice Maeterlinck	1947-49
Benedette Croce	1949-52
Charles Morgan	1953-56
André Chamson	1956-59
Alberto Moravia	1959-62
Victor van Vriesland	1962-65
Arthur Miller	1965-69
Pierre Emmanuel	1969-71
Heinrich Böll	1971-74
V.S. Pritchett	1974-76
Mario Vargas Llosa	1976-79
Per Wästberg	1979-85
Francis King	1985-

III

Some of the many distinguished writers who supported P.E.N. in the formative years. The list is not exhaustive because records are not complete and some P.E.N. secretaries were more diligent in sending news of their progress than others. English names are not included; they can be found in the index. There was never a Russian Centre, but individual Russian supporters of P.E.N. have been included.

Scholem Asch (Poland – Yiddish)
Ramon Pérez de Ayala (Spain)
Henri Barbusse (France)
A. Bihlmans (Latvia)
Johan Bojer (Norway)
Peter Cornelius Boutens (Holland)
Georg Brandes (Denmark)
Ioan A. Bratescu-Voinesti (Roumania)

Ivan Bunin (Russia)
Willa Cather (U.S.A.)
Ivan D. Chichmanov (Bulgaria)
Louis Couperus (Holland)
Benedetto Croce (Italy)
Milan Ćurčin (Jugoslavia)
Gabriele d'Annunzio (Italy)
Jovan Dučić (Jugoslavia)

Anatole France (France)
Robert Frost (U.S.A.)
Ferdinand Goetel (Poland)
Maxim Gorky (Russia)
Lady Gregory (Ireland)
Herbert Grierson (Scotland)
C.M. Grieve (Hugh McDiarmid) (Scotland)
Bertel Gripenberg (Finland)
Angel Guimera (Spain)
Gunnar Gunnarsson (Iceland)
Knut Hamsun (Norway)
Gerhart Hauptmann (Germany)
H. Heyermans (Holland)
Hugo von Hofmannstahl (Austria)
Blasco Ibañez (Spain)
Johannes V. Jensen (Denmark)
Alois Jirasek (Czechoslovakia)
Dom Nicholas Jorga (Roumania)
James Joyce (Ireland)
Aino Kallas (Estonia)
Ellen Key (Sweden)
Helmi Krohn (Finland)
Selma Lagerlöf (Sweden)
Stephen Leacock (Canada)
Sinclair Lewis (U.S.A.)
J.M. Lòpez-Picó (Catalonia)

Salvador de Madariaga (Spain)
Maurice Maeterlinck (Belgium)
Thomas Mann (Germany)
Thomas Masaryk (Czechoslovakia)
Dmitri Merezhkovsky (Russia)
Ivan Mestrovič (Jugoslavia)
Sarah Gertrude Millin (South Africa)
Martin Andersen Nexø (Denmark)
Anders Österling (Sweden)
Louis Piérard (Belgium)
Luigi Pirandello (Italy)
Antol Rado (Hungary)
James Rainis (Latvia)
J. Rakosi (Hungary)
Barbra Ring (Norway)
Hermann Robbers (Holland)
Mazo de la Roche (Canada)
Romain Rolland (France)
Queen Marie of Roumania (Roumania)
Felix Salten (Austria)
Artur Schnitzler (Austria)
Hermann Sudermann (Germany)
Paul Valéry (France)
W.B. Yeats (Ireland)
Stefan Zeromski (Poland)
Emil Zilliacus (Finland)
Oton Zupanič (Jugoslavia)

Index of Names

Brief biographical details have been included wherever possible.